old-fashioned goodness with
VARIABLE POWER MICROWAVE COOKING
from LITTON

Litton Microwave Cooking Products, Minneapolis, Minnesota 55426

LITTON
Microwave Cooking

Greetings from Litton . . .

Now there's a flexible new way to cook with microwaves — variable power. Home economists and engineers have teamed up to produce a microwave oven that lets you select cooking power as you do with a conventional range — a product that consumer interviews show you want and need.

Whether you're short of time or being creative on a weekend, variable power microwave cooking lets you simmer a stew, soften butter, gently cook a custard or scramble an egg in half the usual time — and with the same flexibility as a conventional range. Variable power also lets you do things your range can't do — defrost a steak, heat a cup of coffee in its cup or warm leftovers in minutes right on the plate.

Tell us how you like your variable power microwave oven. Your thoughts and ideas help us develop products and materials YOU want. Write: Litton Microwave Cooking, Minneapolis, Minnesota 55441.

Verna Ludvigson

Verna Ludvigson
Director Consumer Affairs

CONTENTS

Picture on cover: Tomato Beef Stew garnished with sliced tomatoes and parsley, page 92

Photographs in this book illustrate recipes prepared using the variable power microwave oven.

Don't turn this page until you read it! Then read the next three. This is your introduction to a variable power microwave oven — the most exciting cooking appliance since Great Grandma turned in her cook stove for a gas or electric range, Grandpa stopped splitting wood and the family sighed with relief when food still tasted "old-fashioned" good.

A totally new cooking concept needs a careful explanation — even when it's as simple as variable power microwave cooking. So this is not an ordinary introduction. These first pages are designed to help you understand microwaves and how they cook; how variable power works easily for you; what cooking techniques you need to know; what utensils you need to use. Do refer to your Use and Care Manual for instruction for this particular oven.

Cookbook chapters are divided into food categories with **"grey box" keys** outlining microwave cooking techniques used in the recipes. The recipes, developed and tested by home economists, have been carefully selected to make your oven usable every meal of the day, between meals and when company's coming. Flexibility and quality are the recipe selection criteria. There are examples in every microwave technique category — a plus that soon will let you adapt Grandma's recipes and your own.

Now do read on — and turn the pages. Join a new generation of modern cooks who know how to serve up old-fashioned goodness at every meal — in minutes.

Pictured: Glass cooking dishes, straw and paper supplies used in microwave cooking.

STOP! MICROWAVE COOKING STARTS HERE

MICROWAVE COOKING CHAPTER CONTENTS

HOW MICROWAVES COOK

Traditionally, food heats and cooks because of molecular activity caused by a gas flame, burning wood and charcoal or electricity converted to heat energy. This intense heat must be applied to the bottom of a pan of food or used to surround food in an oven with hot air. If food comes in direct contact with these traditional heat sources, it burns before it cooks through.

Now electrical energy can be converted to microwave energy by means of an electron tube called a magnetron. This tube is inside your microwave oven and sends microwaves directly into food.

Microwaves are classified as electromagnetic waves of a non-ionizing frequency. Microwaves travel directly to food without heating the air or the recommended cooking dishes. The cooking process speeds up because it starts as soon as the oven is turned on.

Microwaves move directly to food because they are attracted to the fat, sugar and liquid or moisture molecules causing them to vibrate at a fantastically fast rate. This vibration is heat energy. The vibrating molecules bump and rub others, start these molecules vibrating and set up a chain reaction that moves from the outside edges, where microwaves first come in contact with food, toward the center — cooking as it goes. This chain reaction is called conduction. The molecule vibration, or cooking, continues for several minutes after food comes from a microwave oven and is taken into consideration in microwave recipes.

Microwaves' specific attraction for moisture, fat and sugar in molecules, plus the fast molecule vibration rate this causes, results in the amazing speed of microwave cooking.

USER INSTRUCTIONS

> #### PRECAUTIONS TO AVOID POSSIBLE EXPOSURE TO EXCESSIVE MICROWAVE ENERGY
>
> (a) Do not attempt to operate this oven with the door open since open-door operation can result in harmful exposure to microwave energy. It is important not to defeat or tamper with the safety interlocks.
>
> (b) Do not place any object between the oven front face and the door or allow soil or cleaner residue to accumulate on sealing surfaces.
>
> (c) Do not operate the oven if it is damaged. It is particularly important that the oven door close properly and that there is no damage to the: (1) Door (bent), (2) hinges and latches (broken or loosened), (3) door seals and sealing surfaces.
>
> (d) The oven should not be adjusted or repaired by anyone except properly qualified service personnel.

VARIABLE POWER — A REAL MICROWAVE BONUS

Variable power brings astounding flexibility to microwave cooking, for it lets you choose the speed at which food cooks. It is as convenient as a conventional oven or an electric skillet temperature control. Teamed up with microwave speed, it lets you (bachelor, working wife, mother or grandpa) enjoy outstanding cooking quality and convenience never before available. A variable power microwave oven cooks most food in about half the time necessary in a conventional range. And cool microwave cooking is a real plus in hot weather.

The energy setting words used in these recipes are: WARM, DEFROST, SIMMER, ROAST, REHEAT AND HIGH. These denote major cooking techniques for which a particular microwave speed is used.

HIGH SETTING radiates the most power and should be used to cook foods with high moisture content or foods that require fast, quick cooking to retain natural goodness, flavor and texture. Do not use this setting for "delicate" cooking.

• Cook fish and seafood dishes without butter, egg or sauce made with rich cream or sour cream.
• Quickly heat tender beef roasts; finish cooking on ROAST.
• Cook vegetables, unless recipe calls for butter, cream or egg sauces.
• Cook poultry such as tender young cut-up chicken or small whole birds weighing 3 pounds or under.
• Quickly heat many less tender beef cuts before final cooking on a lower setting.
• Heat beverage liquids until bubbling to dissolve instant mixes or to reheat previously cooked beverages.
• Boil water before cooking rice or pasta.
• Finish cooking cakes and quick breads on this setting to set batter or dough after it raises.
• Cook fresh fruit and fresh fruit desserts that have no eggs or cream.
• Cook savory or dessert sauces made with flour or cornstarch — no cream or eggs.
• Cook fillings made with flour or cornstarch — no cream or eggs.
• Preheat microwave browning grill.

REHEAT SETTING provides a bit less energy which makes it the most-used choice for heating previously cooked foods.

- Heat main dish mixtures made primarily from pre-cooked or canned foods. However, use a lower setting if recipe calls for "critical" ingredients such as eggs, cheese, cream, sour cream, kidney beans or mushrooms.
- Heat precooked rice or pasta mixed with other "non-critical" ingredients.
- Heat cooked fruit and cook or heat precooked fruit desserts with no cream, sour cream or eggs.
- Heat baked goods such as doughnuts, dinner rolls, coffee cake and sweet rolls.
- Heat all canned vegetables and entrées such as stews and spaghetti.
- Heat frozen foods that do not contain eggs, cheese, cream, sour cream, kidney beans or mushrooms.
- Heat fish fillets or fish sticks — precooked and frozen.

ROAST SETTING has many functions because it uses medium energy. It cooks many meats and mixtures with critical ingredients especially well.

- Cook critical ingredient recipes — those containing mushrooms, cheese, sour cream, cream, mayonnaise, eggs, kidney beans, clams or scallops.
- Finish cooking tender beef roasts.
- Start cooking less tender beef on this setting; finish on SIMMER.
- Cook all ground meat.
- Cook most pork and lamb.
- Thaw whole poultry over 4 pounds.
- Cook large, whole chicken or turkey, plus geese, ducks and pheasants.
- Cook sandwiches, especially those with cheese.
- Melt and blend shortening-sugar mixtures.
- Melt butter.
- Sauté finely-cut vegetables in butter.
- Cook frostings with lots of butter.
- Cook candy.
- Cook egg and cheese dishes.
- Bake pie shells.
- Thaw meat over 4 pounds.

SIMMER SETTING is slow and gentle — though about twice as fast as conventional range-top simmering or mid-range oven baking.

- Bake yeast breads.
- Raise cakes and quick bread mixes — batter sets using higher energy on HIGH.
- Cook soft custards and custard-base desserts with eggs.
- Cook less tender beef — during major part of cooking time.
- Total cooking of small veal cuts and final cooking period of large veal cuts.
- Bake bars and cookies.

DEFROST SETTING is used to defrost frozen foods that require a low energy setting and to cook some delicate foods.

- Cook rice or pasta — after water boils on HIGH.
- Cook baked custards and desserts with baked custard bases which cannot be stirred.
- Bake fruitcakes with a dense batter chock full of fruit.
- Thaw meat and poultry under 4 pounds.
- Thaw fish.

WARM SETTING is the gentlest of the gentle in the variable power spectrum.

- Raise yeast breads.
- Keep a main dish warm for about an hour if a meal must wait.
- Soften cream cheese and butter.

The HIGH setting is the fastest cooking, REHEAT and ROAST cook slightly slower, allowing more time for the heat to penetrate the center of foods. SIMMER cooks like mid-heat setting of range burners. DEFROST is yet slower especially good for defrosting frozen foods. Finally, WARM offers the most gentle cooking for delicate softening of butter. The cookbook gives all the cooking techniques for the settings, but you can use any settings in between.

Note:

The symbol * used with some recipes indicates that these recipes are cooked on two or more cooking periods and/or power settings with stirring sometimes suggested at this convenient time (when returning to reset the oven).

STOP! MICROWAVE COOKING STARTS HERE

HOW YOU WILL COOK WITH MICROWAVES

There are two familiar questions to ask yourself in order to become a variable power microwave oven expert.

First: What's to be done with the food you want to microwave — defrost it, heat it or cook it?

Second: What is this food like — volume, or how much; density, or compactness; temperature, before it goes in the microwave, and are any of the ingredients "critical" or sensitive to microwaves?

Answers to these two questions determine cooking time, cooking technique (including things like oven settings, covering, stirring or turning) and utensils used.

The following paragraphs help answer these questions, define necessary microwave cooking techniques and list cooking utensils usable in a microwave oven.

OVEN SETTINGS: This book is designed to show you how to cook with variable power. Settings vary from WARM through HIGH . Cooking time is expressed in minutes and seconds. Check all controls on your oven before beginning to cook. See your Use and Care Manual to make certain that all controls are in the correct position.

DEFROSTING: Defrosting gradually heats frozen foods to change ice molecules into water without beginning the cooking process. The process must be slow. The variable power DEFROST setting automatically reduces the power for even thawing.

HEATING: Heating occurs when microwaves start food molecules vibrating. Porous food like bread quickly heats. Dense food, like meat, should be sliced to heat through without overcooking edges.

COOKING: Cooking is prolonged heating that changes food texture from a raw to a cooked state. Since microwaves are attracted to liquid, fat and sugar, variable power provides energy levels that assure even, quality cooking.

HIGH ALTITUDE COOKING: The usual high altitude adjustments are not necessary in microwave cooking. The only change may be a slight increase in cooking time.

BROWNING: Sear steaks and chops on a microwave browning grill. Large meat items will brown in a microwave oven because the fat attracts microwaves and reaches a high temperature during cooking. Cakes and breads, however, will not brown in the oven. Recipes in this book suggest ingredients to enhance color.

VOLUME: As the volume of food put in the oven increases, the concentration of microwaves in a given food item decreases — so cooking time goes up slightly. For example, one sandwich will heat faster than two.

STARTING TEMPERATURE: Cold food takes longer to cook than room temperature or warm food. Lukewarm tap water heats faster than cold.

DENSITY: Denser, more compact foods take longer to heat than porous foods. This is because microwaves penetrate deeper into porous items creating instant heat throughout. Microwaves first penetrate the outer portion of dense food and the center must be heated by conduction from the hot, outer edges. A slice of meat, for example, heats in 2 to 3 minutes while a slice of bread the same size takes 30 seconds.

ARRANGEMENT: Minimize differences in density, volume or starting temperature of similar-size foods by arranging items in a ring, when possible, so there is no center that must be heated. When food varies in shape or size, place slow-to-heat dense food near the outside of the dish where heating takes place first.

STIRRING: Variable power with its lower energy settings keeps stirring at a minimum. However, stirring reduces cooking time for "critical" foods that must be cooked more slowly. Heated portions are moved from the edges to the center — cool portions to the edges where they cook faster. Stirring also keeps "critical" foods from overcooking at edges.

TURNING FOOD OVER: Turn over meat and other dense pieces of food to make certain it cooks more evenly.

COVERING: Glass covers, plastic wrap, wax paper, glass plates and saucers trap steam and hasten cooking. Remove covers carefully to avoid steam burns. Small pieces of aluminum foil may be used to prevent overcooked spots on large pieces of meat.

CRITICAL INGREDIENTS: This term is used throughout the book and refers to food items that microwave very quickly and can overcook, curdle or "pop." These foods are cheese, eggs, cream, sour cream, condensed milk, mayonnaise, snails, scallops, oysters, kidney beans and mushrooms.

STANDING TIME: Cooking continues after food comes from a microwave oven. It is often advisable to undercook or underthaw food slightly and let the process finish during the standing time as designated in recipes.

ADAPTING RECIPES: Favorite family recipes can be adapted to microwave cooking. Select a similar recipe in this book as a model. Check its "**grey box**" **key** for techniques and tips. Always take "critical" ingredients into consideration. A general conversion chart for adapting recipes is not possible — experiment. See page 180 for information on food expectations.

GLASS UTENSILS: Ovenproof glass or glass ceramic oven-baking dishes are the most-used microwave cooking utensils. These dishes allow microwaves to pass through directly to food. Dishes will remain cool unless cooking is prolonged causing hot food to heat the dish.

Glass, sturdy china and pottery serving dishes can also be used. These should not have silver, gold, platinum or other metal trim which will be damaged by the microwaves.

Fine china is not ovenproof. Do not use it at all if it has a metal signature on the bottom or any other metal trim. Fine china without metal trim may be used to heat precooked foods for short periods of time.

Some paints or glazes used on glass dishes do contain metallic substances and should not be used in a microwave oven.

If in doubt about any glass, pottery or china utensil, place it in the oven on HIGH for 15 to 20 seconds. If the container feels warm when taken from the oven, do not cook or heat in it.

PLASTICS: Dishwasher-safe plastics, usually quite rigid material, can be used for cooking or heating.

Hard plastic trays, picnic ware, thermal cups, mugs and bowls (including the sturdy bowls in which a number of dairy toppings and other products are packaged) may be used in the oven. Melamine ware has a tendency to absorb energy, so you should give it a 15 to 20 second test on HIGH to be certain your particular brand is safe. (See Glass Utensils.)

Plastic foam cups and dishes can be used for heating. Cover loosely to avoid dish distortion.

Plastic baby bottles are safe for heating milk or formulas.

Spatulas and spoons designed for non-stick pans can be left in the oven for short-time periods.

Plastic wrap can be used as a tight covering, but it should be pierced before being removed to prevent steam burns on hands or arms.

Plastic cooking pouches can also be used to heat and/or cook contents, but should be slit before cooking so excess steam can escape.

PAPER: Paper cups, plates, towels, wax paper and paper cartons can be used for heating. Prolonged time in the oven can cause paper to burn. Wax paper can be used as a covering during cooking.

STRAW: Baskets can be used in the oven for the very short time it takes to heat rolls.

METAL: Metal dishes and foil reflect microwaves and inhibit cooking. Gaps in the metal particles of an object can also cause arcing. The walls of a microwave oven are made of smooth, continuous metal with no particle gaps.

Metal objects can be used in the oven under certain conditions although care must be taken that metal does not touch oven surfaces and arc.

Small pieces of aluminum foil can be used to cover spots on large pieces of meat which appear to be overcooking.

Foil TV-type trays can be used if no more than ¾ inch deep because microwaves reflect off the foil and must heat from the top food surface.

Metal skewers and clamps are usable when the proportion of food is much greater than the metal. Chunks of food filling shish kabob skewer microwave well without arcing. Metal clamps and clips on turkeys may be left on during cooking.

Do not use metal twister, it will arc. These sparks may ignite paper and plastic.

WOOD: Moisture in wooden utensils evaporates during microwave cooking and will cause wood to crack. Small items such as a wooden spoon or wood-handled rubber spatula can be left in the oven for short periods of time.

MEAT AND CANDY THERMOMETERS: Only microwave meat thermometers may be used during microwave cooking. Conventional meat and candy thermometers may be inserted to test temperature after food is taken out of the oven. The reason? Mercury in conventional thermometers reflects microwaves and makes them inaccurate.

MICROWAVE ROASTING RACK: This accessory may be purchased from the oven manufacturer. It is used to hold meat above pan drippings during open pan cooking. Inverted glass or pottery saucers (without metal trim) can be used to simulate a rack.

MICROWAVE BROWNING GRILL: The browning grill is an accessory which may be purchased from the oven manufacturer. The unit is preheated in the microwave oven; then food is added to sear and/or brown.

Additional information on utensils may be found in Utensil Chart pages 178-179.

STOP! MICROWAVE COOKING STARTS HERE

Challenge! Fun! A fascinating new way to put delectable meals on the table! That's microwave sequence cooking which allows you to cook one dish after another and serve a hot meal in less than usual time. It's a brand new experience, so home economists have developed traditional breakfast, lunch and dinner menus, then asked a homemaker to prepare them — a gal who'd never turned on a microwave oven before. Use these menus, sequences, tips and options for your first full meals from a microwave oven.

Pictured clockwise from the top: Fresh Fruit Pie, page 146; Scalloped Potatoes, page 13; Broccoli garnished with lemon slices, page 113; Ham Slice in Orange Sauce, page 13.

BREAKFAST

Perked Coffee and/or Milk
Caramel Biscuit Ring-a-Round
Glazed Grapefruit or Juice
Scrambled Eggs
Bacon

Pick a weekend morning and have fun developing this tasty, nutritious microwave breakfast menu in sequence. Breakfast is the key meal of the day — preparing it is easy and orderly in a microwave oven.

Perk the coffee first. Then gather breakfast ingredients, set the table with the morning paper handy — and you're ready for a fascinating microwave cooking experience. Do prepare foods in the order given.

Our homemaker suggests that cooking three microwave dishes in sequence is the most relaxed way to begin cooking microwave meals. If this is your first full microwave meal, substitute juice for grapefruit.

1
Prepare Caramel Biscuit Ring-a-Round Coffee cake, page 136. It takes longer to cook than other foods on the menu, but it will still be warm when bacon and eggs are ready to serve.

2
Get grapefruit ready while coffee cake cooks. Microwave after coffee cake and serve while bacon cooks.

GLAZED GRAPEFRUIT: Remove core and seeds from grapefruit halves; cut edges and between sections. Sprinkle each half with brown sugar; dot with butter or margarine. Microwave on HIGH — 2 halves, 3 to 3½ minutes; 4 halves, 4 to 5 minutes.

3
Layer bacon between paper towels and microwave as directed on page 65.

4
Prepare scrambled eggs, page 101, while bacon cooks. Cook eggs and arrange with bacon on glass platter. Return platter of food to oven to warm bacon on ROAST for about 45 seconds, if desired.

LUNCH

Baked Apple
Cup of Tomato Brew
Reuben Sandwich
Milk

This everyday lunch menu classic is perfect for busy Saturdays when kids and Dad are home and have worked up whopping appetites. Working out three microwave cooking techniques in sequence is a cinch because baked apples are delicious warm or cool and the tomato soup stays hot while sandwiches heat. In fact, our homemaker recommends this as the first microwave meal sequence you try.

She also suggests that it's worth the extra time to check carefully through recipes before beginning meal preparations.

Remember, too, that with speedy microwave cooking it's wise to set the table, assemble ingredients and utensils before you start cooking. Prepare food in order listed.

Baked Apples should be cooked first. These take a little longer than the other foods on the menu and need a cooling time before serving. Prepare and cook apples according to directions on page 151.

Make Tomato Brew next. Soup creations using canned or "from scratch" ingredients are easy to mix and cook in a microwave oven. Use the recipe on page 87. Make certain buttermilk is completely mixed into the other liquids to prevent separation. Store leftover soup (if any) and reheat it for another meal.

3

Prepare Reuben Sandwiches as the soup cooks — there's plenty of time. Toasted bread is always the firmest sandwich base. Place microwave sandwiches on paper towel or napkin to absorb moisture as bread and filling heat.

FOUR REUBEN SANDWICHES: Toast 8 slices of pumpernickel bread. Spread 4 slices with mayonnaise and place on paper towels or napkins. Top each slice with thinly-sliced corned beef, well drained sauerkraut and a slice of Swiss cheese. Place remaining 4 toast slices on top. Microwave on ROAST — 2 sandwiches, 2 to 2½ minutes; 4 sandwiches, 3½ to 4 minutes. These times are guidelines developed with medium-thick sandwiches.

DINNER

Fresh Fruit Pie
Tossed Salad or Fresh Fruit
Scalloped Potatoes
Ham Slice in Orange Sauce
Buttered Broccoli
Perked Coffee and/or Milk

Microwave an "all American" dinner — ham, scalloped potatoes and fruit pie. This menu calls for four dishes cooked in the microwave oven. Before starting, think through the entire menu. And, while you're cooking, check oven setting and timing device before putting the next dish in the oven.

The easy three-recipe cooking sequence for beginning cooks is adaptable to this meal if the pie is baked earlier in the day. If you elect to make a tossed salad, mix greens ahead of time, refrigerate and toss with dressing just before dinner.

Next set the table and get coffee ready to perk; then assemble ingredients and utensils for microwave oven dishes. Now you're ready to fix an outstanding meal much, much faster than usual. Cook food in order given.

1

Early in the day, make and microwave your favorite Fresh Fruit Pie, page 146, or cook a Frozen Fruit Pie, page 167.

2

First dish to prepare and microwave just before dinner is Scalloped Potatoes.

SCALLOPED POTATOES: Peel and thinly slice 4 medium potatoes. Arrange in 3-quart glass casserole. Sprinkle on 1 tablespoon all-purpose flour, 1 teaspoon salt and ¼ cup chopped onion. Pour 1½ cups milk over all. Dot with butter or margarine. Cover with glass lid or plastic wrap. Microwave on HIGH for 10 minutes. Stir; recover, and continue cooking on HIGH for 8 to 10 minutes or until potatoes are tender. Let stand, covered, 5 minutes before serving. If necessary, reheat potatoes, covered, on REHEAT for 3 to 4 minutes or until hot.

3

Prepare ham and sauce while potatoes cook.

HAM SLICE IN ORANGE SAUCE: Trim and score edges of 1-inch-thick ham slice. Place on microwave roasting rack in 2-quart (12 x 7) glass baking dish. Make Orange Sauce by combining 1 tablespoon cornstarch, ⅛ teaspoon ginger and 1 cup orange juice in 2-cup measure; mix well. Brush both sides of ham with some of the sauce. Microwave on ROAST for 10 minutes. Turn ham over and pour on remaining sauce. Continue cooking on ROAST for 5 to 6 minutes or until meat is hot and sauce thickened. Let stand, covered, 5 minutes before serving. Meat is covered during standing time to hold heat while broccoli cooks.

4

Cook and serve broccoli on a glass or pottery serving platter without metal trim. See Fresh and Frozen Vegetable Cooking Chart on page 113.

3 MEALS FROM A MICROWAVE

Fancy dinner or an after school get-together with the kids — a microwave oven lets the cook enjoy her party. Food and drink are hot and delicious in the wink of an eye — often right in serving cups or dishes.

Beverages are particularly easy to make — one serving or several. Use the chart on page 19.

Dips and tiny appetizers are hot in minutes, too. Though appetizer size is somewhat consistent — small — recipe ingredients include a wide variety of meat, fish and cheese. So microwave techniques vary with the food in each recipe. This chapter divides appetizers into three groups: Those with ingredients that are fast and easy to cook; those that need slower cooking, and delicate appetizers that need very low heat and careful watching. **"Grey box" keys offer special helps.**

Try these recipes; then adapt some old favorites.

Pictured from the top: Hot spiced Cider garnished with orange slices, page 19; Spicy Franks, page 16; Cheese and Onion Canapés, page 16; Zippy Cheese Dip, page 17.

SPEEDY APPETIZER KEY: "Non-critical" appetizers and dips microwave nicely on HIGH in a few minutes because the ingredients cook easily without precise timing or watching.

Canapé mixtures mounded on crackers or toast rounds bubble and blend on REHEAT. Ingredients need little or no cooking and the canapés microwave in seconds. Do not assemble these canapés until ready to microwave or crackers and toast become soggy. Appetizers with crusts do not microwave well — pastry is pale and unappealing.

Microwave REHEAT also freshens potato chips, salty crackers and other nibblers in seconds.

Remember that appetizers and dips are made from a wide assortment of foods. Each microwaves in a particular way. When experimenting, check this section plus chapter "keys" of the new recipe's major ingredients for particular microwaving tips. When experimenting, try one or two appetizers alone to verify procedure.

CHEESE AND ONION CANAPES

½ cup mayonnaise or salad dressing
¼ cup grated Parmesan cheese
2 green onions, finely chopped
24 toast rounds

1. Combine all ingredients, except rounds, in small mixing bowl; mix well. Spread mixture on rounds and place in 3-quart (13 x 9) glass baking dish.

2. Microwave on REHEAT for 45 to 55 seconds or until just bubbly. About 24 Canapés

MEXICAN BEAN DIP

4 slices bacon, cut into pieces
1 can (31 oz.) pork and beans in tomato sauce
½ cup sharp Cheddar flavored cheese food
1 teaspoon garlic salt
1 teaspoon chili powder
½ teaspoon salt
2 teaspoons vinegar
2 teaspoons Worcestershire sauce
Cayenne pepper

1. Place bacon pieces in 1½-quart glass casserole.

2. Microwave on HIGH for 3 to 4 minutes or until crisp. Remove bacon pieces, set aside. Place beans in blender and blend until smooth. Pour into bacon drippings in 1½-quart glass casserole. Stir in remaining ingredients, except bacon. Cover with glass lid or plastic wrap.

3. Microwave on HIGH for 7 to 8 minutes or until mixture is hot in center. Sprinkle top with bacon pieces. About 3½ Cups Dip

SPICY FRANKS

1 jar (10 oz.) currant jelly
3 tablespoons prepared mustard
1 lb. skinless franks (about 10)

1. Combine jelly and mustard in 4-cup glass measure.

2. Microwave on HIGH for about 3 minutes or until jelly melts. Beat well with rotary beater or whip to blend in mustard.

3. Cut each frank crosswise into 6 pieces. Stir into jelly mixture and continue cooking on HIGH for 4 to 5 minutes or until franks are hot. Serve in chafing dish with toothpick. About 60 Franks

TIP • Substitute 2 packages (8 oz. each) cocktail franks for skinless franks.

RUMAKI

9 slices bacon, cut in thirds
1 can (5 oz.) water chestnuts
Worcestershire sauce

1. Wrap bacon slice around one water chestnut. Skewer with toothpick. Place in 2-quart (12 x 7) glass baking dish. Sprinkle with Worcestershire sauce.

2. Microwave on HIGH for 10 to 12 minutes or until bacon is crisp. About 27 Appetizers

TIP • Cut large water chestnuts in half.

Mix spread ahead and mound on toast just before cooking.

REGAL CRAB TOASTERS

1 can (6½ oz.) flaked cooked crabmeat, drained
¼ cup shredded Swiss cheese
2 tablespoons chopped celery
2 tablespoons mayonnaise or salad dressing
2 tablespoons milk
1 tablespoon chopped pimento
1 tablespoon finely chopped onion
½ teaspoon lemon juice
⅛ teaspoon salt
Dash pepper
12 to 15 toast rounds

1. Combine all ingredients, except toast rounds, in small glass mixing bowl; mix well. Spread mixture on toast. Place in 2-quart (12 x 7) glass baking dish.

2. Microwave on REHEAT 1 to 1½ minutes or until hot. 12 to 15 Crab Toasters

TIPS • Toast rounds may be homemade or packaged.

• Make Regal Crab Toasters in bowl-shaped natural shells. Spoon crab mixture into shells. Microwave on REHEAT for 1½ to 2 minutes or until hot.

CURRIED SHRIMP*

- 3 tablespoons butter or margarine
- 3 tablespoons all-purpose flour
- ¼ teaspoon curry powder
- ¼ teaspoon salt
- ⅓ cup milk
- ⅓ cup dry white wine
- 1 package (8 oz.) frozen shrimp

1. Place butter in 1½-quart glass casserole.

2. Microwave on ROAST about 1 minute or until melted. Blend in flour, curry powder, salt. Stir in milk and wine; add shrimp. Cover with glass lid or plastic wrap.

3. Microwave on HIGH for 5 minutes. Stir; re-cover, and continue cooking on HIGH for 4 to 5 minutes or until hot.   About 1½ Cups Dip

---

GENTLE-COOK APPETIZER KEY: Micro-wave ROAST is the speed to cook any ap-petizer food or mixture which contains a "criti-cal" ingredient — cheese that may burn; shell-fish that may toughen; mushrooms that may "pop"; meat mixtures that should blend and tender-cook gently.

Microwave appetizers in glass casserole or baking dish with a fitted glass cover or plastic wrap tucked tightly across top of cooking dish.

Bowl-shaped natural shells are also safe at-tractive microwave cooking containers for ap-petizer mixtures. Cover shells tightly with plas-tic wrap. See Coquilles St. Jacques recipe in Fish and Seafood chapter.

When experimenting, check similar recipes in this section plus the chapter "keys" of new recipe's major ingredients.

ZIPPY CHEESE DIP*

- 2 tablespoons butter or margarine
- 2 tablespoons all-purpose flour
- ½ teaspoon dry mustard
- ½ teaspoon Worcestershire sauce
- ¼ teaspoon garlic powder
- Dash Tabasco
- ⅔ cup milk
- 3 cups shredded process American cheese

1. Place butter in 2-quart glass casserole.

2. Microwave on ROAST for about 1 minute or until melted. Blend in flour, dry mustard, Worcester-shire sauce, garlic powder and Tabasco. Stir in milk and cheese. Cover with glass lid or plastic wrap.

3. Microwave on ROAST for 4 minutes. Stir; re-cover, and continue cooking on ROAST for 4 to 5 minutes or until cheese is melted.

    About 2 Cups Dip

TIP ● Reheat dip on ROAST setting if it cools during a party.

Mushrooms stay tender, don't burst, if cooked on ROAST .

MUSHROOMS BOURGUIGNON

- ¼ cup butter or margarine
- 1 lb. fresh mushrooms, cleaned
- 1 cup dry red wine or beef broth
- 1 tablespoon finely chopped green onion
- ½ teaspoon garlic salt
- ½ teaspoon dill weed
- ¼ teaspoon salt
- Dash pepper

1. Place butter in 3-quart (13 x 9) glass baking dish.

2. Microwave on ROAST for about 1½ minutes or until melted. Stir in remaining ingredients. Arrange mushrooms, caps down, in sauce. Cover with glass lid or plastic wrap.

3. Microwave on ROAST for 8 to 10 minutes or until hot.   About 36 Mushrooms

---

Gentle cooking keep these shellfish tender.

CLAMS IN THE SHELL

- ¼ cup water
- 6 fresh clams, thoroughly washed

1. Pour water into 2-quart glass casserole.

2. Microwave on HIGH for 1 to 2 minutes or until boiling. Place clams into boiling water. Cover with glass lid or plastic wrap.

3. Microwave on ROAST for 4 to 5 minutes or until shell opens. Let stand, covered, 2 minutes. Clam meat should be firm when done.

    4 to 5 Servings

TIP ● Substitute oysters for clams.

MEATBALLS IN TOMATO SAUCE

- 1 lb. ground beef
- ¼ cup finely chopped onion
- 1 egg, beaten
- 1 teaspoon salt
- ⅓ cup packed brown sugar
- 1 can (8 oz.) tomato sauce
- 3 tablespoons lemon juice
- ⅛ teaspoon garlic salt

1. Combine ground beef, onion, egg and salt in medium mixing bowl; mix well. Shape into 18 (1-inch) meatballs. Place in 9-inch round glass bak-ing dish. Cover with plastic wrap.

2. Microwave on ROAST for 8 minutes. Drain drippings. Combine remaining ingredients in small mixing bowl. Pour over meatballs and continue cooking on ROAST for 5 to 6 minutes or until piping hot.   18 Meatballs

DELICATE APPETIZER KEY: DEFROST or SIMMER are the microwave settings for appetizers that need special care.

Sometimes these are appetizers cooked in tiny containers that do not allow for much bubbling. Others include ingredients that toughen or "pop" if cooked on too-high heat.

Watch these canapés carefully. It's a good idea to experiment with one before you cook the whole batch.

DEFROST cooks snails and butter sauce in shells without spattering. Lower setting is used as butter has tendency to overflow.

ESCARGOT

½ **cup butter or margarine**
1 **clove garlic, finely chopped**
2 **tablespoons dried parsley flakes**
¼ **teaspoon chervil, if desired**
⅛ **teaspoon pepper**
1 **can (7½ oz.) snails, drained**
Snail shells

1. Cream butter and seasonings in small mixing bowl.

2. Place about ¼ teaspoon seasoned butter in each snail shell; top with snail; fill to rim with seasoned butter. Repeat for each shell.

3. Place escargots (snails on shells) on glass platter.

4. Microwave on DEFROST for 3 to 3½ minutes or until butter begins to bubble.   4 Servings

CHICKEN LIVER PATE

¾ **cup butter or margarine**
¼ **cup chopped green onions**
1 **clove garlic, finely chopped**
½ **teaspoon salt**
¼ **teaspoon nutmeg**
⅛ **teaspoon pepper**
¼ **cup dry sherry or broth**
1 **lb. chicken livers**
2 **tablespoons light cream**

1. Combine all ingredients except cream in 1½-quart glass casserole. Cover with glass lid or plastic wrap.

2. Microwave on SIMMER for 18 to 20 minutes or until liver is done. Stir in cream.

3. Pour mixture into electric blender and blend until smooth. Pour into serving bowl or mold. Cover and chill before serving. Serve with crackers.
About 2½ Cups Pâté

HOT BEVERAGE KEY: Heat beverages quickly — use Microwave HIGH setting. Reheat cooled beverages at the same setting.

Use glass or pottery pitchers, 8-ounce mugs, juice jars, brandy snifters — and everyday 6-ounce coffee cups. Do not use dishes with gold, silver or other metal trim.

Paper "hot" cups, styrofoam cups and even small waxed milk cartons work in a microwave oven. DO OPEN the carton to prevent bulging. DO NOT OVERHEAT or waxed surface will dissolve.

Why keep a coffee pot plugged in all day? Perk coffee, then reheat a cup or two at a time using the directions in the beverage chart next page.

Heat beverages, or water for beverages, almost to a boil for full flavor in the finished drink. Watch milk closely so it does not boil over.

Add instant coffee or tea after water is hot to avoid bitter taste.

TOM AND JERRY

2 **eggs, separated**
1 **cup powdered sugar**
½ **teaspoon vanilla**
½ **cup rum**
½ **cup brandy**
Nutmeg

1. Place egg whites in small mixing bowl. Beat with rotary beater until soft peaks form. Fold in ½ cup powdered sugar. Beat egg yolks with remaining sugar until thickened. Fold in beaten egg whites and vanilla. Cover and refrigerate until serving time. Fill four 8-ounce glass mugs ¾ full of water.

2. Microwave on HIGH for 8 to 9 minutes or until hot and bubbly. Stir 1 heaping tablespoon batter, 1½ tablespoons rum and 1½ tablespoons brandy into each mug of water. Sprinkle with nutmeg; serve.   About 4 (1-Mug) Servings

TOMATO NOGGINS

1 **can (46 oz.) tomato juice**
2 **cans (10½ oz. each) condensed beef broth**
Vodka
1 **lemon, sliced**

1. Combine tomato juice and beef broth in 3-quart glass bowl or pitcher.

2. Microwave on HIGH for 16 to 18 minutes or until hot and bubbly. Pour into nine 8-ounce glass mugs. Stir in vodka to taste. Garnish with lemon slice.   About 9 (1-Mug) Servings

TIP ● Substitute 3 bouillon cubes or 3 teaspoons instant beef bouillon and 2½ cups water for canned beef broth.

Fast warm-up after a winter outing.

HOT SPICED CIDER

    2 quarts apple cider
    4 cinnamon sticks
    16 whole allspice
    16 whole cloves
    2 tablespoons packed brown sugar
    2 lemons, sliced
    2 oranges, sliced

1. Combine all ingredients in 2-quart glass bowl or pitcher.

2. Microwave on HIGH for 16 to 18 minutes or until hot and bubbly. Stir; remove spices, and serve.   About 8 (1-Mug) Servings

TIP • Make 1 serving. Combine ½ cinnamon stick, 2 whole allspice, 2 whole cloves, ½ teaspoon brown sugar, 1 lemon and 1 orange slice in 8-ounce glass mug. Fill with cider. Microwave on HIGH for 2 to 2½ minutes or until hot.

HOT BUTTERED RUM

    1 cup water or apple cider
    1 tablespoon packed brown sugar
    1½ tablespoons rum
    1 teaspoon butter or margarine

1. Fill 10-ounce mug with water or apple cider. Stir in brown sugar.

2. Microwave on HIGH for 2 to 2½ minutes or until hot and bubbly. Add rum and top with butter.
                                            1 Serving

BOUILLON SIPPER

    2 cans (10½ oz. each) condensed beef bouillon
    1⅓ cups hot water
    2 tablespoons dry sherry
    4 lemon slices
    Parsley

1. Combine all ingredients, except lemon and parsley, in 1½-quart glass bowl or pitcher.

2. Microwave on HIGH for 6 to 7 minutes or until hot. Garnish each serving with a lemon slice and parsley.   About 4 (1-Mug) Servings

HOW TO MAKE HOT BEVERAGES

• Microwave on HIGH.

• Microwave hot drinks in glass or pottery cups and serving pitchers without silver or other metal trim.

• Heat ½ pints of milk in the carton. OPEN carton to prevent bulging. DO NOT OVERHEAT or waxed surface will dissolve.

• Heat liquids almost to a boil for best taste.

• WATCH MILK carefully so it does not boil over.

• Add a marshmallow to hot chocolate drinks during the last 10 to 15 seconds of heating.

BEVERAGE	6-OZ. SERVING	MINUTES	8-OZ. SERVING	MINUTES
WATER OR MILK to make regular tea, instant beverages or instant breakfasts	1 cup	2 to 2½	1 mug	3 to 3½
	2 cups	3 to 3½	2 mugs	4 to 5½
	4 cups	5 to 6½	4 mugs	8 to 9
	6 cups	8 to 9	6 mugs	12 to 14
REHEATING COFFEE OR COCOA made with water or milk	1 cup	1½ to 2	1 mug	2 to 2½
	2 cups	2 to 2½	2 mugs	3 to 3½
	4 cups	4 to 5	4 mugs	6 to 7
	6 cups	5 to 6	6 mugs	7 to 8
MILK OR CHOCOLATE MILK in opened ½-pt. waxed carton			1 carton	2 to 2½
			2 cartons	3 to 3½
			4 cartons	5½ to 6
			6 cartons	7½ to 8
MILK OR CHOCOLATE MILK	1-qt. glass pitcher	7 to 8		

Flaky! Tender! Delicate! These are words a cook-who-cares uses to describe outstanding fish and seafood dishes. And taste-testers agree: "Fish and seafood from a microwave oven are some of the best we've ever eaten."

Fish and seafood have always been "last minute" foods to fix. Now, with microwave speed, "minute" means just that — shortening a busy homemaker's kitchen time when a hungry family's waiting or she wants to spend time with guests.

The "grey box" techniques make microwave fish and seafood cooking easy: steam or poach with liquid; oven-cook with little or no liquid; combine with cream or eggs.

Get to know these techniques well — then enjoy some of the most delicious fish and seafood, ever!

Pictured clockwise from the top: Salmon Steaks with Lemon Dill Sauce garnished with parsley, page 30; Seafood Newburg garnished with parsley, page 31; Wine Scampi, made with large shrimp and garnished with snipped parsley, page 25.

FISH/SEAFOOD CHAPTER CONTENTS

HOW TO DEFROST FISH AND SEAFOOD

- Thaw fish and seafood in original closed package in a glass baking dish.

- Microwave on DEFROST setting. This thawing technique sends enough heat into food center to warm and defrost it without starting cooking process at outer edges.

- Let fish or seafood rest 5 minutes in package after removing from oven.

- Rinse whole fish or seafood under cold running water to finish thawing center before cooking.

- Carefully separate fish fillets under cold running water.

FISH/SEAFOOD	WEIGHT	MINUTES
FROZEN FILLETS: Sole, Perch, Pike, Halibut, Whitefish, Snapper, Flounder	1-lb. pkg.	10 to 12
WHOLE FISH	1½ to 1¾ lbs.	13 to 14
SALMON STEAKS	1 lb.	5 to 6
SCALLOPS	12-oz. pkg. / 1-lb. pkg.	4 to 5 / 5 to 6
SHRIMP	8-oz. pkg. / 1-lb. pkg.	3 to 4 / 5 to 6
LOBSTER TAILS	8-oz. pkg.	6 to 7

HOW TO COOK FRESH FISH AND SEAFOOD

- Cook flaky-tender fresh or frozen fish and seafood (thawed) in a microwave oven.

- Thaw fish or seafood before cooking. Use defrosting chart above. Complete thawing under cold, running water.

- Cook fish or seafood in a glass baking dish or casserole. Glass or pottery serving platters may be used if they do not have gold, silver, platinum or other metal trim.

- Place steaks and fillets in baking dish with thicker edges and larger pieces toward outside of baking dish. Arrange small whole fish with tail ends toward center of baking dish.

- Cover cooking dish with a fitted glass lid or plastic wrap tucked tightly across the top. Pierce plastic wrap to allow steam to escape.

- Quick-cook on Microwave HIGH.

- Let fish stand, covered, for 5 minutes to complete cooking.

- Fish is done if it flakes when lifted gently with a fork near center.

FISH/SEAFOOD	WEIGHT	GLASS CONTAINER	MINUTES
FILLETS: Sole, Halibut, Perch, Pike, Whitefish, Flounder, Snapper	1 lb. / 2 lbs.	2-qt. (12 x 7) baking dish	6 to 7 / 8 to 9
WHOLE FISH	1½ to 1¾-lb.	3-qt. (13 x 9) baking dish	10 to 12
SHRIMP OR SCALLOPS	8-oz. pkg.	1-qt. casserole	6 to 7

OVEN-COOKED FISH KEY: Oven-cook fish on Microwave HIGH to retain juices and delicate flavors. DO NOT OVERCOOK!

Oven-cook most any fresh or frozen fish. Use whole fish, fillets or steaks.

Use the Defrost Chart on page 22 to thaw frozen fish. Note that thawing is completed under cold running water.

Substitute steaks for fillets (if desired) with a slight increase in cooking time.

Substitute one kind of fish for another. Sole, perch, halibut, snapper, flounder and whitefish can be interchanged in these recipes.

Fish are usually oven-cooked in a shallow glass baking dish. These dishes do not have a fitted lid. However, most fish is microwave oven-cooked with a cover. Use plastic wrap tightly tucked over baking dish when recipes call for a cover.

Keep thicker edges and larger pieces of fish toward the outside of the cooking dish where food cooks sooner.

Cook fish last when serving with vegetables and/or rice cooked in the microwave oven. The vegetables and rice hold heat and texture longer after cooking.

Test for doneness when you take fish from the oven. Fish should flake when lifted gently with a fork near the center.

Keep fish dishes covered during standing time, so center of fish cooks completely and edges remain moist.

Favorite recipes for both fish and seafood cooked by conventional methods can be adapted to a microwave oven. Use less moisture, butter and cooking time. Compute new amounts and times by checking similar microwave-tested recipes in this section.

Elegant with early garden peas and tiny whole potatoes.

SOLE IN LEMON PARSLEY BUTTER

½ cup butter or margarine
2 tablespoons cornstarch
3 tablespoons lemon juice
1 teaspoon dried parsley flakes
⅛ teaspoon celery salt
Dash pepper
2 lbs. frozen sole fillets, thawed

1. Place butter in 2-quart (12 x 7) glass baking dish.

2. Microwave on ROAST for about 2 minutes or until melted. Blend in cornstarch, lemon juice, parsley, celery salt and pepper. Dip each fillet in seasoned butter. Arrange fillets with thick edges toward outside of dish. Cover with plastic wrap.

3. Microwave on HIGH for 8 to 9 minutes or until fillets flake easily. Let stand, covered, 5 minutes before serving. 6 to 8 Servings

TURBAN OF SOLE

2 tablespoons butter or margarine
½ cup finely chopped celery
¼ cup finely chopped onion
1½ teaspoons dried parsley flakes
¼ teaspoon leaf chervil, if desired
⅛ teaspoon ground thyme
⅛ teaspoon pepper
1 teaspoon lemon juice
1½ cups soft bread cubes
1 lb. frozen sole fillets, thawed

Sauce:
½ can (10¾ oz.) condensed cream of mushroom soup
1 tablespoon chopped pimento
1 tablespoon milk

1. Combine butter, celery, onion, seasonings and lemon juice in medium glass mixing bowl.

2. Microwave on ROAST for about 3 to 4 minutes or until vegetables are partly cooked. Stir in bread cubes; set aside. Butter four 6-oz. custard cups. Line sides and bottom with thin pieces of fish; reserve some pieces of fish for top. Evenly divide stuffing among the 4 custard cups. Top with reserved pieces of fish. Cover with plastic wrap.

3. Microwave on HIGH for 5 to 6 minutes or until fish flakes easily. Let stand, covered, while making sauce. Invert on serving platter before serving. Spoon Sauce over turban and serve.

4. **Sauce:** Combine all ingredients for sauce in 2-cup glass measure. Microwave on HIGH for 1½ to 2 minutes or until mixture is bubbly. 4 Servings

SHRIMP STUFFED TROUT

1 green onion, chopped
¼ cup finely chopped celery
1 tablespoon finely chopped pimento
2 tablespoons butter or margarine
1 tablespoon lemon juice
¼ teaspoon leaf chervil
Dash pepper
1 can (4½ oz.) broken shrimp
1½ cups coarsely crushed dry bread
1 egg, slightly beaten
4 (8 to 10 oz. each) trout

1. Combine green onion, celery, pimento, butter, lemon juice and seasonings in medium glass mixing bowl.

2. Microwave on ROAST for 3 to 4 minutes or until vegetables are partly cooked. Add shrimp, bread crumbs and egg; mix well. stuff each trout with ⅓ to ½ cup dressing. Tie trout with string or secure with toothpicks. Place fish, tail ends toward center, in 3-quart (13 x 9) glass baking dish. Cover with plastic wrap.

3. Microwave on HIGH for 12 to 14 minutes or until trout flakes easily. Let stand, covered, 5 minutes before serving. About 4 Servings

ORANGE 'N SOY FILLETS

> 2 tablespoons soy sauce
> 2 tablespoons thawed frozen orange juice concentrate
> 1 tablespoon lemon juice
> 1 tablespoon catsup
> 1 clove garlic, finely chopped
> 1 lb. frozen fish fillets, thawed

1. Combine soy sauce, orange and lemon juice, catsup and garlic in 2-quart (12 x 7) glass baking dish. Dip fillets in seasoned sauce. Arrange fillets with thick edges toward outside of dish. Cover with plastic wrap.

2. Microwave on HIGH for 6 to 8 minutes or until fish flakes easily. Let stand, covered, 5 minutes before serving. Serve with cooked rice.

3 to 4 Servings

HALIBUT WITH PIQUANT SAUCE

> ¼ cup butter or margarine
> ½ teaspoon dry mustard
> 1½ teaspoons dried parsley flakes
> ⅛ teaspoon garlic powder
> 1½ teaspoon lemon juice
> 1 lb. frozen halibut fillets, thawed

1. Place butter in 1½-quart (10 x 6) glass baking dish.

2. Microwave on ROAST for about 1½ minutes or until melted. Add mustard, parsley flakes, garlic powder and lemon juice. Cut each fillet into 4 pieces. Dip in seasoned butter; arrange with thick edges toward outside of dish. Cover with plastic wrap.

3. Microwave on HIGH for 6 to 7 minutes or until fish flakes easily. Let stand, covered, 5 minutes before serving. 4 Servings

RED SNAPPER AMANDINE*

> 1 lb. frozen red snapper, thawed
> 1 teaspoon lemon juice
> Salt

Sauce:
> ⅓ cup slivered almonds
> ⅓ cup butter or margarine

1. Place red snapper in 1½-quart (10 x 6) glass baking dish. Rub lemon juice on top and salt lightly. Cover with plastic wrap.

2. Microwave on HIGH for 6 to 7 minutes or until fish flakes easily. Let stand, covered, while making sauce.

3. Sauce: Combine almonds and butter in 1-cup glass measure. Microwave on HIGH for about 2 minutes or until melted. Stir and continue cooking on HIGH for 2 to 3 minutes or until lightly browned. Serve over fillets. About 4 Servings

Keep thicker parts toward outside of dish where food cooks sooner, thin edges toward center.

HALIBUT DIVAN

> 1 lb. frozen halibut fillets, thawed
> 1 package (10 oz.) frozen broccoli spears, thawed
> ½ teaspoon tarragon
> 1 can (10¾ oz.) condensed cream of shrimp soup

1. Arrange halibut in 2-quart (8 x 8) glass baking dish with thick edges toward outside of dish. Place broccoli, stalks toward outside of dish, on top of fillets. Sprinkle with tarragon. Cover with plastic wrap.

2. Microwave on HIGH for 12 to 14 minutes or until fish flakes easily and broccoli is tender-crisp. Let stand, covered, while making sauce.

3. Pour soup in 2-cup glass measure or glass serving bowl.

4. Microwave on HIGH for 3 to 4 minutes or until hot. Serve sauce over fillets and broccoli.

About 4 Servings

Standing time key to well-cooked stuffing.

STUFFED WALLEYED PIKE*

> 1½ lbs. fresh whole walleyed pike
> Salt
> 2 tablespoons butter or margarine
> 2 tablespoons chopped green onion
> ⅛ teaspoon dried parsley flakes
> ⅓ cup dry white wine or water
> 1 cup crushed herb seasoned stuffing mix

1. Cut off large fin on back of pike. Sprinkle inside of pike with salt; set aside. Combine butter, onion and parsley in medium glass mixing bowl.

2. Microwave on ROAST for 2 to 3 minutes or until onion is partly cooked; stir in wine and stuffing mix. Stuff and tie with string or fasten with toothpicks. Place fish in 2-quart (12 x 7) glass baking dish. Cover with plastic wrap.

3. Microwave on HIGH for 5 minutes; turn fish, and continue cooking on HIGH for 5 to 6 minutes or until fish flakes easily. Let stand, covered, 5 minutes before serving. About 4 Servings

Pictured: Stuffed Walleyed Pike garnished with parsley and lemon twists, this page.

OVEN-COOKED SHELLFISH KEY:

Oven-cook lobster, shrimp or scampi on Microwave HIGH. Cook snails, clams, scallops and oysters on Microwave ROAST. Lower setting eliminates any chance of "popping." DO NOT OVERCOOK!

Microwave fresh or frozen shellfish. Many recipes call for frozen shellfish because it is nearly always available. However, fresh shellfish can be used.

Defrost frozen shellfish using the chart on page 22. Note that thawing is completed under cold, running water.

Shellfish in the shell cook in the same time as shellfish without a shell.

Snail or bowl-shaped natural shells are safe attractive microwave cooking containers.

When recipe calls for "standing time," follow directions carefully.

Shellfish are sometimes cooked covered. When a recipe calls for a cover, use a fitted glass lid or a tightly-tucked piece of plastic wrap across the top of the cooking casserole or dish.

Cook shellfish last when serving with vegetables or rice cooked in the microwave oven because these two hold heat and texture longer after cooking.

Shellfish finish cooking after being taken from the oven. Keep dish covered so food at center cooks completely and edges stay tender-moist.

WINE SCAMPI*

> 2 tablespoons butter or margarine
> 1 clove garlic, finely chopped
> 3 tablespoons dry white wine
> 1 package (10 oz.) frozen uncooked scampi, thawed
> Parsley

1. Combine butter, garlic and wine in 1½-quart glass casserole.

2. Microwave on ROAST for 2 to 3 minutes or until melted. Add scampi.

3. Microwave on HIGH for 4 minutes. Stir and continue cooking on HIGH for about 2 minutes or until scampi turns pink. Garnish with snipped parsley. Let stand 5 minutes before serving.

2 to 3 Servings

TIP ● Substitute shrimp for the larger scampi in recipe.

SCALLOPED OYSTERS

> ½ cup butter or margarine
> 1½ cups dry bread crumbs
> ½ cup grated Parmesan cheese
> ⅛ teaspoon pepper
> Ground mace
> 2 cans (8 oz. each) oysters, undrained
> ¼ cup dry sherry or water

1. Place butter in 4-cup glass measure.

2. Microwave on ROAST for 2 to 2½ minutes or until melted. Blend in bread crumbs, cheese, pepper and mace. Arrange half of crumb mixture in bottom of 1½-quart (10 x 6) glass baking dish. Spoon oysters evenly over crumbs. Pour oyster liquid and sherry over all. Top with remaining crumbs.

3. Microwave on ROAST for 9 to 10 minutes or until oysters are hot. Let stand 5 minutes before serving.

4 to 6 Servings

TIP ● Substitute canned whole clams for oysters.

STEAMED OR POACHED FISH KEY: Steam or poach fish in a microwave oven on HIGH. DO NOT OVERCOOK!

Try whole fish, fillets or steaks.

Steaks may be substituted for fillets with a slight increase in cooking time.

Sole, perch, halibut, snapper, flounder and whitefish may be interchanged in these recipes.

Use fresh or frozen fish. Defrost frozen fish using the chart on page 22. Note that thawing is completed under cold running water.

Fish is always poached or steamed in a flat glass dish which does not have its own lid. Since a cover is needed, tightly tuck plastic wrap over top of dish.

Arrange fish so larger pieces and thicker edges are toward the outside of the cooking dish where food cooks sooner.

Microwave a fish dish last when serving with vegetables and/or rice cooked in a microwave oven because these hold heat and texture longest.

Test for doneness when fish comes from the oven. It should flake when lifted gently with a fork near the center.

Fish finishes cooking during standing time. Keep fish covered so edges stay moist, center cooks completely.

Favorite recipes for both fish and seafood cooked by the conventional methods can be cooked in a microwave — but these will need less moisture, butter and cooking time. Adapt by checking similar microwave-tested recipes in this section.

Serve with fruit and you can put a meal on the table in about 20 minutes.

FILLETS WITH LEMON RICE

    1½ cups quick-cooking rice
    ¼ cup chopped onion
    1 teaspoon salt
    1 teaspoon dried parsley flakes
    ½ teaspoon ground thyme
    2 tablespoons lemon juice
    1¼ cups water
    1 lb. frozen fish fillets, thawed
    2 tablespoons butter or margarine
       Dash paprika

1. Combine rice, onion, salt, parsley, thyme, lemon juice and water in 2-quart glass casserole. Arrange fillets on top of rice mixture with thick edges toward outside of dish. Dot with butter; sprinkle with paprika. Cover with glass lid or plastic wrap.

2. Microwave on HIGH for 10 to 12 minutes or until fish flakes easily. Let stand, covered, 5 minutes before serving.   About 4 Servings

Bay leaf adds a special flavor.

SAUCY SOLE IN WINE*

    1 lb. frozen sole fillets, thawed
    2 teaspoons all-purpose flour
    ⅓ cup dry white wine or water
    ½ teaspoon salt
    2 green onions, sliced
    1 teaspoon dried parsley flakes
    ½ bay leaf
    2 tablespoons milk

1. Arrange fillets in 1½-quart (10 x 6) glass baking dish with thick edges toward outside of dish. Combine flour and wine in small mixing bowl. Add salt, onions, parsley and bay leaf. Pour over fillets. Cover with plastic wrap.

2. Microwave on HIGH for 4 minutes. Spoon sauce over fish again; recover, and continue cooking on HIGH for 3 to 4 minutes or until fillets flake easily. Let stand, covered, 5 minutes before serving.   About 4 Servings

SALMON WITH MUSHROOM STUFFING

    4 salmon steaks, cut ¾ inch thick
    ¼ teaspoon salt
    ¼ cup butter or margarine
    ¼ cup chopped onion
    ½ cup chopped celery
    3 cups soft bread cubes
    2 cups fresh sliced mushrooms
    2 teaspoons dried parsley flakes
    ¼ teaspoon salt
    ⅛ teaspoon pepper
    1 tablespoon lemon juice
    ½ cup milk

1. Arrange salmon steaks in 2-quart (12 x 7) glass baking dish with thick edges toward outside of dish. Sprinkle with salt; set aside. Combine butter, onion and celery in large glass mixing bowl.

2. Microwave on ROAST for 3 to 4 minutes or until vegetables are partly cooked. Stir in bread cubes, mushrooms, parsley, salt, pepper and lemon juice; mix well. Sprinkle on top of salmon steaks. Pour milk over all. Cover with plastic wrap.

3. Microwave on HIGH for 12 to 14 minutes or until salmon flakes easily. Let stand, covered, 5 minutes before serving. Garnish with lemon slices.   About 4 Servings

A tender classic – do not overcook.

POACHED FISH

     3 **cups water**
     ¼ **cup vinegar**
     ¼ **cup finely chopped carrot**
     ¼ **cup finely chopped onion**
     2 **teaspoons salt**
     5 **peppercorns**
     1 **tablespoon dried parsley flakes**
     1 **bay leaf**
     ⅛ **teaspoon ground thyme**
     2 **lbs. frozen fish, thawed**

1. Combine all ingredients except fish in 2-quart (12 x 7) glass baking dish.
2. Microwave on HIGH for 16 to 18 minutes or until boiling. Strain broth and return to baking dish. Arrange fish with thick edges toward outside of dish. Cover with plastic wrap and continue cooking on HIGH for 8 to 10 minutes or until fish flakes easily. Let stand, covered, 5 minutes. Remove from broth and serve.   About 4 Servings

TIPS • To eliminate need to strain broth, tie carrots, onion, peppercorns, parsley and bay leaf in small square of cheese cloth and remove after cooking.

    • Poach whole fish or larger pieces of un-boned fish.

Lower ROAST setting is used at first so mushrooms will not pop.

MUSHROOM-LEMON FILLETS

     ¼ **cup butter or margarine**
     2 **cups sliced fresh mushrooms**
     ¼ **cup sliced green onion**
     2 **tablespoons all-purpose flour**
     1 **teaspoon salt**
     1 **teaspoon dried parsley flakes**
     1 **teaspoon grated lemon peel**
     ⅛ **teaspoon pepper**
     1 **cup milk**
     2 **lbs. frozen fish fillets, thawed**

1. Place butter, mushrooms and onion in 2-quart (12 x 7) glass baking dish.

2. Microwave on ROAST for 3 to 4 minutes or until onion is partly cooked. Blend in flour, salt, parsley flakes, lemon peel and pepper. Stir in milk; mix well. Cover with plastic wrap and continue cooking on ROAST for 6 to 7 minutes or until mixture bubbles. Stir well. Arrange fillets with thick edges toward outside of dish. Spoon sauce over fillets. Cover with plastic wrap.

4. Microwave on HIGH for 11 to 12 minutes or until fish flakes easily. Let stand, covered, 5 minutes before serving.   6 to 8 Servings

TIP • Substitute 1 can (4 oz.) mushroom stems and pieces, drained, for fresh mushrooms.

Try sole, whitefish or halibut.

CREOLE FISH

     2 **tablespoons butter or margarine**
     ¼ **cup chopped onion**
     ½ **cup chopped celery**
     ¼ **cup chopped green pepper**
     ¼ **teaspoon salt**
     ½ **teaspoon leaf basil**
     1 **lb. frozen fish fillets, thawed**
     1 **can (10¾ oz.) condensed tomato soup**

1. Combine butter, onion, celery, green pepper, salt and basil in 1½-quart (10 x 6) glass baking dish.

2. Microwave on ROAST for 3 to 4 minutes or until onion is partly cooked. Arrange fillets in seasoned butter with thick edges toward outside of dish. Spoon soup over fillets. Cover with plastic wrap.

3. Microwave on HIGH for 7 to 8 minutes or until fillets flake easily. Let stand, covered, 5 minutes before serving.   About 4 Servings

Canned salmon makes this supper dish superb.

TENDER-CRISP VEGETABLES WITH SALMON

     4 **medium carrots, thinly sliced**
     3 **stalks celery, sliced ¼ inch thick**
     6 **small onions, cut in half**
     1 **cup water**
     1 **teaspoon salt**
     3 **tablespoons all-purpose flour**
     1 **cup milk**
     1 **can (16 oz.) salmon, undrained and flaked**
     1 **tablespoon Worcestershire sauce**
Dash pepper
     ½ **cup shredded Cheddar cheese**

1. Combine carrots, celery, onions, water and salt in 2-quart glass casserole. Cover with glass lid or plastic wrap.

2. Microwave on HIGH for 10 to 12 minutes or until vegetables are partly cooked. Combine flour and milk in medium mixing bowl; mix well. Stir in flaked salmon, Worcestershire sauce and pepper. Mix into vegetables; recover.

3. Microwave on HIGH for 11 to 12 minutes or until vegetables are tender-crisp and sauce thickened. Stir in cheese. Let stand, covered, 5 minutes before serving.   4 to 6 Servings

STEAMED OR POACHED SHELLFISH KEY:
Juicy, tender lobster and shrimp or scampi should be steamed or poached on Microwave HIGH. Cook snails, scallops, clams and oysters on Microwave ROAST to prevent "popping."

Check the chart on page 22 when defrosting frozen shellfish. Fresh shellfish, however, may be used in these recipes.

Cooking time is the same whether fish are in or out of the shell because shell does not absorb heat.

Shellfish is steamed or poached, covered, in a glass casserole with a fitted lid or tightly-tucked piece of plastic wrap.

Microwave shellfish dishes last when serving with vegetables or rice cooked in a microwave oven. These have a longer holding time after being taken from the oven.

Keep shellfish dishes covered during standing time so fish center cooks completely and edges stay moist.

GARNISHES FOR FISH AND SEAFOOD

- Lemon or orange slices

- Toasted almonds

- Finely chopped green onions, including tops

- Dried or fresh parsley

- Fresh tomato slices

- Dried leaf basil or marjoram

SAUCES FOR FISH AND SEAFOOD

- Drawn or melted butter

- Cucumber, Hollandaise, tartar, cocktail or dill

FRESH LOBSTER

    ½ **cup water**
    ½ **teaspoon salt**
  1½ **lb. fresh lobster, pegged**

1. Combine water and salt in 4-quart casserole.

2. Microwave on HIGH for 2 to 3 minutes or until water boils. Place lobster in casserole. Cover with glass lid or plastic wrap.

3. Microwave on HIGH for 10 to 12 minutes or until shell turns red. Let stand, covered, for 2 minutes. Split tail; if meat is still translucent in center continue cooking 1 to 2 more minutes. Serve with melted or drawn butter.   1 to 3 Servings

FROZEN LOBSTER TAILS, THAWED

1. Split each 9-ounce tail through top shell. Pull lobster meat out of shell; place on top, but leave connected to shell end. Brush with melted butter or margarine. Sprinkle with paprika. Arrange in 2-quart (12 x 7) glass baking dish. Cover with plastic wrap.

2. Microwave on HIGH:
    1 lobster tail — 4 to 5 minutes;
    2 lobster tails — 7 to 8 minutes;
    4 lobster tails — 11 to 12 minutes.
Let stand, covered, 5 minutes before serving.

Check chart for defrosting instructions.

SHRIMP CURRY

    ¼ **cup butter or margarine**
    ¼ **cup chopped onion**
    ½ **cup chopped celery**
    2 **tablespoons chopped green pepper**
    3 **tablespoons all-purpose flour**
    2 **teaspoons curry powder**
    1 **teaspoon instant chicken bouillon**
    ½ **cup water**
    ½ **cup milk**
    1 **package (12 oz.) frozen uncooked shrimp, thawed**

1. Combine butter, onion and celery in 2-quart glass casserole.

2. Microwave on ROAST for 3 to 4 minutes or until vegetables are partly cooked. Stir in remaining ingredients. Cover with glass lid or plastic wrap.

3. Microwave on HIGH for 13 to 14 minutes or until shrimp turns pink. Serve over hot rice.
    4 to 6 Servings

TIPS • If serving curry with rice, cook rice in microwave oven while mixing together other ingredients. Cook curry while rice rests, covered.

    • Condiments to pass with curry: toasted coconut, chopped peanuts, pickle relish, chunky sliced green onions, raisins or crumbled crisp bacon.

Careful covering is secret to tender shrimp, fluffy rice.

SHRIMP FLAMENCO*

    1 package (6 oz.) herb seasoned rice mix
    1 can (16 oz.) tomatoes, undrained
    2 tablespoons butter or margarine
    1 cup water
    1 package (12 oz.) frozen uncooked shrimp, thawed
    1 can (10¾ oz.) condensed cream of chicken soup
    2 tablespoons milk
    1 tablespoon dry white wine or lemon juice
    ½ teaspoon salt
    Dash cayenne pepper
    1 tablespoon dried parsley flakes

1. Combine rice mix, tomatoes, butter and water in 2-quart glass casserole. Cover with glass lid or plastic wrap.

2. Microwave on HIGH for 6 minutes; stir.

3. Microwave on DEFROST for 12 to 15 minutes or until rice is tender. Let stand, covered, until shrimp is cooked. Combine shrimp, soup, milk, wine and seasonings in 1½-quart glass casserole. Cover with glass lid or plastic wrap.

4. Microwave on HIGH for 5 minutes. Stir and continue cooking on HIGH for 3 to 4 minutes. Let stand, covered, 5 minutes before serving. Serve over hot rice mixture.   4 to 5 Servings

Cooking time is the same whether seafood is in or out of the shell.

SWEET 'N SOUR SHRIMP

    ¼ cup sugar
    3 tablespoons cornstarch
    ½ teaspoon ground ginger
    1 teaspoon paprika
    2 tablespoons soy sauce
    ¼ cup vinegar
    1 can (13¼ oz.) pineapple tidbits
    1 package (12 oz.) frozen uncooked shrimp, thawed
    3 green onions, finely sliced
    ¼ cup sliced celery
    1 green pepper, cut into strips
    1 medium tomato, chopped

1. Combine sugar, cornstarch, ginger, paprika, soy sauce and vinegar in 2-quart glass casserole; mix well. Stir in remaining ingredients except tomato. Cover with glass lid or plastic wrap.

2. Microwave on HIGH for 13 to 14 minutes or until shrimp turns pink. Stir in tomato. Let stand, covered, 5 minutes before serving.

    4 to 6 Servings

> **FISH WITH EGGS OR CREAM KEY:** Cook fish dishes made with cream or eggs on Microwave ROAST. Slower cooking keeps sauce mixtures from separating. DO NOT OVERCOOK!
>
> Whole fish, fillets, steaks or canned fish cook well in a microwave.
>
> Substitute steaks for fillets, if desired, with a slight increase in cooking time.
>
> Interchange sole, perch, halibut, snapper, flounder and whitefish in these recipes.
>
> Either fresh or frozen fish may be used. Defrost frozen fish using the chart on page 22.
>
> Arrange fish so larger pieces and thicker edges are toward the outside of the glass baking dish or casserole.
>
> Creamed or egg mixtures are usually covered tightly. Use a fitted glass lid or plastic wrap stretched tautly across top of cooking dish.
>
> Cook a fish dish last when serving with vegetables and/or rice cooked in a microwave oven because these hold heat and texture longer.
>
> Test for doneness when fish is taken from the oven. It should flake when lifted gently with a fork near the center.
>
> Fish finishes cooking during standing time. Keep fish covered so edges stay moist, center cooks completely.
>
> Adapt favorite, conventional fish and seafood recipes to microwave cooking. Use less moisture, butter and cooking time — check similar microwave-tested recipes in this section to compute new amounts and times.

Also good made with canned tuna.

SALMON IN THE ROUND

    3 eggs
    1 can (16 oz.) red salmon, drained and flaked
    1 cup dry bread crumbs
    ½ cup chopped celery
    ¼ cup chopped green pepper
    2 tablespoons finely chopped onion
    1 tablespoon lemon juice
    ¾ cup milk

1. Break eggs into 1½-quart glass casserole; stir with fork. Stir in remaining ingredients; mix well.

2. Microwave on ROAST for 18 to 20 minutes or until mixture is set in center. Let stand 5 minutes before serving.   About 6 Servings

TIP ● Substitute 2 cans (7 oz. each) tuna for salmon.

ROAST setting keeps cream sauce smooth.

FISH FILLETS IN CUCUMBER SAUCE

    1 medium cucumber, unpeeled and
       chopped
    ½ teaspoon dill weed
    2 tablespoons butter or margarine
    1 can (10¾ oz.) condensed cream of
       mushroom soup
    ⅓ cup sour cream
    1 medium tomato chopped
    2 tablespoons butter or margarine
    ½ teaspoon salt
    2 lbs. frozen fish fillets, thawed

1. Combine cucumber, dill weed and 2 tablespoons butter in 4-cup glass measure.

2. Microwave on ROAST for 3 to 4 minutes or until
butter is melted. Stir in soup, sour cream and tomato; set aside. Combine butter and salt in 2-quart
(12 x 7) glass baking dish.

3. Microwave on ROAST for about 1 minute or
until melted. Arrange fish with thick edges toward
outside of dish. Pour sauce over fish. Cover with
plastic wrap.

4. Microwave on ROAST 18 to 20 minutes or until
fish flakes easily. Let stand, covered, 5 minutes before serving.   6 to 8 Servings

SALMON STEAKS WITH LEMON DILL SAUCE*

    4 salmon steaks, ¾ inch thick
    1 medium onion, sliced
    1 teaspoon instant chicken bouillon
    1 tablespoon lemon juice
    1 teaspoon dill weed
    ½ teaspoon salt
    1 cup water

Sauce:
    2 tablespoons butter or margarine
    2 tablespoons all-purpose flour
    ½ teaspoon salt
    ½ cup light cream
    2 tablespoons lemon juice

1. Arrange salmon steaks in 2-quart (12 x 7) glass
baking dish with thick edges toward outside of dish.
Top with onion, instant bouillon, lemon juice, dill, salt
and water. Cover with plastic wrap.

2. Microwave on HIGH for 10 to 12 minutes or
until fish flakes easily. Let stand, covered, 5 minutes
and serve with hot Sauce. Garnish with parsley.

3. Sauce: Place butter in 2-cup glass measure.

4. Microwave on ROAST for about 1 minute or
until melted. Blend in flour and salt. Stir in cream,
lemon juice, fish liquid; mix until smooth.

5. Microwave on ROAST for 3 minutes. Stir and
continue cooking on ROAST for 2 to 3 minutes or
until mixture bubbles.   About 4 Servings

SHELLFISH WITH CREAM OR EGGS KEY:
Shellfish cooked with cream or eggs needs the
lower Microwave ROAST setting to keep
sauces from separating. DO NOT OVERCOOK!
    Use the chart on page 22 when defrosting
frozen shellfish. Fresh shellfish, however, may
be substituted in these recipes.
    Shellfish with cream or egg sauces are usu-
ally cooked in a glass casserole with a fitted lid
or a taut cover of plastic wrap.
    Microwave shellfish dishes last when serving
with vegetables or rice cooked in a microwave
oven. These have a longer holding time after
cooking.
    Keep shellfish dishes covered during stand-
ing time so food in center of dish cooks completely and edges stay moist.

*Frozen breaded scallops do not need to be thawed
or covered during cooking.*

SCALLOPS WITH DEVILED SAUCE

    2 packages (7 oz. each) frozen breaded
       scallops
    ¾ cup milk
    2 teaspoons snipped chives
    2 teaspoons Dijon mustard
    ¼ cup sour cream

1. Place frozen scallops on glass serving platter.

2. Microwave on ROAST for 6 to 8 minutes or until
piping hot. Combine milk, chives, mustard and sour
cream in 2-cup glass measure; mix well.

3. Microwave on ROAST for 2 to 3 minutes or until
mixture thickens slightly. Let stand, covered, 5
minutes. Pour sauce over scallops or into gravy boat
to pass with scallops.   4 Servings

TIP ● Substitute 1 teaspoon dry mustard for Dijon
mustard.

SEAFOOD THERMIDOR

    1 can (10¾ oz.) condensed cream of
       shrimp soup
    1 can (4 oz.) sliced mushrooms, drained
    1 can (6½ oz.) cooked lobster meat,
       drained and diced
    ¼ cup milk
    ¼ teaspoon dry mustard
    Cayenne pepper
    Grated Parmesan cheese
    Dash paprika

1. Combine all ingredients, except cheese and paprika, in large mixing bowl; mix well. Spoon into 4
individual glass casseroles or natural baking shells.
Sprinkle with Parmesan cheese and paprika.

2. Microwave on ROAST for 6 to 7 minutes or until
bubbly. Let stand 5 minutes before serving.
                                 About 4 Servings

Cook and serve in natural shells for a pretty dish.

COQUILLES ST. JACQUES*

¼ cup butter or margarine
¼ cup chopped celery
1 can (4 oz.) sliced mushrooms, drained
2 medium green onions, sliced
2 tablespoons chopped green pepper
2 tablespoons all-purpose flour
½ teaspoon salt
⅛ teaspoon pepper
1 bay leaf
½ cup dry white wine
1 lb. sea scallops
1 tablespoon chopped pimento
¼ cup light cream
1 egg yolk

Buttered Bread Crumbs:
2 tablespoons butter or margarine
2 tablespoons dry bread crumbs
2 tablespoons grated Parmesan cheese

1. Combine butter, celery, mushrooms, onions and green pepper in 2-quart glass casserole.

2. Microwave on ROAST for 3 to 4 minutes or until onion is tender. Stir in flour, salt, pepper, bay leaf and wine; mix well. Add scallops and pimento.

3. Microwave on ROAST for 6 minutes. Stir and continue cooking on ROAST for 2 to 3 minutes or until thickened. Mix together in small bowl, cream and egg yolk; stir into scallop mixture.

4. Microwave on ROAST for 2 to 3 minutes or until piping hot. Remove bay leaf. Spoon into 4 natural shells or 1-cup glass serving dishes.

5. Sprinkle about 1 tablespoon Buttered Bread Crumbs on each serving. Microwave on REHEAT for 1 to 2 minutes or until heated through. Let stand, covered, 5 minutes before serving.

6. Buttered Bread Crumbs: Place 2 tablespoons butter in 1-cup glass measure.

7. Microwave on ROAST for 1 to 1½ minutes or until melted. Stir in bread crumbs and Parmesan cheese.   4 Servings

Make sure final cooking is on lower, ROAST setting.

SCALLOPS POULETTE*

¼ cup butter or margarine
1 tablespoon finely chopped onion
¼ cup unsifted all-purpose flour
½ teaspoon salt
⅛ teaspoon pepper
½ cup dry white wine or chicken broth
1 can (4 oz.) mushroom stems and pieces, drained
1 package (12 oz.) frozen sea scallops, thawed
1 bay leaf
½ cup light cream
1 egg yolk
1 teaspoon dried parsley flakes

1. Combine butter and onion in 2-quart glass casserole.

2. Microwave on ROAST for 3 to 4 minutes or until onions are partly cooked. Blend in flour, salt and pepper. Stir in wine, mushrooms, scallops and bay leaf. Cover with glass lid or plastic wrap.

3. Microwave on ROAST for 5 minutes. Stir and continue cooking on ROAST for 5 to 6 minutes or until scallops are fork tender. Combine cream and egg yolk in small mixing bowl. Gradually stir into hot mixture. Recover.

4. Microwave on ROAST for 3 to 4 minutes or until hot. Let stand, covered, 5 minutes before serving. Add parsley and serve.   About 4 Servings

Make ahead and reheat for a party.

SEAFOOD NEWBURG*

¼ cup butter or margarine
1½ tablespoons all-purpose flour
½ teaspoon salt
1½ cups light cream
2 egg yolks
¼ cup dry sherry or water
1 package (12 oz.) cooked lobster, crab or shrimp

1. Place butter in 1½-quart glass casserole.

2. Microwave on ROAST for 2 to 3 minutes or until melted. Blend in flour and salt. Combine cream and egg yolks; mix well. Stir into flour mixture to form smooth paste. Add sherry and seafood. Cover with glass lid or plastic wrap.

3. Microwave on ROAST for 6 minutes. Stir and continue cooking on ROAST for 5 to 6 minutes or until mixture thickens. Let stand, covered, 5 minutes before serving. Serve over toast points, patty shells or cooked rice.   5 to 6 Servings

Delicate flavor! Tender juicy meat! Crunchy crumb coatings and savory sauces! A microwave oven offers a wealth of versatility to those who enjoy nutritious chicken, turkey and other poultry.

Time-saving microwave techniques vary with size of bird; whether cut up or whole; sauced or crumb coated; how tender and/or fat. The **cooking chart and "grey box"** keys outline each microwave cooking method in detail.

Giblets are a gourmet bonus. Save and microwave these into delicious broth for soups or gravy — there's a recipe in the soup chapter.

A microwave oven is especially helpful when defrosting poultry — check the chart in this chapter for exact instructions.

Take the time to become familiar with these recipes — then enjoy adapting other special recipes to microwave cooking.

Pictured top to bottom: Roast Duckling, page 44; Stuffin' Mix Chicken, page 40; Ruby Red Cranberry Stuffing, page 45.

POULTRY/GAME BIRD CHAPTER CONTENTS

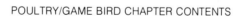

HOW TO DEFROST POULTRY

● Thaw poultry in its original wrapping including metal clip. Place in a large flat glass baking dish to catch drippings.

● Whole poultry and parts weighing 4 pounds and over are thawed on ROAST.

● Whole poultry and parts weighing under 4 pounds are thawed on DEFROST. This defrosting technique sends enough heat into meat to warm and defrost center without starting cooking process at outer edges.

● Start whole birds thawing with breast side up. See chart for specific oven settings and times.

● Poultry should be icy in center when taken from the microwave oven.

● Finish thawing by immersing poultry in cold water. If not completely thawed, poultry will take longer to cook and will not cook evenly.

● Remove loosened giblets from whole birds and set aside for gravy or soup broth. See soup chapter for directions.

POULTRY	WEIGHT	SETTING	TIME
CHICKEN			
Whole, fryer	2 to 3-lb.	DEFROST	20 to 25 min.
Whole, roasting	3 to 4-lb.	DEFROST	25 to 30 min.
Cut Up	2½ to 3-lb.	DEFROST	14 to 16 min.
Breasts	4 to 6 (½ lb. ea.)	DEFROST	15 to 17 min.
Drumsticks and Thighs	4 (½ lb. ea.)	DEFROST	8 to 10 min.
Drumsticks	about 1 lb.	DEFROST	7 to 8 min.
Thighs	about 1 lb.	DEFROST	7 to 8 min.
Wings	1½ lbs.	DEFROST	6 to 8 min.
Stewing Hen, cut up	2½ to 3-lb.	DEFROST	25 to 30 min.
Liver and/or Hearts	8 ozs. 2 lbs.	DEFROST	5 to 6 min. 9 to 10 min.
TURKEY			
Whole	8 to 12-lb.	ROAST	15 min., rest 10 min.; turn over; 15 min. Stand in cold water about 1 hr.
	12 to 16-lb.	ROAST	20 min., rest 10 min.; turn over; 20 min. Stand in cold water about 1½ hrs.
	16 to 20-lb.	ROAST	15 min., rest 10 min.; turn over; 15 min., rest 10 min.; repeat once. Stand in cold water about 2 hrs.

POULTRY	WEIGHT	SETTING	TIME
Breast, Bone-In	4 to 8-lb.	ROAST	10 min.; rest 10 min.; turn over; 10 min. Stand in cold water about 10 min.
Drumsticks	1 to 2-lb. 2 to 3-lb.	DEFROST	15 to 20 min. 25 to 30 min.
Thigh	1 to 2-lb.	DEFROST	15 to 20 min.
Wings	2 to 3-lb.	DEFROST	20 to 25 min.
CAPON Whole	6 to 8-lb.	ROAST	15 min., rest 10 min.; turn over; 15 min. Stand in cold water about 1 hr.
DUCKLING Whole	4 to 5-lb.	ROAST	10 min., rest 10 min.; turn over; 10 min. Stand in cold water for about 30 min.
GOOSE Whole	9 to 11-lb.	ROAST	20 min., rest 10 min.; turn over; 20 min. Stand in cold water about 1 hr.
PHEASANT Cut up	2 to 3-lb.	DEFROST	12 to 15 min.
ROCK CORNISH GAME HEN Whole	2 (12 oz. ea.) 4 (12 oz. ea.)	DEFROST	15 to 18 min. 20 to 25 min.

HOW TO COOK POULTRY

● Poultry should be completely thawed before cooking. See defrosting chart in this chapter.

● Season meat to taste before cooking.

● Place large whole poultry in 3-quart (13 x 9) glass baking dish; small whole birds and poultry pieces in 2-quart (12 x 7) glass baking dish.

● Use a microwave roasting rack in the dish when cooking whole birds.

● Arrange pieces of poultry with skin side up and thick edges toward outside of dish.

● Metal clip holding drumsticks may be left in place on large whole birds during cooking. Pop-out "doneness indicators" may be left in birds but will not indicate doneness in microwave cooking.

● Most whole poultry is cooked uncovered.

● When two different settings are mentioned, use HIGH during first cooking period; ROAST during the second.

● Stuffing does not increase cooking time.   *(Continued, next page)*

• Foil may be used to cover portions of the meat that appear to be drying during cooking. Do not allow foil to touch oven interior or the microwaves will arc and pit oven surfaces.

• Chicken and turkey pieces cooked without sauce or crumb coating should be covered during cooking and standing time. Use tightly-tucked plastic wrap or wax paper. Pierce wrap before removing it so steam escapes slowly and does not burn hands.

• Poultry weighing 10 pounds or less should be turned over once during cooking; when over 10 pounds, turn over three times.

• A microwave meat thermometer, registering 170° F. when bird comes from the oven, is an accurate test for doneness with whole birds. When a bird must be turned (Rock Cornish Game Hens are not), insert thermometer into thick part of the thigh after bird is turned the last time. DO NOT use a regular meat thermometer in a microwave oven.

• Other doneness tests: Meat and juices are no longer pink when bird is sliced between leg and body. Leg and thigh meat of small birds is tender when pinched. A conventional meat thermometer, inserted in thickest part of thigh meat after bird comes from oven, registers 170° F. At the end of cooking time. It is a good idea to check doneness in both thighs in birds weighing 10 pounds or more.

• Poultry skin may be crisped by placing it under a conventional oven broiler for a few minutes before standing time.

• Standing time is ESSENTIAL to complete cooking. Allow whole birds or pieces totaling 10 pounds or less to stand 5 to 10 minutes after being taken from oven. Birds and pieces over 10 pounds should stand 10 to 15 minutes — internal temperature will rise 10° F. to 15° F.

• Cover whole birds tightly with foil during standing time. Cover cut-up poultry with glass lid, plastic wrap or wax paper.

• Duck and goose are fatty meats. Drain excess fat from dish during cooking to prevent spatters and burning.

POULTRY	WEIGHT	FIRST SETTING	SECOND SETTING	APPROXIMATE COOKING TIME
CHICKEN*				
Whole, fryer	2 to 3-lb.	HIGH	HIGH	8 min. per lb.
Whole, roasting	3 to 4-lb.	HIGH	ROAST	9 min. per lb.
Cut Up	2 to 3-lb.	HIGH	HIGH	8 min. per lb.
Parts	1 to 2 lbs.	HIGH	HIGH	8 min. per lb.
TURKEY*				
Whole	8 to 10-lb.	HIGH	ROAST	8 min. per lb.
	10 to 14-lb.	HIGH	ROAST	9 min. per lb.
Breast, bone-in	4 to 5-lb.	ROAST	ROAST	11 min. per lb.
Parts	2 to 3-lb.	ROAST	ROAST	15 min. per lb.
CAPON*				
Whole	6 to 8-lb.	HIGH	ROAST	8 min. per lb.
DUCKLING*				
Whole	4 to 5-lb.	ROAST	ROAST	10 min. per lb.
GOOSE*				
Whole	9 to 11-lb.	ROAST	ROAST	10 min. per lb.
PHEASANT*				
Cut Up	2 to 3-lb.	ROAST	ROAST	8 min. per lb.
ROCK CORNISH GAME HEN*				
Whole	4 (12 oz. ea.)	HIGH	HIGH	9 min. per lb.

HOW TO COOK A FEW CHICKEN PIECES

- Microwave 1 tablespoon butter on ROAST setting until melted.
- Roll chicken piece in melted butter, then in seasoned dry bread crumbs.
- Place chicken, skin side down, in glass pie plate or flat baking dish.
- Turn chicken piece(s) over halfway through cooking time.
- Microwave on HIGH until fork tender.

CHICKEN PIECE	WEIGHT	SETTING	TIME
1 WING OR DRUMSTICK	4-oz.	HIGH	4 to 4½ min.
1 THIGH OR BREAST	5 to 6-oz.	HIGH	5 to 6 min.
3 INDIVIDUAL PIECES Assorted	14-oz.	HIGH	10 to 11 min.
1 THIGH-LEG (2 PIECES ATTACHED)	9-oz.	HIGH	7 to 8 min.
1 QUARTER	10-oz.	HIGH	8 to 9 min.

WHOLE CHICKEN AND CAPON KEY: Small tender whole chicken, 3 pounds and under, may be cooked quickly on Microwave HIGH. Whole chicken and capon over 3 pounds begins cooking on HIGH to heat meat through. Then continues on ROAST to tenderize meat and keep it juicy.

Thaw poultry completely before cooking. See defrosting chart in this chapter.

Stuffing will not increase cooking time.

Arrange birds, breast side down on microwave roasting rack, to hold them above drippings.

Place rack in flat glass baking dish to catch juices.

Turn poultry over once halfway through cooking when weight is under 10 pounds. See cooking chart for larger birds.

Drain fat from dish in which goose or duck are cooking halfway through cooking period. Draining prevents spatters and possible burning.

Foil may be used to cover portions of meat which appear to be drying during cooking. Do not let foil touch oven interior or arcing and pitting may result.

Skin may be crisped under a conventional oven broiler. Broil just a few minutes then let bird stand as recipe directs.

Standing time is essential to assure a well cooked bird. Follow directions carefully. Internal temperature will rise about 15° F. during standing time.

A microwave meat thermometer inserted in the thickest part of the thigh registers doneness at 170° F. at the end of cooking time. Insert thermometer after bird is turned in the oven. DO NOT use conventional meat thermometer in a microwave oven.

Other doneness tests: Meat and juices are no longer pink when bird is sliced between leg and body. A conventional meat thermometer, inserted in thickest part of the thigh AFTER bird comes from oven, registers 170° F.

ROAST CHICKEN WITH ONIONS AND APPLES

4 to 4½-lb. whole roasting chicken
Salt
Pepper
1 medium apple, peeled, cored and quartered
1 medium onion, quartered
1 medium onion, chopped
1 cup applesauce

1. Sprinkle body cavity with salt and pepper. Place quartered apple and onion in cavity. Tie legs together and wings to body. Place chicken, breast side down on microwave roasting rack, in 2-quart (12 x 7) glass baking dish.

2. Microwave on HIGH for 18 minutes. Combine chopped onion and applesauce in medium bowl. Turn breast side up; pour on applesauce mixture.

3. Microwave on ROAST for 18 to 20 minutes or until microwave meat thermometer registers 170° F. Let stand, covered with foil, 5 to 10 minutes before serving.   4 to 6 Servings

Check internal temperature at end of standing time – it should register about 185° F.

ROAST CAPON*

6 lb. whole capon
4 cups prepared stuffing

1. Wash capon; set aside giblets. Fill neck opening and body cavity with stuffing. Secure openings with toothpicks or metal skewers. Tie legs together and wings to body. Place capon, breast side down on microwave roasting rack, in 2-quart (12 x 7) glass baking dish.

2. Microwave on HIGH for 24 minutes. Turn breast side up.

3. Microwave on ROAST for 24 to 26 minutes or until microwave meat thermometer registers 170° F. after cooking. Let stand, covered with foil, 5 to 10 minutes before serving.   6 to 8 Servings

HOME STYLE BARBECUE CHICKEN*

¼ cup cooking oil
½ cup vinegar
1 tablespoon salt
1 teaspoon poultry seasoning
⅛ teaspoon pepper
2½ to 3-lb. whole frying chicken

1. Combine all ingredients, except chicken, in 2-cup glass measure; mix well. Place chicken, breast side down on microwave roasting rack, in 2-quart (12 x 7) glass baking dish. Brush with barbecue sauce.

2. Microwave on HIGH for 12 minutes. Turn breast side up; brush with remaining sauce, and continue cooking on HIGH for 10 to 15 minutes or until microwave meat thermometer registers 170° F. Let stand, covered with foil, 5 minutes before serving.   4 to 6 Servings

STUFFED CORNISH GAME HENS

¼ cup butter or margarine
1 teaspoon paprika
4 whole Rock Cornish Game Hens (12 oz. each)
1 teaspoon salt
Almond stuffing, page 45

1. Place butter and paprika in 2-cup glass measure.

2. Microwave on ROAST for about 1½ minutes or until melted; set aside.

3. Salt body cavities of hens. Fill each hen with stuffing. Tie legs together and wings to body. Arrange, breast side up and drumsticks toward center of microwave roasting rack, in 2-quart (12 x 7) glass baking dish. Brush with seasoned melted butter.

4. Microwave on HIGH for 30 to 35 minutes or until microwave meat thermometer registers 170° F. Let stand 5 minutes before serving.   4 Servings

CUT UP CHICKEN KEY: nearly all cut up chicken is cooked on Microwave HIGH. Quick cooking is possible because pieces are small and tender. However, when cream is added to a chicken sauce, the dish is cooked on ROAST to prevent separation and curdling.

Chicken should be completely thawed or it will take longer to cook. See defrosting chart on page 34.

Arrange chicken in a flat glass baking dish with thick edges and large pieces toward outside of dish where they will microwave faster.

Start cooking chicken skin side down; then turn over once to assure even cooking.

Chicken coated with a crumb mixture is cooked uncovered so it crisps.

Chicken cooked in sauce is covered with plastic wrap or wax paper during the first cooking period to blend flavors.

Remove cover during last cooking period to crisp skin surface. Chicken in cream sauce is an exception. Cover these mixtures throughout cooking. Pierce wrap before removing to prevent steam burns.

Standing time is important to assure complete cooking. Follow directions in recipes. Chicken is ready to eat when it is fork tender.

Chicken should always be completely thawed before cooking.

BOMBAY CHICKEN*

¼ cup butter or margarine
1 tablespoon curry powder
¼ teaspoon ginger
2½ to 3-lb. frying chicken, cut up
Salt
Pepper
1 medium onion, chopped
1 greening apple, peeled, cored and chopped
½ cup raisins
2 cups hot cooked rice

1. Place butter in 2-quart (12 x 7) glass baking dish.

2. Microwave on ROAST for about 1½ minutes or until melted. Stir in curry powder and ginger. Place chicken pieces, skin side down and thick edges toward outside, in curried butter. Sprinkle with salt and pepper; top with onion, apple and raisins. Cover with plastic wrap.

3. Microwave on HIGH for 20 minutes. Turn chicken over and continue cooking on HIGH for 5 to 6 minutes or until chicken is fork tender. Let stand 5 minutes before serving. Stir cooked rice into hot seasoned drippings. Serve with chicken.
          4 to 6 Servings

TIP • Final cooking is done without a cover to "crisp" skin.

ORANGE BURGUNDY CHICKEN*

  2½ **to 3-lb. frying chicken, cut up**
   ½ **cup orange marmalade**
   ½ **cup orange juice**
   ½ **cup dry red wine**
   2 **tablespoons cornstarch**
   2 **tablespoons packed brown sugar**
   1 **tablespoon lemon juice**
   1 **teaspoon salt**

1. Arrange chicken pieces, skin side down and thick edges toward outside, in 2-quart (12 x 7) glass baking dish. Combine remaining ingredients in medium mixing bowl; pour over chicken. Cover with plastic wrap.

2. Microwave on HIGH for 20 minutes. Turn chicken over and continue cooking on HIGH for 5 to 6 minutes or until chicken is fork tender. Let stand 5 minutes before serving.   4 to 6 Servings

Pictured top to bottom: Stuffed Cornish Game Hens garnished with mandarin oranges and parsley, page 38; Orange Burgundy Chicken, this page.

Cover during first part of cooking makes saucy chicken tender in a hurry.

OVEN ORANGE CHICKEN*

  2½ **to 3-lb. frying chicken, cut up**
   ¼ **cup chopped onion**
   ¼ **cup chopped green pepper**
   ⅓ **cup orange juice**
   ⅓ **cup catsup**
   2 **tablespoons all-purpose flour**
   2 **tablespoons soy sauce**
   1 **teaspoon prepared mustard**
   ½ **teaspoon salt**
   ½ **teaspoon garlic powder**
   ¼ **teaspoon pepper**
   2 **oranges, sliced**

1. Place chicken pieces, skin side down and thick edges toward outside, in 2-quart (12 x 7) glass baking dish. Sprinkle on onion and green pepper. Combine remaining ingredients, except orange slices, in small mixing bowl; pour over chicken. Cover with plastic wrap.

2. Microwave on HIGH for 20 minutes. Turn chicken over; place orange slices on top, and continue cooking on HIGH for 5 to 6 minutes or until fork tender. Let stand 5 minutes before serving.
    4 to 6 Servings

SHERRIED CHICKEN*

  2½ **to 3-lb. frying chicken, cut up**
    Salt
    Pepper
   1 **medium onion, sliced**
   2 **slices bacon, cut into pieces**
   ¼ **cup dry sherry**

1. Arrange chicken pieces, skin side down and thick edges toward outside, in 2-quart (12 x 7) glass baking dish. Sprinkle with salt and pepper. Add onion and uncooked bacon. Pour sherry over chicken. Cover with plastic wrap.

2. Microwave on HIGH for 20 minutes. Turn chicken over and continue cooking on HIGH for 5 to 6 minutes or until fork tender. Let stand 5 minutes before serving.   4 to 6 Servings

TIP • Cook chicken, uncovered, during last cooking time to "crisp" skin.

CHICKEN FOR BARBECUING

  2½ **to 3-lb. frying chicken, quartered**
    Bottled barbecue sauce

1. Place chicken, skin side down and thick edges toward outside, in 2-quart (12 x 7) glass baking dish.

2. Microwave on HIGH for 15 minutes. Remove from oven. Brush both sides of each chicken piece with barbecue sauce. Place chicken, skin side down, on barbecue grill over hot coals. Grill 15 to 20 minutes; turn occasionally, and brush with remaining barbecue sauce until chicken is fork tender.
    4 to 6 Servings

TIP • If barbecue grill has a hood, follow manufacturer's directions for barbecuing chicken.

CHICKEN AND CELERY BAKE

2½ to 3-lb. frying chicken, cut up
1 can (10¾ oz.) condensed cream of
   celery soup
¼ cup sour cream
Paprika
Hot cooked rice

1. Arrange chicken pieces, skin side down and thick edges toward outside, in 2-quart (12 x 7) glass baking dish. Cover with plastic wrap.

2. Microwave on HIGH for 10 minutes; drain. Combine soup and sour cream. Turn chicken over; pour on sauce; sprinkle with paprika, and recover.

3. Microwave on ROAST for 24 to 25 minutes or until chicken is fork tender. Let stand, covered, 5 minutes. Serve over hot rice.   5 to 6 Servings

CHICKEN WITH DRIED BEEF

3 whole chicken breasts (1 lb. each), halved
1 can (10¾ oz.) condensed cream of
   mushroom soup
½ cup sour cream
1 jar (2½ oz.) dried beef, cut into pieces
1 tablespoon dried parsley flakes

1. Place chicken breasts, skin side down and thick edges toward outside in 2-quart (12 x 7) glass baking dish. Cover with plastic wrap.

2. Microwave on HIGH for 10 minutes; drain. Combine remaining ingredients in medium mixing bowl. Turn chicken over; pour on sauce; recover.

3. Microwave on ROAST for 15 to 16 minutes or until chicken is fork tender. Let stand, covered, 5 minutes before serving.   About 6 Servings

CRUNCHY CHICKEN*

⅓ cup butter or margarine
1 clove garlic, finely chopped
¾ cup dry bread crumbs
1 tablespoon dried parsley flakes
1 teaspoon salt
¼ teaspoon poultry seasoning
⅛ teaspoon pepper
2½ to 3-lb. frying chicken, cut up

1. Place butter and garlic in 2-quart (12 x 7) glass baking dish.

2. Microwave on ROAST for about 2 minutes or until melted. Combine remaining ingredients, except chicken, in flat dish. Roll chicken in seasoned butter, then in crumb mixture. Place chicken pieces, skin side down and thick edges toward outside, in buttered baking dish. Sprinkle with remaining bread crumbs.

3. Microwave on HIGH for 12 minutes. Turn chicken over and continue cooking on HIGH for 10 to 12 minutes or until fork tender. Let stand 5 minutes before serving.   4 to 6 Servings

STUFFIN' MIX CHICKEN*

¼ cup butter or margarine
1 cup crushed seasoned stuffing mix
Hbs ¼ cup dried parsley flakes
½ teaspoon paprika
½ teaspoon leaf oregano
⅛ teaspoon leaf basil
1 teaspoon salt
⅛ teaspoon pepper
2½ to 3-lb. frying chicken, cut up
   garlic salt

1. Place butter in 2-quart (12 x 7) glass baking dish.

2. Microwave on ROAST for about 1½ minutes or until melted. Combine remaining ingredients, except chicken, in flat dish. Roll chicken pieces in melted butter, then in seasoned crumbs. Place chicken pieces, skin side down and thick edges toward outside, in buttered baking dish.

3. Microwave on HIGH for 12 minutes. Turn chicken over, and continue cooking on HIGH for 10 to 12 minutes *6-8 min* or until chicken is fork tender. Let stand 5 minutes before serving.   4 to 6 Servings

CHICKEN IN SEASONED CRUMBS*

3 tablespoons cooking oil
2½ to 3-lb. frying chicken, cut up
1 package (2⅜ oz.) seasoned coating mix

1. Brush chicken with oil. Pour coating mix into shallow dish. Roll chicken pieces in seasoned coating. Place chicken pieces, skin side down and thick edges toward outside, in 2-quart (12 x 7) glass baking dish.

2. Microwave on HIGH for 12 minutes. Turn chicken over and continue cooking on HIGH for 10 to 12 minutes or until fork tender. Let stand 5 minutes before serving.   4 to 6 Servings

TIP ● Substitute crushed corn flakes for mix.

HERBED CHICKEN BREASTS

¼ cup butter or margarine
¼ teaspoon garlic powder
¼ teaspoon pepper
⅛ teaspoon leaf oregano
1 teaspoon salt
2 whole chicken breasts (1 lb. each), halved
¼ cup dry white wine or water

1. Place butter in 2-quart (12 x 7) glass baking dish.

2. Microwave on ROAST for about 1½ minutes or until melted. Add seasonings to butter; mix well. Roll chicken breasts in seasoned butter. Place skin side down and thick edges toward outside, in buttered baking dish. Cover with plastic wrap.

3. Microwave on HIGH for 10 minutes. Turn chicken over; pour wine over all, and continue cooking on HIGH for 6 to 8 minutes or until fork tender. Let stand 5 minutes before serving.   4 Servings

Do not cover during final cooking time.

Thigh-legs in one piece are available at meat counter.

LEMON CHICKEN WINGS*

   ¼ **cup butter or margarine**
   2 **tablespoons all-purpose flour**
   1 **tablespoon lemon juice**
   1 **green onion, finely chopped**
   ½ **teaspoon paprika**
   ¼ **teaspoon salt**
   ⅛ **teaspoon ground thyme**
   Dash pepper
   ¾ **lb. chicken wings**

1. Place butter in 2-quart (8 x 8) glass baking dish.

2. Microwave on ROAST for about 1½ minutes or until melted. Stir in remaining ingredients, except chicken wings. Fold chicken wing tip under drumstick joint. Coat wings with lemon butter. Place wings, thick edges toward outside, in baking dish. Cover with plastic wrap.

3. Microwave on HIGH for 8 minutes. Turn wings over and continue cooking on HIGH for 5 to 6 minutes or until fork tender. Let stand 5 minutes before serving.   2 to 3 Servings

TIPS • Recipe may be doubled. Microwave chicken wings in 2-quart (12 x 7) glass baking dish on HIGH for 10 minutes. Turn wings over and continue cooking on HIGH for 8 to 10 minutes or until fork tender. Let stand 5 minutes before serving.

    • Serve for appetizers or as a main course.

BUTTERY CHICKEN THIGHS

   1 **tablespoon butter or margarine**
   ¼ **cup finely chopped onions**
   4 **chicken thighs (5 oz. each)**
   Salt
   Pepper
   1 **jar (2½ oz.) mushroom stems and pieces, drained**
   ¼ **cup dry white wine or water**

1. Place butter and onions in 2-quart (8 x 8) glass baking dish.

2. Microwave on ROAST for about 1½ minutes or until onion is partly cooked. Place chicken thighs, skin side down and thick edges toward outside, in butter-onion mixture. Season with salt and pepper. Cover with plastic wrap.

3. Microwave on HIGH for 15 minutes. Turn chicken over; add mushrooms and wine, and continue cooking on HIGH for 3 to 4 minutes or until thighs are fork tender. Let stand 5 minutes before serving.   2 to 3 Servings

TIP • Cook, uncovered, during final cooking time to "crisp" skin.

SWEET 'N SOUR CHICKEN THIGH-LEGS

   4 **chicken thigh-legs (9-oz. each)**
   1 **teaspoon poultry seasoning**
   2 **teaspoons salt**
   ¼ **teaspoon pepper**
   1 **can (10¾ oz.) condensed cream of mushroom soup**
   1 **can (4 oz.) mushroom stems and pieces, drained**
   ½ **cup sour cream**
   ½ **cup dry sherry or water**
   ½ **teaspoon finely chopped garlic**

1. Place chicken thigh-legs, skin side down and thick edges toward outside, in 2-quart (12 x 7) glass baking dish. Season with poultry seasoning, salt and pepper. Cover with plastic wrap.

2. Microwave on HIGH for 15 minutes; drain. Combine remaining ingredients in small mixing bowl. Turn chicken over; pour on cream soup mixture; recover, and continue cooking on ROAST for 6 to 8 minutes or until fork tender. Let stand, covered, 5 minutes before serving.

    About 4 Servings

> **STEWED CHICKEN KEY:** Stewed chicken is similar to soup. Microwave first in HIGH to heat quickly; then reduce to SIMMER to tenderize the tougher meat with slow cooking. Check the Soup Key for detailed techniques.

OLD-FASHIONED CHICKEN 'N NOODLES*

   1 **cup chopped celery**
   3 **green onions, chopped**
   1 **medium tomato, quartered**
   1 **tablespoon dried parsley flakes**
   2 **teaspoons salt**
   Dash pepper
   2½ **lbs. stewing chicken, cut up**
   3 **cups water**
   1½ **cups uncooked egg noodles**

1. Combine all ingredients, except noodles, in 3-quart glass casserole. Cover with glass lid or plastic wrap.

2. Microwave on HIGH for 15 minutes. Turn chicken pieces over.

3. Microwave on SIMMER for 50 to 60 minutes or until chicken is fork tender. Remove chicken from broth; stir in noodles; recover, and continue cooking on DEFROST for 12 to 14 minutes or until noodles are tender. Remove chicken from bones. Return chicken meat to broth; recover, and continue cooking on SIMMER for 3 to 4 minutes or until hot. Let stand, covered, 5 minutes before serving.

    4 to 6 Servings

ROAST TURKEY KEY: Roast up to 14-pound whole turkeys in a microwave oven. Start birds on HIGH to warm meat through; then continue cooking on ROAST to help meat cook evenly and stay juicy.

Microwave boneless turkey breasts on ROAST to insure even cooking.

Check the poultry cooking chart in this chapter for specific directions.

ROAST TURKEY BREAST*

   3 to 4-lb. frozen bone-in turkey breast, thawed
   ¼ cup currant jelly

1. Place turkey breast, top side down on microwave roasting rack, in 2-quart (12 x 7) glass baking dish. Cover tip end of breast with foil during first part of cooking.

2. Microwave on ROAST for 17 minutes. Turn breast side up; spread with jelly, and continue cooking on ROAST for 18 to 20 minutes or until c-microwave meat thermometer registers 170° F. let stand, covered with foil, 10 minutes before carving.

            6 to 8 Servings

TIP ● Good served with Ruby Red Cranberry Stuffing, page 45.

Pictured clockwise from the top: Roast Turkey, this page; Turkey Noodle Bake, page 83; Easy Chicken Rice, page 82.

Move thermometer from thigh to breast for a double doneness test.

ROAST WHOLE TURKEY*

   12 lb. frozen turkey, thawed
   Salt
   Stuffing, if desired
   Melted butter or margarine

1. Wash completely thawed turkey; set aside giblets. Sprinkle inside of cavity with salt. Stuff cavity and neck opening, if desired. Secure opening with toothpicks or metal skewers. Tie drumsticks together and wings to body with string.

2. Place bird, breast side down on microwave roasting rack, in 3-quart (13 x 9) glass baking dish. Brush with butter. (Microwave 9 minutes per pound as directed in chart, page 36.)

3. Microwave on HIGH for 27 minutes. Turn breast side up and continue cooking on HIGH for 27 minutes. Turn breast side down. Some areas may cook more rapidly than others; cover these with foil to slow down cooking.

4. Microwave on ROAST for 27 minutes. Turn breast side up; insert microwave meat thermometer in thickest part of thigh, and continue cooking on ROAST for 27 minutes or until thermometer registers 165° F. to 170° F. in thigh and 175° F. when inserted in breast meat. Let stand, covered with foil, 10 to 15 minutes before serving. Temperature will increase 10 to 15° F. during this time.

            About 12 Servings

TURKEY PARTS KEY: Microwave turkey parts on ROAST so they will be juicy and fork tender.

Turkey must be completely thawed before cooking. See defrosting chart on page 35.

Microwave in a flat glass baking dish.

Place turkey parts skin side down and arrange with thickest portions toward outside of dish where they cook faster. Why? It takes microwaves longer to penetrate to center of a dish of food.

Note that a small amount of liquid is added to steam and tenderize turkey meat.

Cover dish with plastic wrap or wax paper tightly tucked at edges to hold steam and insure tender meat. Pierce wrap before removing so steam escapes slowly and does not burn hands.

Turn turkey parts over once to insure even cooking.

Let turkey stand, covered, after removing it from the oven. Cooking is completed during this time and meat should be fork tender.

Turning pieces cooks meat evenly.

BARBECUE TURKEY DRUMSTICKS*

>   1 package (2 to 2½ lb.) frozen drumsticks, thawed
>   1 cup bottled barbecue sauce

1. Place turkey drumsticks, thick end toward outside, in 2-quart (12 x 7) glass baking dish. Pour barbecue sauce on top. Cover with plastic wrap.

2. Microwave on ROAST for 25 minutes. Turn drumsticks over; recover, and continue cooking on ROAST for 20 to 25 minutes or until fork tender. Let stand, covered, 5 minutes before serving.

2 to 3 Servings

Standing time is essential to complete cooking.

SAVORY TURKEY THIGH*

>   1 package (1 to 1½ lb.) frozen turkey thigh, thawed
>   ⅛ teaspoon garlic salt
>   ¼ cup water

1. Place thigh, skin side down, in 2-quart (8 x 8) glass baking dish. Sprinkle with garlic salt. Pour water into bottom of dish. Cover with plastic wrap.

2. Microwave on ROAST for 10 minutes. Turn thigh over; recover, and continue cooking on ROAST for 10 to 12 minutes or until fork tender. Let stand, covered, 5 minutes before serving.

3 to 4 Servings

TURKEY THIGHS WITH WALNUT SAUCE

>   1 package (1½ to 2 lb.) frozen turkey thighs, thawed, deboned, skinned and quartered lengthwise
>   2 tablespoons all-purpose flour
>   ½ cup water
>   ¼ cup finely chopped onion
>   ½ teaspoon garlic salt
>   ⅛ teaspoon ground colves
>   ⅛ teaspoon cinnamon
>   ¼ teaspoon salt
>   1 bay leaf
>   1 tablespoon dried parsley flakes
>   ½ cup chopped walnuts

1. Place quartered thighs in 1½-quart (10 x 6) glass baking dish. Cover with plastic wrap.

2. Microwave on ROAST for 15 minutes. Combine remaining ingredients in small mixing bowl; set aside. Turn thighs over; pour on sauce; recover, and continue cooking on ROAST for 10 to 11 minutes or until fork tender. Let stand, covered, 5 mintues before serving.

4 Servings

OLD-FASHIONED TURKEY DRUMSTICKS*

>   1 package (2 to 2½ lb.) frozen turkey drumsticks, thawed
>   1 teaspoon salt
>   ½ teaspoon tarragon
>   ⅛ teaspoon pepper
>   2 tablespoons water

1. Place turkey drumsticks, thick end toward outside, in 2-quart (12 x 7) glass baking dish. Sprinkle with seasonings and water. Cover with plastic wrap.

2. Microwave on ROAST for 20 minutes. Turn drumsticks over; recover, and continue cooking on ROAST for 10 to 15 minutes or until meat is fork tender. Let stand, covered, 5 minutes before serving.

2 to 3 Servings

TURKEY WINGS WITH VEGETABLES

>   1 package (2½ to 3 lb.) frozen turkey wings, thawed and cut into 2 pieces at large joint
>   ½ cup chopped onion
>   2 medium tomatoes, quartered
>   1 teaspoon salt
>   ½ teaspoon leaf basil
>   ⅛ teaspoon pepper
>   1 bay leaf

1. Place turkey wing pieces, thick pieces toward outside, in 2-quart (12 x 7) glass baking dish. Cover with plastic wrap.

2. Microwave on ROAST for 25 minutes. Turn wings over; add vegetables and seasonings; recover, and continue cooking on ROAST for 25 to 30 minutes or until meat is fork tender. Let stand, covered, 5 minutes before serving.

2 to 3 Servings

DUCK, GOOSE AND PHEASANT KEY: Duck, goose and pheasant microwave best on ROAST because fat rendered from the meat during cooking will spatter less — and because these less tender meats have better texture when cooked slowly and gently.

Place whole birds, breast side down, on a microwave roasting rack which holds meat above fat and drippings.

Place rack in a flat glass baking dish.

Quartered or cut up birds are cooked without a rack in a glass casserole or baking dish with thick pieces and edges of meat toward the outside where they cook faster.

Turn birds as recipe specifies to assure even cooking.

Drain fat from pan halfway through cooking to prevent messy oven spatters and possible smoking.

Pheasant is often cooked in sauce and with a cover to keep the naturally dry meat moist.

Crisper outer skin results if birds are placed under a conventional oven broiler for a few minutes before standing time.

Whole birds are cooked if a microwave meat thermometer registers 170° F. when meat is taken from the oven. Cut-up or quartered birds should be fork tender.

Covering birds during standing time is important to complete cooking — follow recipe directions. Internal temperature will rise about 15° F.

See poultry charts at the beginning of this chapter for specific defrosting and cooking times.

Always use a glass dish under the rack to catch drippings.

ROAST GOOSE*

    9 lb. frozen domestic goose, thawed
    1 teaspoon salt
    3 to 4 medium apples, quartered
    8 to 10 dried prunes
    1 teaspoon leaf marjoram

1. Wash goose; remove giblets. Sprinkle inside of cavity with salt. Fill cavity with apples and prunes. Sprinkle with marjoram. Secure openings with toothpicks or metal skewers. Tie legs together and wings to body.

2. Place goose, breast side down on microwave roasting rack, in 3-quart (13 x 9) glass baking dish.

3. Microwave on ROAST for 45 minutes. Turn goose breast side up and continue cookıng on ROAST for 45 to 50 minutes or until microwave meat thermometer inserted in thickest part of thigh meat registers 170° F. Let stand, covered with foil, 10 minutes before serving.   About 10 Servings

ROAST setting insures moist tender meat.

ROAST DUCKLING*

    4 to 5-lb. young duckling
    1 orange, quartered
    1 onion, quartered
    ¼ cup plum preserves

1. Stuff orange and onion quarters into duckling neck and body cavity. Secure openings with toothpicks or metal skewers. Tie legs together and wings to body. Place duckling, breast side down on microwave roasting rack, in 2-quart (12 x 7) glass baking dish. Spread duckling back with half of plum preserves.

2. Microwave on ROAST for 23 to 25 minutes. Turn duckling over; spread with remaining preserves, and continue cooking on ROAST for 20 to 22 minutes or until microwave meat thermometer registers 170° F. when bird is taken from the oven. Let stand, covered with foil, 10 minutes before serving.   4 to 6 Servings

Microwave cooking rack holds ducks above juices.

APRICOT-GLAZED DUCK WITH*
WILD RICE STUFFING

    1 package (6 oz.) seasoned white and wild
      rice mix
    2½ cups water
    ¾ cup chopped mixed dried fruit
    1 medium onion, chopped
    2 wild Mallard ducks (2 lb. each)
    ¼ cup apricot preserves

1. Combine seasoned rice mix, water, dried fruit and onion in saucepan; cook as directed on rice package.

2. Clean ducks; wash, and pat dry. Stuff ducks with rice mixture; fasten openings with toothpicks or metal skewers; lace shut with string.

3. Place ducks, breast side down on microwave roasting rack, in 2-quart (12 x 7) glass baking dish.

4. Microwave on ROAST for 20 minutes. Turn ducks over; drain fat from pan. Brush ducks with apricot preserves and continue cooking on ROAST for 18 to 20 minutes or until meat and juices are no longer pink when duck is cut between leg and body. Let stand, covered with foil, 5 minutes before serving.   4 Servings

TIPS • For crisper skin, put ducks under conventional oven broiler for a few minutes before standing period.

 • Substitute 1 (4 to 5 lb.) young duckling for wild Mallard ducks.

Slower ROAST setting keeps pheasant meat moist.

SMOTHERED PHEASANT*

2 tablespoons butter or margarine
1 pheasant (2 lb.), cut up
All-purpose flour
Salt
Pepper
⅛ teaspoon celery salt
¼ teaspoon ground sage
½ cup thinly sliced carrots
¼ cup finely chopped onion
⅓ cup milk

1. Place butter in 2-quart (12 x 7) glass baking dish.

2. Microwave on ROAST for about 1 minute or until melted. Roll pheasant in flour. Place, thick edges toward outside, in buttered baking dish. Season with salt, pepper, celery salt and sage. Top with carrots and onion. Cover with plastic wrap.

3. Microwave on ROAST for 10 to 12 minutes. Turn pheasant over; recover, and continue cooking on ROAST for 8 to 10 minutes. Add milk; recover, and continue cooking on ROAST for 2 to 3 minutes or until fork tender. Let stand, covered, 5 minutes before serving.   3 to 4 Servings

---

STUFFINGS KEY: Stuffings prepared for whole fowl are cooked on Microwave ROAST to melt butter, soften vegetables and begin cooking process. Then mixture is spooned into the bird.

Stuffings cooked in a glass casserole are assembled and cooked on ROAST; then covered and cooked on SIMMER to finish cooking and blend flavors.

Covering is important for casserole stuffings — bread must not dry out.

Casserole stuffings need standing time to complete heating and cooking.

Most stuffings may be used with any poultry — and many are good with pork. Do check how much stuffing a recipe yields and adjust it to fit the bird.

Stuffings do not add to the cooking time of whole poultry.

STUFFING MIX

½ cup butter or margarine
1 cup water
1 package (8 oz.) crushed, seasoned stuffing mix

1. Combine butter and water in 2-quart glass casserole.

2. Microwave on ROAST for 4 to 5 minutes or until melted. Stir in stuffing mix. Stuff poultry.
                              Stuffs 5 to 8-Lb. Bird

ALMOND STUFFING

¾ cup butter or margarine
½ cup chopped celery
¼ cup chopped onion
½ cup chopped almonds
4 cups soft bread cubes
1 tablespoon dried parsley flakes
¼ teaspoon salt
1 teaspoon instant chicken bouillon
⅓ cup water

1. Combine butter, celery and onion in medium mixing bowl.

2. Microwave on ROAST for 4 to 5 minutes or until vegetables are partly cooked. Stir in remaining ingredients; mix well. Stuff poultry.
    Stuffs 4 Cornish Hens or 4 to 5-lb. Roasting Chicken

BASIC BREAD STUFFING

⅔ cup butter or margarine
¼ cup finely chopped onion
½ teaspoon salt
½ teaspoon poultry seasoning
¼ teaspoon pepper
8 cups dried bread cubes
2 to 4 tablespoons water, depending on dryness of bread

1. Place butter and onion in 2-quart glass baking dish.

2. Microwave on ROAST for 4 to 5 minutes or until butter is melted. Stir in remaining ingredients; mix well. Stuff poultry.   Stuffs 4 to 6-lb. Bird

Cook casserole stuffings on SIMMER so bread doesn't dry out.

RUBY RED CRANBERRY STUFFING

¼ cup butter or margarine
½ cup chopped onion
½ cup chopped celery
2 cups finely chopped tart apple
1 cup whole cranberry sauce
⅓ cup raisins
1 package (8 oz.) seasoned cornbread stuffing mix

1. Combine butter, onion and celery in 2-quart glass casserole.

2. Microwave on ROAST for about 4 minutes or until vegetables are partly cooked. Stir in remaining ingredients; mix well. Stuff poultry.
                              Stuffs 5 to 8-lb. Bird

TIP ● To cook as a casserole dish, blend ½ cup orange juice into above ingredients. Place in buttered 2-quart glass baking dish or casserole. Cover with glass lid or plastic wrap. Microwave on SIMMER for 12 to 15 minutes or until hot. Let stand, covered, 5 minutes before serving.   4 to 6 Servings

American homemakers like to feed their families meat at least once a day — so microwave meat cooking know-how is an intriguing essential for oven owners.

This chapter outlines newest developments.

Basic techniques for beef, fresh and cured pork, sausage, lamb, veal, variety meats — even venison and rabbit — are spelled out carefully.

Read the cooking chart and "grey box" keys. Try recipes, evaluate results — then enjoy the challenge of experimenting with the kind and quality meat you buy. Remember that meat age, marbling size and shape vary from purchase to purchase.

Pictured clockwise from the top: Center Rib Pork Roast with Cherry Sauce, page 61; Boneless Rump Roast, page 52; Orange Glaze Leg O'Lamb, page 67.

MEAT CHAPTER CONTENTS

HOW TO DEFROST MEAT

● Thaw meat in its original wrapping. Place wrapped meat in a flat glass baking dish to catch drippings.

● Meat weighing 4 pounds and over is thawed on ROAST; under 4 pounds thaws on DEFROST.

● Turn large cuts during defrosting as specified in chart.

● Meat should be icy in center when removed from oven. Edges will begin cooking if microwaves thaw meat completely.

● Standing time in package is necessary to complete thawing.

CUT	WEIGHT	SETTING	DEFROSTING TIME	APPROXIMATE STANDING TIME (at room temperature)
BEEF				
Rib roast, rolled*	7 to 8-lb.	ROAST	8 min.; turn Repeat 3 times.	2 hrs.
	3 to 4-lb.	DEFROST	30 to 35 min.	1 hr.
Rib Roast, standing*	5 to 6-lb.	ROAST	8 min.; turn. Repeat 3 times.	2 hrs.
Sirloin Tip Roast*	4 to 5-lb.	ROAST	8 min.; turn. Repeat 2 times.	2 hrs.
Rump Roast, boneless*	6 to 7-lb.	ROAST	10 min. turn; 8 to 10 min.	2 hrs.
	3 to 4-lb.	DEFROST	20 to 22 min.	1 hr.
Rump Roast, bone in	3 to 4-lb.	DEFROST	20 to 22 min.	1 hr.
Chuck Arm Roast	4 to 4½-lb.	ROAST	10 to 12 min.	10 min.
Chuck Roast	3 to 4-lb.	DEFROST	12 to 16 min.	10 min.
Beef Blade Roast	2¾ to 3¼-lb.	DEFROST	18 to 20 min.	5 min.
Rib Eye Steak	2 to 3-lb.	DEFROST	8 to 10 min.	5 min.
Sirloin Steak	1¾ to 2-lb.	DEFROST	12 to 15 min.	5 min.
Round Steak	1¾ to 3-lb.	DEFROST	12 to 15 min.	5 min.
Flank Steak	1¼ to 1½-lb.	DEFROST	9 to 10 min.	5 min.
Cubed Steak	8 oz.	DEFROST	3 to 4 min.	5 min.
Short Ribs	2 to 3 lbs.	DEFROST	8 to 10 min.	5 min.
Stew Meat	1¾ to 2 lbs.	DEFROST	8 to 10 min.	5 min.
Ground beef	1 lb.	DEFROST	8 to 10 min.	5 min.
	2 lbs.	DEFROST	18 to 20 min.	5 min.
Brisket, fresh	3¼ to 3½-lb.	DEFROST	15 to 20 min.	1 hr.
Brisket, corned	2¾ to 3-lb.	DEFROST	14 to 16 min.	30 min.

CUT	WEIGHT	SETTING	DEFROSTING TIME	APPROXIMATE STANDING TIME (at room temperature)
VARIETY MEATS				
Liver	8 ozs.	DEFROST	5 to 6 min.	5 min.
	1 lb.	DEFROST	6 to 7 min.	5 min.
Tongue*	2¼ to 2½-lb.	DEFROST	8 min.; turn; 8 min.	5 min.
Kidney	2-lb.	DEFROST	6 to 8 min.	5 min.
PORK				
Loin Roast, boneless*	4 to 5-lb.	ROAST	10 min.; turn; 5 to 6 min.	1 hr.
Loin Roast, center rib*	4 to 5-lb.	ROAST	10 min.; turn; 5 to 6 min.	1 hr.
Tenderloin	1¾ to 2-lb.	DEFROST	12 to 15 min.	5 min.
Loin Chops, 1-in. thick	3 to 3½ lbs.	DEFROST	10 to 15 min.	10 min.
Chops, ½-in. thick	1½ lbs.	DEFROST	10 to 15 min.	5 min.
Blade Steak	1¼ to 1½-lb.	DEFROST	5 to 10 min.	5 min.
Shoulder steak	2½-lb.	DEFROST	15 to 20 min.	5 min.
Spareribs, country style	2 to 3 lbs.	DEFROST	15 to 20 min.	5 min.
Spareribs	2¾ to 3 lbs.	DEFROST	15 to 20 min.	5 min.
Cubed	1½ lbs.	DEFROST	8 to 10 min.	5 min.
Hocks	1 to 2 lbs.	DEFROST	8 to 10 min.	5 min.
Ground, fresh	1 lb.	DEFROST	8 to 10 min.	5 min.
Ground, ham	1 lb.	DEFROST	8 to 10 min.	5 min.
LAMB				
Leg Roast*	4 to 4½-lb.	ROAST	10 min.; turn; 10 min.	1 hr.
Shoulder Roast*	3¼ to 3½-lb.	ROAST	10 min.; turn; 5 to 6 min.	1 hr.
Steaks	2 to 2½ lbs.	DEFROST	8 to 10 min.	5 min.
Spareribs	2¼ to 2½ lbs.	DEFROST	8 to 10 min.	5 min.
Shanks	1 lb.	DEFROST	5 to 8 min.	5 min.
Cubed	1 lb.	DEFROST	7 to 8 min.	5 min.
Ground	1 lb.	DEFROST	5 to 7 min.	5 min.
Patties	1½ lbs.	DEFROST	7 to 9 min.	5 min.

(Continued, next page)

CUT	WEIGHT	SETTING	DEFROSTING TIME	APPROXIMATE STANDING TIME (at room temperature)
VEAL				
Rump Roast, bone in *	2½ to 3-lb.	DEFROST	10 to 15 min.	30 min.
	5 to 6-lb.	ROAST	10 min.; turn; 8 to 10 min.	1 hr.
Chops	1 to 2 lbs.	DEFROST	12 to 15 min.	5 min.
Steak	1 lb.	DEFROST	7 to 8 min.	5 min.
Ground	1 lb.	DEFROST	5 to 7 min.	5 min.
VENISON				
Rump Roast, bone in	3 to 3½-lb.	DEFROST	15 to 18 min.	1 hr.
Chops	1¼ lbs.	DEFROST	7 to 8 min.	5 min.
RABBIT				
Cut up	2 to 2½-lb.	DEFROST	20 to 22 min.	5 min.

HOW TO ROAST MEATS

- Microwave fresh or completely thawed frozen meat. See defrosting chart page 48.

- Season meat to taste. Place meat, fat side down on microwave roasting rack, in 2-quart (12 x 7) glass baking dish.

- Microwave on "first setting" for half of the total cooking time.

- Turn meat, fat side up. Meat weighing 7 pounds or over should be turned 3 times during cooking.

- Microwave on "second setting" for second half of cooking time. Check for desired doneness as specified in chart.

- Use a microwave meat thermometer in a microwave oven during cooking. DO NOT use a conventional meat thermometer in a microwave oven; insert this kind as soon as meat comes from oven.

- Let meat stand, covered with foil, about 10 minutes before serving. Temperature will rise about 15° F. during standing time as meat continues to cook to final desired doneness.

CUT AND WEIGHT	FIRST SETTING	SECOND SETTING	DONENESS WHEN MEAT COMES FROM OVEN	APPROXIMATE COOKING TIME
BEEF				
Rib Roast, rolled * 3 to 4-lb.	HIGH	ROAST	rare — 125° F. medium — 145° F. well done — 155° F.	8 to 9 min. per lb. 10 to 11 min. per lb. 12 to 13 min. per lb.
Rib Roast, standing * 5 to 6-lb.	HIGH	ROAST	rare — 125° F. medium — 145° F. well done — 155° F.	7 to 8 min. per lb. 8 to 9 min. per lb. 10 to 11 min. per lb.
Sirloin Tip Roast * 4 to 5-lb.	HIGH	ROAST	rare — 125° F. medium — 145° F. well done — 155° F.	8 to 9 min. per lb. 10 to 11 min. per lb. 12 to 13 min. per lb.

CUT AND WEIGHT	FIRST SETTING	SECOND SETTING	DONENESS WHEN MEAT COMES FROM OVEN	APPROXIMATE COOKING TIME
Rump Roast, boneless * 3 to 4-lb.	ROAST	SIMMER	rare — 125° F. medium — 145° F. well done — 155° F.	11 to 12 min. per lb. 13 to 14 min. per lb. 15 to 16 min. per lb.
Rump Roast, bone in * 3 to 4-lb.	ROAST	SIMMER	rare — 125° F. medium — 145° F. well done — 155° F.	11 to 12 min. per lb. 13 to 14 min. per lb. 15 to 16 min. per lb.
PORK Loin Roast, boneless * 4 to 5-lb.	HIGH	ROAST	well done — 155° F.	10 to 11 min. per lb.
Loin Roast, center rib cut * 4 to 5-lb.	HIGH	ROAST	well done — 155° F.	10 to 11 min. per lb.
Ham, boneless, ready to eat * 2 to 3-lb. 4 to 5-lb. 6 to 8-lb.	ROAST ROAST ROAST	ROAST ROAST ROAST	heated — 120° F. heated — 120° F. heated — 120° F.	12 to 13 min. per lb. 11 to 12 min. per lb. 9 to 10 min. per lb.
Ham, shank of leg, ready to eat * 7 to 8-lb.	ROAST	ROAST	heated — 120° F.	8 to 9 min. per lb.
Ham, canned * 3-lb. 5-lb.	ROAST ROAST	ROAST ROAST	heated — 120° F. heated — 120° F.	10 to 11 min. per lb. 8 to 9 min. per lb.
LAMB Leg Roast * 4 to 4½-lb.	ROAST	ROAST	well done — 160° F.	10 to 11 min. per lb.
Shoulder Roast, rolled * 3 to 4-lb.	ROAST	ROAST	well done — 160° F.	9 to 10 min. per lb.
VEAL Rump Roast, bone in * 2½ to 3-lb.	ROAST	SIMMER	well done — 155° F.	20 to 21 min. per lb.
VENISON Rump Roast, bone in * 3 to 3½-lb.	ROAST	ROAST	well done — 155° F.	12 to 13 min. per lb.

ROAST BEEF KEY: Microwave tender beef roasts, such as sirloin tip and rib, on Microwave HIGH during first half of cooking time. This setting heats meat through quickly. Microwave on ROAST during final cooking period so meat stays tender and is thoroughly cooked.

Microwave less tender beef roasts, such as rump roast, on ROAST, then SIMMER. Lower settings allow longer cooking to tenderize meat.

Microwave fresh or completely thawed frozen beef roasts. See defrosting chart on page 48.

Season meat to taste. Place, fat side down on microwave roasting rack, in a flat glass baking dish. Rack keeps meat above drippings.

Beef roasts weighing 7 pounds or over should be turned over 3 times to assure even cooking.

Cook roasts to desired doneness using a microwave meat thermometer and the meat doneness chart on this page as a guide.

Note that the 10-minute standing time is very important because meat continues to cook after it comes from the oven and internal temperature should rise about 15° F. Cover dish of meat with foil during standing time to hold in heat.

A microwave meat thermometer can be used in the oven during cooking. Insert it after meat is turned the last time. DO NOT use a conventional meat thermometer in a microwave oven. Check doneness with this kind of thermometer by inserting it as soon as roast comes from the oven.

Roasting times in the following recipes are for rare meat. Adjust cooking time for medium or well-done roasts. See chart on page 50.

BONELESS RUMP ROAST*

3½ to 4-lb. boneless beef rump roast
2 teaspoons salt
1 teaspoon dry mustard
¼ teaspoon garlic powder
¼ teaspoon pepper

Sauce:
1 tablespoon catsup
1 teaspoon Worcestershire sauce
½ cup dry red wine or broth

1. Sprinkle roast with seasonings. Place roast, fat side down on microwave roasting rack, in 2-quart (12 x 7) glass baking dish.

2. Microwave on ROAST for 20 minutes. Turn fat side up. Pour Sauce over roast.

3. Microwave on SIMMER for 20 to 24 minutes or until rare doneness. Let stand, covered with foil, 10 minutes before serving.

4. **Sauce:** Combine catsup, Worcestershire sauce and wine in small mixing bowl.   9 to 12 Servings

Thaw meat completely before cooking.

ROLLED PRIME RIB ROAST WITH MADEIRA SAUCE*

3 to 4-lb. rolled beef rib roast
1 teaspoon salt
¼ teaspoon pepper

Madeira Sauce:
1 teaspoon salt
½ teaspoon pepper
1 can (10½ oz.) condensed beef broth
¼ cup Madeira wine

1. Place roast, fat side down on microwave roasting rack in 2-quart (12 x 7) glass casserole. Season with salt and pepper.

2. Microwave on HIGH for 16 minutes. Turn fat side up.

3. Microwave on ROAST for 12 to 16 minutes or until rare doneness. Let stand, covered with foil, 10 minutes before serving. Serve with Madeira Sauce.

4. **Madeira Sauce:** Combine all ingredients in 2-cup measure. Stir into hot meat drippings; mix well.
9 to 12 Servings

TIPS ● STANDING RIB ROAST and BONELESS SIRLOIN TIP ROAST: Use same technique as above. See meat roasting chart, page 50, for time and doneness tests.

● Allow ¼ to ⅓ pound boneless meat or ½ to ⅔ pound bone-in meat per serving.

INTERNAL TEMPERATURE GUIDE FOR ROAST BEEF DONENESS

Rare — 125° F. when meat is removed from oven. Temperature will increase to about 140° F. during standing time.

Medium — 145° F. when meat is removed from oven. Temperature will increase to about 160° F. during standing time.

Well Done — 155° F. when meat is removed from oven. Temperature will increase to about 170° F. during standing time.

Pictured top to bottom: Potted Beef, page 54; Veal Meatballs, page 69; Canadian Bacon with Fruit Sauce, page 64.

POT ROAST BEEF KEY: Microwave the less tender large meat cuts called pot roasts using a technique similar to braising — HIGH for short quick heating, then SIMMER with added moisture for thorough cooking and tenderizing.

Frozen roasts should be completely thawed. See defrosting chart on page 48.

Pot roasts seem to cook most evenly and tenderize best when divided lengthwise into 4 pieces, this allows meat to be easily turned over and rearranged in dish during cooking. A useful technique since microwaves cook food at the edges of the dish first.

Place seasoned roast in a flat glass baking dish. Cover throughout cooking with plastic wrap or wax paper tucked tightly across top of dish. Pierce plastic wrap before removing it to prevent steam burns.

Rearrange and turn meat over twice during cooking. Add sauce mixtures called for in the recipe when meat is turned the first time and setting changes from HIGH to SIMMER

Meat should be fork tender when removed from oven.

Meat must stand, covered, for 10 minutes to complete cooking.

Turning meat allows even cooking.

CORNED BEEF 'N CABBAGE DINNER*

> 2¾ to 3-lb. corned beef brisket with
>   seasonings
> 1½ cups water
>   2 medium onions, quartered
>   3 carrots, sliced
>   3 potatoes, quartered
>   1 cabbage, cut into 8 wedges

1. Place corned beef brisket in 3-quart glass casserole; add water, and sprinkle with seasonings included with meat. Cover with glass lid or plastic wrap.

2. Microwave on HIGH for 10 to 12 minutes or until boiling. Turn meat over.

3. Microwave on SIMMER for about 1½ hours or until fork tender. Turn meat over; add remaining ingredients; recover.

4. Microwave on SIMMER for 30 to 45 minutes or until vegetables are tender. Let stand, covered, 5 minutes before serving.   About 6 Servings

TIP ● Substitute a mixture of 1 bay leaf, ½ teaspoon peppercorn and ½ teaspoon garlic salt for envelope of seasonings.

Frozen roasts should thaw completely before cooking.

POTTED BEEF*

> 3½ to 4-lb. beef chuck roast,
>   cut into 4 pieces
>   1 large onion, sliced
>   1 cup finely chopped celery
>   2 teaspoons salt
>   ¼ teaspoon pepper
>   1 bay leaf
>   1 can (4 oz.) mushroom stems
>   and pieces, drained
> 1½ cups sliced carrots
>   3 medium potatoes, quartered

1. Place cut roast in 3-quart (13 x 9) glass baking dish. Cover with plastic wrap.

2. Microwave on HIGH for 10 minutes. Drain; turn meat over; rearrange, and recover.

3. Microwave on SIMMER for 45 minutes. Turn meat over. Add remaining ingredients; recover, and continue cooking on SIMMER for 40 to 45 minutes or until fork tender. Let stand, covered, 10 minutes before serving.   6 to 8 Servings

QUICK-COOK TENDER BEEF STEAK KEY: Tender steak, such as sirloin and tenderized minute steaks, cook fast and retain full flavor on Microwave HIGH .

The microwave browning grill accessory can be used to sear these steaks on HIGH as directed in the manufacturer's instruction booklet.

When tender beef steak pieces are rolled and stuffed and/or a sauce is added, final cooking period is at ROAST to cook and blend flavors.

Frozen steak should be completely thawed before cooking. See defrosting chart at the beginning of this chapter.

Cook tender beef steak directly on the microwave browning grill when called for in a recipe. Other cooking dishes used must be glass. Covers should be fitted glass lids, plastic wrap or wax paper. Pierce plastic wrap before removing it to prevent steam burns.

Stir, turn or rearrange steak as called for in a recipe to assure even cooking.

Standing time, when called for, is important. It assures complete cooking.

These tender steak recipes are models for favorites from a homemaker's recipe box.

These strips of tender beef cook quickly.

SUKIYAKI

- 1½ to 2-lb. beef sirloin steak, cut into thin strips
- ½ cup soy sauce
- ½ cup water
- 3 tablespoons sugar
- 1 can (4 oz.) mushroom stems and pieces, drained
- ½ cup sliced green onion
- 1 can (5 oz.) water chestnuts, drained and sliced
- 1 can (5 oz.) bamboo shoots, drained
- 1 can (16 oz.) bean sprouts, drained

1. Combine steak, soy sauce, water and sugar in 2-quart (12 x 7) glass baking dish. Cover with plastic wrap. Marinate 3 to 4 hours at room temperature.

2. Place remaining ingredients in rows across meat and sauce with mushrooms and onions in center rows; recover.

3. Microwave on HIGH for 10 to 12 minutes. Let stand, covered, 2 minutes before serving.

4 to 6 Servings

Pictured top to bottom: Beef Bourguignon, page 56; Sukiyaki, this page.

SIRLOIN ROLL UPS A LA JUICE

- 1½ lbs. beef sirloin thinly sliced into 8 equal portions and pounded
- 1 teaspoon garlic salt
- ½ teaspoon salt
- ½ cup finely chopped green onion
- 1 can (4 oz.) mushroom stems and pieces, drained
- 1 teaspoon instant beef bouillon
- ½ cup water
- ¼ cup sour cream
- 1 medium tomato, sliced
- Hot cooked rice

1. Season pounded steaks with garlic salt and salt. Spoon 1 tablespoon each of chopped onion and mushrooms in center of each steak. Roll up; secure with tooth picks. Preheat microwave browning grill in oven on HIGH as directed in instruction booklet. Place rolls on hot grill.

2. Microwave on HIGH for 5 minutes. Turn rolls over and continue cooking on HIGH for 3 to 5 minutes or until browned. Remove rolls to 2-quart (8 x 8) glass baking dish. Combine bouillon and water in 2-cup measure. Pour over meat. Cover with plastic wrap.

3. Microwave on ROAST for 10 to 12 minutes or until meat is fork tender. Let stand, covered, 5 minutes before serving. Remove meat rolls to serving platter. Blend sour cream with meat juices and pour over meat. Garnish with tomato slices; serve over hot rice.

About 4 Servings

RIB STEAKS ON MICROWAVE BROWNING GRILL

> **2** beef rib steaks (1 lb. each), trim off fat
> **2** tablespoons butter or margarine, if desired
> **Salt**
> **Pepper**

1. Preheat microwave browning grill in oven on HIGH as directed in instruction booklet. Place butter on hot grill to melt. Place steaks on hot grill.

2. Microwave on HIGH for 4 minutes. Turn steaks over and continue cooking on HIGH for 3 to 4 minutes or to desired doneness.   2 Steaks

---

BRAISED BEEF KEY: Pieces, strips and cubes of less tender beef, such as round and chuck, microwave into flavorful entrées. Use Microwave HIGH for quick cooking and then SIMMER for flavorful blending of sauces which provide the moisture needed to tenderize meat.

Although shortribs are from the beef rib, high fat and bone content, plus sauce and vegetable additions, make them suitable to the braising and draining technique used for less tender meat cuts.

Note that cooking times vary with cut of beef, shape of pieces and other ingredients added to the recipe.

Meat should be completely thawed before cooking. See defrosting chart in this chapter.

Coating meat pieces with flour before cooking tends to help meat retain juices.

Pound meat well when called for in a recipe. Use the edge of a saucer or a meat mallet.

Score pieces of meat that must be rolled or which need tenderizing. Do this by making shallow criss-cross cuts on both sides of the meat with a sharp knife.

Cover less tender meat during cooking and standing time to trap steam, hasten cooking and tenderize. Place meat in a glass baking dish or casserole with fitted glass lid, plastic wrap or wax paper stretched tightly across top of dish. Pierce plastic wrap before removing it to prevent steam burns.

Stir or rearrange meat during cooking as recipe directs to assure even cooking.

Drain, when directed, to remove excess fat and moisture.

Meat should be fork tender when it comes from the oven. Follow standing time directions carefully.

When planning to adapt a favorite dish, use a similar recipe in this section as a model. Note that less moisture and fat need to be added in microwave meat cooking.

BEEF BOURGUIGNON

> **1½** to 1¾-lb. beef sirloin steak, cut into 1½-inch cubes
> **¼** teaspoon salt
> **2** tablespoons all-purpose flour
> **1** envelope (1¼ oz.) dehydrated onion soup mix
> **⅔** cup dry red wine
> **1** can (4 oz.) mushroom stems and pieces, drained
> **1** green pepper, cut into strips
> **1** can (16 oz.) whole onions, drained

1. Combine steak cubes, salt, flour, soup mix and wine in 2-quart glass casserole. Cover with glass lid or plastic wrap.

2. Microwave on HIGH for about 5 minutes or until no longer pink. Stir in remaining ingredients; recover.

3. Microwave on SIMMER for 12 to 15 minutes or until fork tender. Let stand, covered, 5 minutes before serving.   About 6 Servings

SWISS STEAK*

> **2** tablespoons butter or margarine
> **2** tablespoons all-purpose flour
> **1** teaspoon salt
> **¼** teaspoon pepper
> **¼** teaspoon dry mustard
> **1½** to 2-lb. boneless beef round steak, cut into serving pieces
> **1** medium onion, sliced
> **¼** cup packed brown sugar
> **½** cup catsup

1. Place butter in 2-quart (12 x 7) glass baking dish.

2. Microwave on ROAST for 1 minute or until melted. Combine flour, salt, pepper and mustard in plate. Coat meat in seasoned flour. Arrange seasoned meat in melted butter. Cover with glass lid or plastic wrap.

3. Microwave on HIGH for about 5 minutes or until no longer pink. Turn meat over. Place onion rings on top. Combine catsup and brown sugar in 2-cup measure. Pour over meat. Cover with plastic wrap.

4. Microwave on SIMMER for 20 minutes. Rearrange meat; recover, and continue cooking on SIMMER for 20 to 25 minutes or until fork tender. Let stand, covered, 5 minutes before serving.   About 4 Servings

Cover tightly to hasten cooking and tenderizing.

BEEF STROGANOFF

¼ cup butter or margarine
4 medium onions, thinly sliced
1 tablespoon dry mustard
1 tablespoon sugar
2 teaspoons salt
1 teaspoon pepper
2 cans (4 oz. each) mushroom stems
    and pieces, drained
2 to 2¼-lb. boneless beef round steak,
    cut into thin strips
1 cup sour cream
Hot buttered noodles

1. Combine butter, onion, dry mustard, sugar, salt and pepper in 3-quart glass casserole. Cover with glass lid or plastic wrap.

2. Microwave on ROAST for about 6 minutes or until onion is partly cooked. Stir in beef; recover.

3. Microwave on HIGH for about 16 minutes or until no longer pink. Stir in mushrooms; recover.

4. Microwave on SIMMER for 20 minutes. Mix in sour cream; recover, and continue cooking on SIMMER for 4 to 5 minutes or until heated through. Serve with buttered noodles. Let stand, covered, 5 minutes before serving.   6 to 8 Servings

Added moisture tenderizes stew meat.

RAGOUT OF BEEF*

2 lbs. cubed beef stew meat
2 medium potatoes, cubed
2 medium carrots, sliced
2 medium onions, cut into
    6 pieces each
1 can (16 oz.) stewed tomatoes
½ cup strong cold coffee
1 teaspoon salt
¼ teaspoon pepper
1 can (16 oz.) peas, undrained
¼ cup unsifted all-purpose flour

1. Place meat in 3-quart glass casserole. Cover with glass lid or plastic wrap.

2. Microwave on HIGH for about 8 minutes or until meat is no longer pink. Stir in remaining ingredients, except peas and flour; recover.

3. Microwave on SIMMER for 45 minutes; stir. Recover and continue cooking on SIMMER for 45 to 50 minutes. Blend juice from peas with flour to make a smooth paste. Stir into meat mixture along with peas; mix well. Recover and continue cooking on SIMMER for 3 to 4 minutes or until hot. Let stand, covered, 5 minutes before serving.
                              6 to 8 Servings

HIGH setting starts cooking process quickly.

BEEF WITH SAUERKRAUT*

1 lb. boneless beef chuck roast,
    cubed
1 teaspoon salt
¼ teaspoon pepper
1 large onion, thinly sliced
½ teaspoon garlic salt
1 teaspoon dill weed
1 teaspoon paprika
½ cup water
¼ cup sour cream
1 can (8 oz.) sauerkraut, drained

1. Place meat in 2-quart glass casserole. Cover with glass lid or plastic wrap.

2. Microwave on HIGH for 8 minutes. Add remaining ingredients, except sour cream and sauerkraut; recover.

3. Microwave on SIMMER for 20 minutes. Stir and continue cooking on SIMMER for 10 to 15 minutes or until fork tender. Blend in sour cream and sauerkraut. Recover and continue cooking on SIMMER for 4 to 5 minutes. Let stand, covered, 5 minutes before serving.   4 to 6 Servings

Stirring assures even cooking.

BEEF HAWAIIAN

2 tablespoons cooking oil
2½ to 2¾-lb. boneless beef round steak,
    cut into thin strips
1 tablespoon soy sauce
1 teaspoon salt
½ teaspoon pepper
½ cup packed brown sugar
¼ cup vinegar
3 tablespoons cornstarch
1 can (13¼ oz.) pineapple chunks,
    undrained
1 medium green pepper, cut into thin strips
2 tomatoes, cut into wedges

1. Measure oil in 2-quart glass casserole.

2. Microwave on HIGH for 2 to 3 minutes or until hot. Stir in beef and continue cooking on HIGH for about 6 minutes or until no longer pink. Stir in soy sauce, salt, pepper. brown sugar and vinegar. Cover with glass lid or plastic wrap.

3. Microwave on SIMMER for 20 minutes. Blend cornstarch and pineapple juice in 2-cup measure. Stir into meat mixture. Mix in pineapple chunks, green pepper and tomatoes. Recover and continue cooking on SIMMER for 8 to 10 minutes or until hot and meat is fork tender. Let stand, covered, 5 minutes before serving.   4 to 6 Servings

MEXICAN ESTAFADO

1½ to 1¾-lb. boneless beef round steak,
    cut into 1-inch cubes
1 large onion, finely chopped
1 can (8 oz.) tomato sauce
3 tablespoons vinegar
1 bay leaf
1 teaspoon leaf oregano
½ teaspoon garlic salt
Salt
Pepper
¼ cup jalapena chile relish

1. Place meat in 2-quart glass casserole. Cover with glass lid or plastic wrap.

2. Microwave on HIGH for about 8 minutes or until no longer pink. Stir in remaining ingredients; recover.

3. Microwave on SIMMER for 40 to 45 minutes or until fork tender. Let stand, covered, 5 minutes before serving.   4 to 6 Servings

SUCCULENT BEEF RIBS*

2½ to 3 lbs. beef short ribs,
    trim off fat
1 cup sliced onion
1 clove garlic, finely chopped
1 teaspoon salt
1 teaspoon thyme
1 bay leaf
½ teaspoon pepper
1 can (10¾ oz.) condensed
    beef broth

1. Cut ribs in half lengthwise. Place in 2-quart (12 x 7) glass baking dish. Cover with plastic wrap.

2. Microwave on HIGH for 10 minutes. Drain. Add remaining ingredients; recover.

3. Microwave on SIMMER for 25 minutes. Stir and continue cooking on SIMMER for 20 to 25 minutes or until fork tender. Let stand, covered, 5 minutes before serving.   2 to 4 Servings

---

BRAISED FIBEROUS BEEF KEY: Fiberous beef cuts, such as fresh beef brisket and flank steak, microwave on SIMMER. This constant low heat tenderizes and eliminates shrinkage.

    Frozen meat should be completely thawed before cooking. See defrosting chart at beginning of chapter.

    Cook meat, covered with plastic wrap or wax paper, in a low glass baking dish. Pierce plastic wrap before removing it to prevent steam burns.

    Turn meat once during cooking.

    Meat should be fork tender when taken from the oven.

DELECTABLE FLANK STEAK

1½ to 2-lb. beef flank steak
Salt
Pepper
2 tablespoons butter or margarine
2 tablespoons finely chopped onion
¼ cup finely chopped celery
2 cups soft bread cubes
¼ teaspoon ground sage
Water, if necessary
1 can (10¾ oz.) condensed
    tomato soup
Parsley

1. Pound flank steak well. Season with salt and pepper; set aside. Combine butter, onion and celery in medium glass mixing bowl.

2. Microwave on ROAST for about 3 minutes or until onion and celery are partly cooked. Stir in bread cubes and sage. Moisten with water if necessary. Spread stuffing lengthwise down center of flank steak. Roll up lengthwise. Tie with strings in 3 or 4 places. Place in 1½-quart (10 x 6) glass baking dish. Cover with plastic wrap.

3. Microwave on SIMMER for 20 minutes. Pour soup over meat. Sprinkle with snipped parsley and continue cooking on SIMMER for 4 to 5 minutes or until fork tender. Let stand, covered, 5 minutes before serving.   4 to 6 Servings

Use REHEAT to warm up the cooked brisket.

FRESH BEEF BRISKET*

3 to 3½-lb. fresh beef brisket
2 teaspoons garlic salt
1 envelope (1¼ oz.) dehydrated onion
    soup mix

1. Sprinkle both sides of meat with garlic salt. Place in 3-quart (13 x 9) glass baking dish. Cover with plastic wrap.

2. Microwave on SIMMER for 45 minutes. Turn meat over; recover, and continue cooking on SIMMER for 40 to 45 minutes or until fork tender. Remove meat to platter; cover, and chill several hours. Dissolve onion soup mix in hot meat juices; set aside. When ready to serve, slice meat and place in reserved seasoned juices in 3-quart (13 x 9) glass baking dish. Cover with plastic wrap.

3. Microwave on REHEAT for 8 to 10 minutes or until heated through. Let stand, covered, 5 minutes before serving.   About 8 Servings

Pictured left to right: Beef Stuffed Peppers, page 61; Ground Beef Patties, page 59 or 60; Frozen Tater Tots, page 166.

GROUND BEEF KEY: Ground beef, mainstay of American dinner tables, microwaves into juicy patties on HIGH — turns into outstanding meatball, meatloaf and stuffed vegetable dishes on even-cooking ROAST.

Meat should be completely thawed before cooking. See defrosting chart on page 48.

Cook ground beef patties uncovered, on a microwave browning grill, a glass pie plate, dinner plate or serving platter (without silver or other metal trim).

Microwave most other ground beef dishes in glass casseroles or baking dishes with fitted glass lids, tight coverings of plastic wrap or wax paper.

Drain off excess fat and moisture as directed in a recipe, to preserve flavor and sauce consistency.

Rearrange or stir ground beef dishes thoroughly when called for in a recipe so the entire mixture cooks evenly.

Follow standing time directions carefully. Food continues to cook after it comes from a microwave oven.

GROUND BEEF PATTIES ON MICROWAVE BROWNING GRILL

- **1 lb. ground beef**
- **1 teaspoon salt**
- **¼ teaspoon pepper**
- **1 tablespoon finely chopped onion**

1. Combine all ingredients in medium glass mixing bowl; mix well. Shape into 4 patties. Preheat microwave browning grill in oven on HIGH as directed in instruction booklet. Place patties on browning grill.

2. Microwave on HIGH for 2 minutes. Turn patties over and continue cooking on HIGH for 2½ to 3 minutes or to desired doneness.   4 Patties

TIPS ● Make ITALIAN-STYLE PATTIES by stirring ½ teaspoon leaf oregano and ¼ teaspoon leaf basil into basic recipe. Microwave as directed in basic recipe. Top with shredded Mozzarella cheese.

● Make FRENCH-STYLE PATTIES by basting meat with ¼ cup dry red wine after first cooking time. Top with 1 can (4 oz.) mushroom stems and pieces, drained, and continue cooking on HIGH for 3 to 4 minutes or until desired doneness. Sprinkle with snipped parsley.

● Make CHEDDAR CHEESE PATTIES. Top each patty with 2 tablespoons shredded Cheddar cheese and 1 teaspoon catsup after first cooking time. Continue cooking as directed in basic recipe.

● Make BLEU CHEESE PATTIES. Combine ¼ cup crumbled Bleu cheese, ½ cup sour cream and 2 tablespoons finely chopped onion. Spoon 2 tablespoons cheese mixture on each patty after first cooking time. Continue cooking as directed in basic recipe.

HOW TO COOK GROUND BEEF PATTIES

● Season 1 pound ground beef with 1 teaspoon salt and ¼ teaspoon pepper. Shape patties.

● Place patty(ies) on 9-inch glass pie plate, dinner plate or platter without silver or other metal trim.

● Microwave on HIGH . Turn once halfway through cooking period.

● When serving surround patties with hot cooked rice or mashed potatoes to absorb flavorful meat juices — or if preferred, drain on paper towel.

PATTIES	WEIGHT	SETTING	MINUTES
1	4-oz.	HIGH	2 to 2½
2	4-oz. ea.	HIGH	3 to 3½
4	4-oz. ea.	HIGH	4½ to 5
6	4-oz. ea.	HIGH	6½ to 7

SEASONED INDIVIDUAL MEAT LOAVES

    2 lbs. ground beef
 1½ cups herb-seasoned stuffing mix
    1 egg
 1½ teaspoon salt
    ¼ teaspoon pepper
    ¼ cup finely chopped onion
    1 can (8 oz.) tomato sauce

1. Combine all ingredients in medium mixing bowl. Form into 8 individual meat loaves. Place in 2-quart (12 x 7) glass baking dish. Cover with plastic wrap.

2. Microwave on ROAST for 20 to 25 minutes or until well done. Let stand, covered, for 5 minutes before serving.   6 to 8 Servings

RANCH MEAT LOAF

 1½ lbs. ground beef
    2 cups soft bread cubes
    ½ cup finely chopped celery
    ½ cup catsup
    ¼ cup finely chopped green pepper
 1½ teaspoons salt
    1 egg, beaten

1. Combine all ingredients in medium mixing bowl; mix well. Pat into 8 x 4 glass loaf dish.

2. Microwave on ROAST for 25 to 30 minutes or until well done in center. Let stand, covered, 5 minutes before serving.   5 to 6 Servings

TIP ● Drizzle with catsup and garnish with parsley.

SALISBURY STEAKS

 1½ lbs. ground beef
    ½ cup cooked rice
    ¼ cup chopped green pepper
    2 green onions, sliced
    1 teaspoon salt
    1 teaspoon dried parsley flakes
    ½ teaspoon garlic salt
    ¼ teaspoon pepper
    1 egg

Sauce:
    1 can (10¾ oz.) condensed beef consomme
    1 can (4 oz.) mushroom stems and pieces, drained
    ⅓ cup catsup
    1 tablespoon cornstarch
    ¼ teaspoon leaf basil
    1 teaspoon Worcestershire sauce

1. Combine all ingredients, except Sauce ingredients, in medium mixing bowl. Shape into 6 rounded patties. Place in 1½-quart (10 x 6) glass baking dish. Cover with plastic wrap.

2. Microwave on ROAST for 8 minutes. Drain and rearrange steaks. Pour Sauce over steaks; recover, and continue cooking on ROAST for 8 to 10 minutes. Let stand, covered, 5 minutes.

3. Sauce: Combine all ingredients in 4-cup measure.   About 6 Servings

SESAME MEATBALL DINNER

    1 lb. ground beef
    1 cup shredded raw potatoes
    1 tablespoon dried parsley flakes
    ½ teaspoon salt
    ¼ teaspoon pepper
    1 small onion, finely chopped
    2 tablespoons sesame seeds
    1 egg, beaten
    2 cups water
 1½ tablespoons instant beef bouillon
    2 tablespoons cornstarch
    2 tablespoons water

1. Mix all ingredients except water, beef bouillon and cornstarch in medium mixing bowl. Shape into 12 (1½-inch) meatballs; set aside.

2. Combine 2 cups water and instant beef bouillon in 2-quart glass casserole. Cover with glass lid or plastic wrap.

3. Microwave on HIGH for 6 to 7 minutes or until boiling. Add meatballs; recover.

4. Microwave on ROAST for 8 minutes. Stir in a mixture of cornstarch and 2 tablespoons water; recover.

5. Microwave on ROAST for 3 to 4 minutes or until sauce is thickened. Let stand, covered, 5 minutes before serving.   About 4 Servings

BEEF-STUFFED PEPPERS

- 3 **large sweet green peppers, cut in half lengthwise**
- 1 **lb. ground beef**
- 1 **cup quick-cooking rolled oats**
- 1 **egg, slightly beaten**
- 1 **small onion, finely chopped**
- 1 **can (8 oz.) tomato sauce**
- 1 **tablespoon Worcestershire sauce**
- 1 **teaspoon salt**
- ⅓ **cup water**

[handwritten: ½, ½ 4 slice bread, 1 tbs, ½, ⅛ tsp garlic powd, moz cheese]

1. Place peppers in 2-quart (12 x 7) glass baking dish; set aside. Combine remaining ingredients, except water, in medium bowl; mix well. Spoon meat mixture into green pepper halves. Pour water in bottom of dish. Cover with plastic wrap.

2. Microwave on ROAST *[handwritten: high]* for 22 to 24 minutes or until done. Let stand, covered, 5 minutes before serving.   About 6 Servings

TIP • Top with catsup or chili sauce.

[handwritten: 1 cans tomato sace (15oz) + H₂O 1/2 cup, 2 tbs prestos - pizza, 1½ tsp sugar]

ROAST FRESH PORK KEY: A microwave oven cooks large pork cuts thoroughly — keeps them tender and juicy. Start cooking on Microwave HIGH to heat meat through quickly. Lower setting to ROAST during last half of cooking to assure evenly done meat.

Thaw meat completely before cooking. See defrosting chart on page 49.

Boneless and bone-in roasts cook in about the same time in open flat glass baking dishes. Place meat on a microwave roasting rack to hold it above drippings.

Microwave roasts, fat side down first; turn smaller roasts over halfway through cooking. If roast weighs 7 pounds or more, turn it over 3 times during cooking.

Glazes and sauces "dress up" roast pork. Bone-in roasts are especially attractive because of browned appearance.

Pork is removed from the oven when internal temperature reaches 160° F. so meat does not overcook. Insert a microwave meat thermometer in roast center when meat is turned the last time.

Let meat stand, covered with foil, to finish cooking and raise internal temperature about 15° F. Pork is done when internal temperature reaches 170° F. (New standards)

Other doneness tests: When roast center is cut, juices run clear and meat is no longer pink. Or a conventional meat thermometer may be inserted after meat is taken from the oven. DO NOT use this thermometer in a microwave oven.

Smaller pork cuts are done when meat is no longer pink and juices run clear. Thorough cooking is important but do not overcook.

CENTER RIB PORK ROAST WITH CHERRY SAUCE *

- 4 **to 5-lb. pork loin center rib roast**

Cherry Sauce:
- ½ **cup cherry preserves**
- ¼ **cup dark corn syrup**
- 2 **tablespoons vinegar**
- ⅛ **teaspoon salt**
- ⅛ **teaspoon nutmeg**
- ⅛ **teaspoon cinnamon**
- ⅛ **teaspoon ground cloves**
  Dash pepper

1. Place roast, fat side down on microwave roasting rack, in 2-quart (12 x 7) glass baking dish.

2. Microwave on HIGH for 24 minutes. Turn fat side up.

3. Microwave on ROAST for 20 to 24 minutes or until microwave meat thermometer inserted in center of meat reaches 160° F. Let stand, covered with foil, 15 minutes before serving or until internal temperature reaches 170° F. Slash pork roast between ribs; place on serving platter. Pour hot Cherry Sauce over meat.

4. **Cherry Sauce:** Combine all ingredients in 2-cup glass measure.

5. Microwave on HIGH for 3 to 4 minutes or until bubbly.   6 to 8 Servings

TIP • BONELESS PORK ROAST: Use same technique as above. See meat roasting chart, page 51, for time and doneness tests.

SMALL CUT FRESH PORK KEY: Fresh pork is great! It is uniformly tender so most small cuts cook well on Microwave ROAST.

Tenderloin, chops, steaks, patties, cubes, strips — even ribs and hocks — come out of a microwave oven juicy and tender. Always buy finely-textured lean firm pork.

Meat should be completely thawed before cooking unless specified in a recipe.

Trim excess fat from meat before cooking.

Use glass baking dishes or serving casseroles without silver or other metal trim.

All cuts are tightly covered to hasten cooking and to assure tenderness. Use glass lids, plastic wrap or wax paper.

Most recipes call for turning or stirring so meat cooks evenly.

Draining, when called for in a recipe, removes excess fat and moisture. Some dishes with sauces, stuffings or very lean pork are not drained because fat and drippings are a desirable addition.

Standing time, covered, is essential to thorough cooking. Pork is done when juices run clear, meat is no longer pink and is fork tender.

HOW TO COOK PORK CHOPS ON A MICROWAVE BROWNING GRILL

- Preheat microwave browning grill in oven on HIGH as directed in manufacturer's instruction booklet.

- Place chop(s) on preheated browning grill.

- Turn once half way through cooking.

- Let stand 3 minutes on hot microwave browning grill before serving.

PORK CHOPS	WEIGHT	SETTING	MINUTES
1 (½-in. thick)	3-oz.	HIGH	3½ to 4
2 (½-in. thick)	3-oz. ea.	HIGH	5 to 6

STUFFED PORK CHOPS

  ½ cup milk
  ¼ cup butter or margarine
  2 cups dry seasoned bread stuffing
  1 envelope (⅝ oz.) brown gravy mix
  8 thin rib pork chops (about 1½ lbs.), trim off fat

1. Combine milk and butter in medium glass mixing bowl.

2. Microwave ROAST for 2 to 3 minutes until butter is melted. Stir in bread stuffing and mix well; set aside. Sprinkle one side of 4 chops with half of dry gravy mix; place seasoned side down in 2-quart (8 x 8) glass baking dish. Spoon dressing on top of each chop. Place remaining chops on top of dressing. Sprinkle with remaining gravy mix. Cover with plastic wrap.

3. Microwave on ROAST for 12 to 15 minutes or until fork tender. Let stand, covered, 5 minutes before serving. About 4 Servings

Drain chops part way through cooking to remove excess fat and moisture.

CENTER CUT CHOP SPECIAL

  3 slices bacon, diced
  1 cup finely chopped onion
  2 cloves garlic, finely chopped
  ¼ cup soy sauce
  3 tablespoons lemon juice
  1 tablespoon honey
  1 teaspoon chili powder
  ½ teaspoon salt
  ½ teaspoon curry powder
  4 (¾-inch-thick) loin pork chops (about 1½ lbs.), trim off fat

1. Combine bacon, onion, garlic in 2-cup glass measure.

2. Microwave on HIGH for 4 to 5 minutes or until bacon is crisp. Combine with remaining ingredients except chops; set aside. Place chops in 2-quart (8 x 8) glass baking dish. Cover with plastic wrap.

3. Microwave on ROAST for 10 minutes. Drain and turn chops over. Pour seasoned sauce over chops. Recover and continue cooking on ROAST for 12 to 15 minutes or until fork tender. Let stand, covered, 5 minutes before serving.
About 4 Servings

Pan juices blend with sauce to create a savory dish.

SWEET AND SOUR PORK

  1½ lbs. cubed lean pork
  2 tablespoons cornstarch
  3 tablespoons soy sauce
  ¼ cup packed brown sugar
  ¼ cup vinegar
  1 teaspoon salt
  ¼ teaspoon ground ginger
  1 can (13¼ oz.) pineapple chunks, undrained
  1 small onion, thinly sliced
  1 medium green pepper, cut into strips

1. Toss together pork and cornstarch in 2-quart glass casserole. Stir in remaining ingredients, except green pepper. Cover with glass lid or plastic wrap.

2. Microwave on ROAST for 25 minutes. Stir in green pepper. Recover and continue cooking on ROAST for 5 to 10 minutes or until fork tender. Let stand, covered, 5 minutes before serving.
4 to 6 Servings

Pictured clockwise from the top: Stuffed Pork Chops garnished with parsley, this page; Sweet and Sour Pork, this page; Boneless Baked Ham garnished with cloves, page 51.

OVEN BAKED SPARERIBS WITH APPLE CIDER

> 3 lbs. Country-Style pork spareribs,
>   cut into serving pieces,
>   trim off fat
> 2 teaspoons leaf basil
> 1 teaspoon paprika
> ½ teaspoon salt
> ¼ teaspoon leaf majoram
> ⅛ teaspoon pepper
> 1 medium onion, sliced
> ½ cup apple cider

1. Place ribs in 2-quart (12 x 7) glass baking dish. Cover with plastic wrap.

2. Microwave on ROAST for 15 minutes. Drain and turn ribs over. Add remaining ingredients. Re-cover and continue cooking on ROAST for 25 to 30 minutes or until fork tender. Let stand, covered, 5 minutes before serving.   About 4 Servings

PORK HOCKS AND CABBAGE

> 1 to 2 fresh pork hocks (about 1¼ lbs.),
>   sawed into serving pieces
> 2 cups water
> ½ medium cabbage, quartered
> 1 teaspoon salt
> ¼ teaspoon pepper
> 2 teaspoons caraway seeds

1. Place hocks in 2-quart glass casserole. Cover with glass lid or plastic wrap.

2. Microwave on ROAST for 20 minutes. Turn meat over. Add remaining ingredients. Recover and continue cooking on ROAST for 20 to 25 minutes or until fork tender. Let stand, covered, 5 minutes before serving.   2 to 3 Servings

PORK PATTIES WITH APPLESAUCE

> 2 eggs, slightly beaten
> 1 lb. ground pork
> 1 cup dry bread crumbs
> ¼ cup finely chopped celery
> 1 teaspoon salt
> 1 teaspoon Worcestershire sauce
> ¼ teaspoon pepper
> ¼ teaspoon ground sage
> 1½ cups applesauce

1. Combine all ingredients, except applesauce, in medium mixing bowl. Shape into 6 patties. Place in 2-quart (12 x 7) glass baking dish. Cover with plastic wrap.

2. Microwave on ROAST for 10 minutes. Drain and turn patties over. Spoon applesauce on top of each patty. Recover and continue cooking on ROAST for 4 to 6 minutes or until no longer pink in center. Let stand, covered, 5 minutes before serving.   2 to 4 Servings

Cover assures ribs' tenderness.

BARBECUED SPARERIBS

> 3 lbs. pork spareribs, cut into serving
>   pieces, trim off fat
> 1 medium onion, finely chopped
> 1 clove garlic, finely chopped
> ¼ cup vinegar
> ¾ cup chili sauce
> 1 can (8 oz.) tomato sauce
> 2 tablespoons packed brown sugar
> 1 tablespoon Worcestershire sauce
> 1 teaspoon salt
> ¼ teaspoon pepper

1. Place ribs in 3-quart (13 x 9) glass baking dish. Cover with plastic wrap.

2. Microwave on ROAST for 15 minutes. Drain and turn ribs over. Arrange onion and garlic on top. Add mixture of remaining ingredients. Recover and continue cooking on ROAST for 25 to 30 minutes or until fork tender. Let stand, covered, 5 minutes before serving.   5 to 6 Servings

TIP • Outdoor barbecuing is fast and easy. Prepare and microwave ribs as directed through first cooking period. Place drained ribs on grill over hot coals. Make sauce of remaining ingredients; brush ribs. Turn ribs and continue brushing with sauce until tender.

No bone, no waste – easy to serve.

PORK TENDERLOIN IN ORANGE SAUCE

> ¼ cup butter or margarine
> 1 medium onion, finely chopped
> 2 tablespoons sugar
> 1 tablespoon cornstarch
> 2 teaspoons salt
> 1 teaspoon grated orange peel
> ⅛ teaspoon pepper
> 1 bay leaf
> ¼ cup orange juice
> ⅓ cup dry sherry
> 2 pork tenderloins (about 1 lb. each)

1. Place butter and onion in 2-quart (12 x 7) glass baking dish.

2. Microwave on ROAST for 3 minutes. Stir in remaining ingredients, except pork. Coat pork tenderloin in sauce. Cover with plastic wrap.

3. Microwave on ROAST for 25 to 30 minutes or until meat is fork tender. Let stand, covered, 5 minutes. Slice diagonally to serve.   6 to 8 Servings

TIP • Tuck thin ends of pork tenderloin under larger portion of meat for more uniform cooking.

CURED PORK KEY: Ham, Canadian bacon, smoked pork chops — all these cured meats come from the market partially or fully cooked. This means they'll microwave evenly on ROAST .

Ground ham, however, can be cooked more quickly on Microwave REHEAT .

Cook large pieces of cured ham on a microwave roasting rack set in a flat glass baking dish.

Microwave smaller cuts of cured pork in a glass baking dish or casserole. Cover, when specified, with glass lid, plastic wrap or wax paper to speed heating and cooking.

Some dishes do not require covering because a roasting technique is employed. Do cover these dishes with foil during standing time to assure thorough heating and cooking.

Turn larger pieces of meat over during cooking. Check the meat chart on page 51.

If an area on a roast appears to be drying during cooking, cover it with foil. Do not let foil touch oven surface or arcing and pitting may result.

Allow ¼ to ⅓ pound boneless ham per serving, ½ to ⅔ pound bone-in ham per serving.

BONELESS BAKED HAM WITH CARAWAY HONEY GLAZE*

    3½ to 3¾-lb. ready-to-eat boneless ham
    2 tablespoons honey
    1 teaspoon prepared mustard
    ½ teaspoon caraway seeds

1. Place ham, fat side down on microwave roasting rack, in 2-quart (12 x 7) glass baking dish.

2. Microwave on ROAST for 21 minutes. Turn fat side up. Brush with mixture of honey, mustard and caraway seeds. Continue cooking on ROAST for 21 to 23 minutes or until heated through.

3. Let stand, covered with foil, about 10 minutes before serving.   10 to 14 Servings

BONE-IN PINEAPPLE GLAZE HAM*

    7 to 8-lb. ready-to-eat bone-in
      ham shank
    1 can (15¼ oz.) crushed pineapple,
      undrained
    ⅓ cup packed brown sugar

1. Place ham, cut side down on microwave roasting rack, in 3-quart (13 x 9) glass baking dish.

2. Microwave on ROAST for 20 minutes. Turn ham on one side and continue cooking on ROAST for 20 minutes. Turn ham to other side. Mix crushed pineapple and brown sugar. Pour sauce over ham and continue cooking on ROAST for 15 to 20 minutes or until heated through. Let stand, covered with foil, about 10 minutes before serving.   10 to 14 Servings

Glaze forms when meat is uncovered.

CANADIAN BACON WITH FRUIT SAUCE

    1 cup halved mixed dried fruit
    1 cup water
    ½ cup plum preserves
    1½ to 1¾-lb. whole Canadian Style bacon

1. Combine dried fruit and water in small glass mixing bowl.

2. Microwave on HIGH for 5 to 6 minutes or until boiling. Stir in plum preserves. Make 6 to 8 serving slashes in bacon; do not slice through. Place in 2-quart (8 x 8) glass baking dish. Spoon fruit sauce between slices and over top of Canadian bacon.

3. Microwave on ROAST for 15 to 18 minutes or until hot. Let stand 5 minutes before serving.
                                        About 6 Servings

CENTER CUT HAM WITH APRICOTS

    3 to 3¼-lb. center cut ham slice,
      2 inches thick, trim off fat
    1 can (16 oz.) apricots, undrained
    ¼ cup packed brown sugar
    2 tablespoons cornstarch
    2 tablespoons vinegar
    ¼ teaspoon nutmeg
    2 tablespoons butter or margarine

1. Score edges of ham slice; place in 2-quart (12 x 7) glass baking dish. Combine apricot juice, brown sugar, cornstarch, vinegar and nutmeg in small mixing bowl; pour over ham. Top with apricots and dot with butter.

2. Microwave on ROAST for 20 to 25 minutes or until ham is hot and sauce thickened. Let stand 5 minutes before serving.   6 to 8 Servings

Meat is certain to be "done" and hot through when allowed to stand, covered.

HAM 'N YAM

    ¾ to 1-lb. ham slice, ¼-inch thick,
      trim off fat
    1 can (18 oz.) vacuum-packed sweet
      potatoes
    ⅓ cup raisins
    2 tablespoons packed brown sugar
    ¼ cup red currant jelly
    2 tablespoons orange juice

1. Place ham slice in 2-quart (8 x 8) glass baking dish. Arrange sweet potatoes around ham slice. Combine remaining ingredients and pour over ham and sweet potatoes. Cover with plastic wrap.

2. Microwave on ROAST for 12 to 14 minutes or until heated through. Let stand, covered, 5 minutes before serving.   About 3 Servings

MINI HAM LOAVES

- **1 lb. ground ham**
- **1 lb. ground pork**
- **2 cups dry bread crumbs**
- **1 cup milk**
- **2 eggs, beaten**
- **½ teaspoon ground sage**

Sauce:
- **¼ cup vinegar**
- **¼ cup water**
- **¾ cup packed brown sugar**
- **½ teaspoon dry mustard**
- **2 tablespoons cornstarch**

1. Combine all ingredients, except Sauce ingredients in medium mixing bowl; mix well. Shape into 8 individual loaves. Arrange in 2-quart (12 x 7) glass baking dish. Cover with plastic wrap.

2. Microwave on ROAST for 15 minutes. Drain. Pour Sauce over ham loaves. Recover and continue cooking on ROAST for 5 to 6 minutes or until meat is done.

3. Sauce: Combine all ingredients in 2-cup measure.   6 to 8 Servings

TIP ● Garnish with chopped green pepper and canned drained mandarin oranges.

BACON AND SAUSAGE KEY: Bacon crisps on Microwave HIGH.

Precooked sausage cooks quickly on REHEAT.

Fresh sausage needs slower more even cooking. Use Microwave ROAST.

A microwave browning grill is a great accessory when it comes to browning and quickly cooking fresh or precooked pork sausage. See manufacturer's instruction booklet.

A barbeque grill technique allows sausage kabobs to microwave very well on a microwave roasting rack placed in a flat glass dish to catch drippings — try it.

Cook all sausage mixtures in glass casseroles or baking dishes. Small amounts of bacon and pork sausage can be placed on paper napkins or towels to absorb grease. Paper will not absorb all grease from larger quantities of bacon or sausage. Drain off excess grease before serving.

A cover keeps sausage meat moist and tender. Use a fitted glass lid, plastic wrap or wax paper tucked tightly across top of the cooking dish.

Turning and rearranging sausage keeps meat cooking evenly and quickly since microwaves cook first at the edges of a dish. Uncooked sausage is the most "touchy." Remove links or patties from oven as they finish cooking.

HOW TO COOK BACON

● Place 1 to 4 bacon strips between paper napkin or towel on glass or pottery plate or baking dish without silver or other metal trim. Paper absorbs nearly all grease. Cook larger quantities of bacon without paper, if desired.

● Microwave on HIGH until crisp.

● Remove paper, if used, and serve. Drain away excess grease.

● Times may vary according to brand, slice thickness and/or cure of bacon. It is recommended that cooking time be reduced for smaller or extra-thin bacon slices.

BACON SLICES	SETTING	MINUTES
2	HIGH	2 to 2½
4	HIGH	4 to 4½
6	HIGH	5 to 6
8	HIGH	8 to 9

Microwave fresh sausage on HIGH when using browning grill.

HOW TO COOK PORK SAUSAGE ON MICROWAVE BROWNING GRILL

● Preheat microwave browning grill in oven on HIGH as directed in manufacturer's instructions.

● Place sausage on preheated grill.

● Microwave on HIGH. Turn sausage over and rearrange halfway through cooking.

● Cook fresh pork sausage until no longer pink in center.

● Brown precooked sausage until hot; serve.

PORK SAUSAGE	SETTING	MINUTES
FRESH LINKS 8-oz. pkg.	HIGH	6 to 6½
PRECOOKED LINKS OR PATTIES 8-oz. pkg.		
Frozen	HIGH	3 to 3½
Refrigerated	HIGH	1½ to 2

HOW TO MICROWAVE PRECOOKED PORK SAUSAGE

• Place sausage links or patties on paper napkin or paper towel on glass plate.

• Microwave on REHEAT until hot; serve.

PORK SAUSAGE	SETTING	TIME
PRECOOKED LINKS OR PATTIES Frozen:		
2	REHEAT	1 to 1½ min.
3	REHEAT	1¾ to 2 min.
4	REHEAT	2 to 2½ min.
Refrigerated: **2**	REHEAT	15 to 30 sec.
3	REHEAT	30 to 45 sec.
4	REHEAT	1 to 1½ min.

SAUSAGE LINKS WITH BEANS

  ½ **lb. fresh pork sausage links in casing, cut into quarters**
  1 **small onion, finely chopped**
  ¼ **cup chopped celery**
  2 **tablespoons packed brown sugar**
  2 **tablespoons prepared mustard**
  1 **tablespoon Worcestershire sauce**
  1 **can (6 oz.) tomato paste**
  1 **can (16 oz.) pork and beans, undrained**

1. Combine all ingredients in 1½-quart glass casserole. Cover with glass lid or plastic wrap.

2. Microwave on ROAST for 12 to 14 minutes or until done. Let stand, covered, 5 minutes before serving. About 4 Servings

POLISH SAUSAGE ATOP CARAWAY SAUERKRAUT*

  1 **package (32 oz.) refrigerated sauerkraut**
  2 **teaspoons caraway seeds**
  1 **medium apple, cored and finely sliced**
  1 **lb. precooked Polish sausage**

1. Drain sauerkraut. Place in 2-quart (8 x 8) glass baking dish. Stir in caraway seeds and apples. Place sausage on top. Cover with plastic wrap.

2. Microwave on REHEAT for 10 minutes. Turn sausage over; recover, and continue cooking on REHEAT for 5 to 7 minutes. Let stand, covered, 5 minutes before serving. 3 to 4 Servings

BRATWURST IN BEER

  6 **uncooked bratwurst (about 1 lb.)**
  ½ **cup finely chopped onion**
  2 **tablespoons butter or margarine**
  1 **can (12 oz.) beer, room temperature**

1. Place bratwurst in 8-inch round glass baking dish. Add remaining ingredients. Cover with plastic wrap.

2. Microwave on ROAST for 5 to 6 minutes or until done. Let stand, covered, 5 minutes before serving. About 3 Servings

Metal skewers, like metal spoons, may be used in a microwave oven.

RING BOLOGNA KABOBS

  1 **ring (16 oz.) bologna, cut into ¾-inch chunks**
  1 **can (8¼ oz.) pineapple chunks, drained**
  1 **can (16 oz.) whole potatoes, drained**
  1 **green pepper, cut into 1-inch pieces**
  Pitted ripe olives
  ¼ **cup orange marmalade**
  Cherry tomatoes

1. Alternate bologna slices, pineapple chunks, potatoes, green pepper and olives on metal kabob skewers. Arrange on microwave roasting rack in 2-quart (12 x 7) glass baking dish. Spread marmalade over kabobs.

2. Microwave on REHEAT for 8 to 9 minutes or until hot. Spear tomatoes on ends just before serving. About 4 Servings

Pictured: Ring Bologna Kabobs, this page; Cooked Rice, page 106.

LAMB KEY: Today's lamb is marketed at a young age, so flavor's delicate and meat's tender. Microwave cooking on ROAST retains these key qualities.

Lamb should be completely thawed before cooking in a microwave oven. See defrosting chart on page 49.

Cook larger roasts, uncovered, on a microwave roasting rack. Set rack in shallow glass baking dish to catch drippings. Turn roasts as specified in roasting chart, on page 50, to make certain meat cooks evenly.

Lamb steaks may be cooked uncovered, too, because they cook so quickly. Other small cuts of lamb should be covered to assure complete cooking plus tenderness. Microwave in glass casseroles or baking dishes covered tightly with glass lids, plastic wrap or wax paper. Pierce plastic wrap before removing it to prevent steam burns.

A microwave meat thermometer is the most accurate doneness test for large cuts. It should register 165° F. when meat comes from oven. Foil covering during standing time allows internal temperature to rise about 15° F. and complete cooking. Small cuts of lamb are done when meat is fork tender.

ROAST setting preserves delicate flavor yet cooks quickly.

ORANGE GLAZE LEG O' LAMB*

4 to 4½-lb. leg of lamb roast
½ cup orange juice
½ cup orange marmalade
2 teaspoons ground ginger

1. Place roast, fat side down on a microwave roasting rack, in 2-quart (12 x 7) glass baking dish.

2. Microwave on ROAST for 25 minutes. Turn meat over and continue cooking on ROAST for 20 to 25 minutes or until meat thermometer inserted in meat registers 165° F. Pour mixture of orange juice, marmalade and ginger over roast during last 10 minutes of cooking time. Let stand, covered with foil, 10 minutes or until internal temperature reaches 180° F.   6 to 8 Servings

TIPS • Save lamb bone to make soup.
• LAMB SHOULDER ROAST: Use same techniques as above. See meat roasting chart, page 51, for time and doneness tests.

Open dish cooking crisps edges a bit.

CRUMBLED BLEU TOPPED LAMB STEAKS*

4 (¼-inch-thick) lamb shoulder steaks (about 2 lbs.), trim off fat
½ cup crumbled Bleu cheese
2 green onions, chopped
¼ teaspoon salt

1. Place steaks in 2-quart (12 x 7) glass baking dish.

2. Microwave on ROAST for 10 minutes. Turn meat over. Continue cooking on ROAST 6 to 8 minutes or until steak is no longer pink. Drain and top each steak with a mixture of cheese, onion and salt. Continue cooking on ROAST for 3 to 5 minutes or until cheese is bubbly.   About 4 Servings

A meal-in-minutes.

CHILI LAMB PATTIES

4 ground lamb patties (about 1½ lbs.)
½ cup chili sauce
¼ cup dried parsley flakes
2 tablespoons prepared mustard
2 tablespoons vinegar
½ teaspoon garlic salt

1. Place lamb patties in 1-quart glass casserole. Cover with glass lid or plastic wrap.

2. Microwave on ROAST for 10 minutes. Drain; turn patties over, and pour a mixture of remaining ingredients over top. Recover and continue cooking on ROAST for 4 to 5 minutes or until done. Let stand, covered, 5 minutes before serving.
                About 4 Servings

Tender morsels of lamb barbecue well under a cover.

DEVILED LAMB SPARERIBS

2½ to 3 lbs. lamb spareribs, slash between ribs, trim off fat
½ cup chili sauce
½ cup lemon juice
2 tablespoons Worcestershire sauce
1 tablespoon prepared mustard
2 teaspoons salt
¼ teaspoon pepper
½ teaspoon paprika

1. Place ribs, fat side down, in 2-quart (12 x 7) glass baking dish. Cover with plastic wrap.

2. Microwave on ROAST for 10 minutes. Combine remaining ingredients in 2-cup measure. Drain and turn meat over. Pour sauce over meat. Recover and continue cooking on ROAST for 15 to 18 minutes or until meat is fork tender. Let stand, covered, 5 minutes before serving.   3 to 4 Servings

CURRIED LAMB MEATBALLS

- 1 lb. ground lamb
- 1 clove garlic, finely chopped
- 1 medium onion, sliced
- 1 stalk celery, sliced
- 2 tablespoons all-purpose flour
- 1½ teaspoons curry powder
- 1 teaspoon salt
- 2 teaspoons instant chicken bouillon
- ¼ cup chutney
- 1 teaspoon prepared mustard
- ¾ cup water

1. Combine ground lamb and garlic in medium mixing bowl; mix well. Shape into 16 to 18 (1-inch) lamb balls. Place in 2-quart (12 x 7) glass baking dish. Add onion and celery. Cover with plastic wrap.

2. Microwave on ROAST for 5 minutes. Combine remaining ingredients in 4-cup measure; mix well. Drain and rearrange lamb balls; pour on sauce. Recover and continue cooking on ROAST for 8 to 10 minutes or until hot. Let stand, covered, 5 minutes before serving.   About 4 Servings

Pictured top to bottom: Liver Bacon and Onions, page 70; Curried Lamb Meatballs, this page. Condiments are raisins, pickle relish and chopped peanuts.

Cover and standing time help tenderize meat.

LAMB SHANKS

- 2 tablespoons all-purpose flour
- 1 teaspoon salt
- ½ teaspoon pepper
- ¼ teaspoon garlic salt
- 4 lamb shanks (2½ to 3 lbs.)
- ½ cup chopped onion
- 1 cup thinly sliced carrots
- 1 tablespoon dried parsley flakes
- ½ teaspoon leaf rosemary
- 1 teaspoon salt
- 1 can (10½ oz.) condensed beef consommé

1. Combine flour, salt, pepper and garlic salt in 9-inch glass pie dish. Roll lamb shanks in seasoned flour; place in 2-quart (12 x 7) glass baking dish. Cover with plastic wrap.

2. Microwave on ROAST for 20 minutes. Turn meat over. Stir in remaining ingredients. Recover and continue cooking on ROAST for 20 to 25 minutes or until fork tender.   About 4 Servings

VEAL KEY: Veal, meat from specially fed beef calves, is delicately flavored and textured. Start larger roasts heating through on ROAST; reduce heat to SIMMER to gently cook and retain tenderness. Check meat chart at the beginning of this chapter for roasting times.

Small cuts of veal cook quickly enough to retain flavor and texture. Use the SIMMER setting throughout cooking.

Ground veal, as with ground beef and pork, cooks well on a higher setting — ROAST in this case.

Roast large cuts of veal on a microwave roasting rack set in a glass baking dish to catch drippings — see meat roasting chart. Braise large bone-in cuts. Use Braised Veal Rump Roast recipe, this page, as a guide.

Cook smaller veal cuts in a flat glass baking dish or casserole. Cover tightly with a glass lid, plastic wrap or wax paper to preserve meat's juiciness. Pierce plastic wrap before removing it to prevent steam burns.

Turn meat when specified to assure even cooking.

Remove veal from the oven when it is fork tender.

Follow standing time directions carefully so meat cooks completely.

VEAL CUTLETS IN WHITE WINE

- ¼ **cup butter or margarine**
- 1 **clove garlic, finely chopped**
- 5 **veal cutlets (about 1½ lbs.)**
- **Salt**
- **Pepper**
- 1 **tablespoon instant beef bouillon**
- 1 **medium onion, thinly sliced**
- ¼ **cup dry white wine**
- 1 **tablespoon dried parsley flakes**

1. Place butter and garlic in 2-quart (12 x 7) glass baking dish.

2. Microwave on ROAST for about 2 minutes or until butter melts. Coat veal in garlic butter and arrange in dish. Add remaining ingredients. Cover with plastic wrap.

3. Microwave on SIMMER for 25 to 30 minutes or until meat is fork tender. Let stand, covered, 5 minutes before serving.   4 to 5 Servings

TIP • Substitute chops for cutlets.

The soup-base gravy with this roast is something special – try it with a beef rump roast, too.

BRAISED VEAL RUMP ROAST

- 2⅓ **to 3-lb. bone-in veal rump roast**
- 1 **can (10¾ oz.) condensed beef and barley vegetable soup**
- 1 **teaspoon salt**
- ¼ **teaspoon pepper**
- 1 **tablespoon dried parsley flakes**
- ½ **teaspoon leaf thyme**
- 1 **bay leaf**
- 2 **tablespoons all-purpose flour**

1. Place roast, fat side down, in 3-quart glass casserole. Cover with glass lid or plastic wrap.

2. Microwave on ROAST for 30 minutes. Turn meat over. Drain juice into measuring cup; set aside. Add remaining ingredients, except flour; recover.

3. Microwave on SIMMER for 30 to 35 minutes or until fork tender. Let stand, covered, 5 minutes before serving. Remove roast to platter. Blend flour with juice drained from roast. Stir into hot seasoned meat drippings; mix well.

4. Microwave on HIGH for 1 to 2 minutes or until thickened. Serve gravy over roast.
About 4 Servings

VEAL MEATBALLS IN SPICY SAUCE

- 2 **tablespoons butter or margarine**
- 2 **lbs. ground veal**
- ¼ **cup dry bread crumbs**
- 1 **clove garlic, finely chopped**
- 2 **teaspoons prepared mustard**
- ⅛ **teaspoon white pepper**

Sauce:
- 1 **can (6 oz.) tomato paste**
- ⅔ **cup water**
- ½ **cup wine vinegar**
- ¼ **cup lemon juice**
- 2 **tablespoons Worcestershire sauce**
- ½ **cup packed brown sugar**
- 1 **teaspoon dry mustard**
- 1 **teaspoon salt**
- ¼ **teaspoon chili powder**

1. Place butter in 2-quart (12 x 7) glass baking dish.

2. Microwave on ROAST for about 1½ minutes or until melted. Combine remaining ingredients, except Sauce ingredients, in medium mixing bowl. Shape into 18 (1-inch) balls and place in melted butter. Cover baking dish with plastic wrap.

3. Microwave on ROAST for 8 minutes. Drain and rearrange. Pour Sauce over meatballs. Recover and continue cooking on ROAST 8 to 10 minutes or until hot and center meatballs are no longer pink. Let stand, covered, 5 minutes before serving.

4. **Sauce:** Combine sauce ingredients in 4-cup glass measure; mix well.   4 to 6 Servings

VARIETY MEAT KEY: A homemaker's concern for top notch nutrition means liver, tongue and kidney dishes should become microwave oven favorites. SIMMER setting retains the fine texture and outstanding flavor of these low-fat meats. Liver is especially delicate and needs gentle cooking to prevent "popping."

Microwave meat that is completely thawed. See defrosting chart on page 49.

All variety meats are cooked, covered, in glass casseroles or baking dishes. Cover dishes tightly with glass lids, plastic wrap or wax paper. Pierce plastic wrap before removing it to prevent steam burns.

Liver should be cooked quickly — only until meat loses its pink color. Do not overcook. Cooked liver slices may be reheated on SIMMER.

Tongue — whether a hot entrée or sliced on a buffet cold cut platter — needs longer cooking to tenderize and season it. Turn whole tongue three times to assure even cooking.

Kidney stews are classics and vegetables may be varied; but this microwave technique will be a new favorite.

Standing times are essential to tender evenly-cooked variety meats — observe these carefully.

KIDNEY CASSEROLE

1½ lbs. beef kidney, trimmed and
    cut into small pieces
2 tablespoons butter or margarine
2 carrots, thinly sliced
2 teaspoons salt
¼ teaspoon leaf chervil
1 can (10¾ oz.) peas, undrained
1 jar (16 oz.) whole onions, undrained
1 can (4 oz.) mushroom stems and pieces,
    drained

1. Wash kidneys well before placing in 2-quart glass casserole. Add butter, carrots, seasonings and juice from peas and onions. Cover with glass lid or plastic wrap.

2. Microwave SIMMER for 20 minutes. Stir in peas, onions and mushrooms. Recover and continue cooking on SIMMER for 10 to 12 minutes. Let stand, covered, 5 minutes before serving.

6 to 8 Servings

TIP • Pan juices may be thickened by stirring in 2 tablespoons all-purpose flour. Microwave on HIGH for 1 to 2 minutes or until thickened.

LIVER BACON AND ONIONS

4 slices bacon
2 medium onions, sliced
1 lb. baby beef liver, sliced
Salt
Pepper

1. Place bacon between paper napkin or towel in 2-quart (12 x 7) glass baking dish.

2. Microwave on HIGH for 4 to 4½ minutes or until crisp. Remove bacon and drain. Coat liver slices with bacon drippings. Arrange in baking dish. Add onions. Cover with plastic wrap.

3. Microwave on SIMMER for 12 to 14 minutes or until meat loses pink color. Crumble bacon on top. Let stand, covered, 5 minutes before serving.

About 4 Servings

TONGUE IN CRANBERRY SAUCE *

2½ to 3-lb. beef tongue, washed
1 large onion, quartered
2 bay leaves
5 whole cloves
1 stalk celery, sliced
1 tablespoon salt
4 cups water

Sauce:
1 cup tongue cooking liquid
1 can (16 oz.) whole cranberry sauce
¼ cup packed brown sugar
1 teaspoon clove
1 teaspoon lemon juice

1. Place tongue in 3-quart glass casserole. Stir in remaining ingredients, except Sauce ingredients. Cover with glass lid or plastic wrap.

2. Microwave on HIGH for 15 minutes. Turn meat over.

3. Microwave on SIMMER for 30 minutes. Turn meat over again. Recover and continue cooking on SIMMER for 30 minutes. Turn meat over again. Recover and continue cooking on SIMMER for 30 minutes or until fork tender. Drain and reserve 1 cup liquid for sauce. Run cold water over tongue to cool. Immediately remove skin and membrane. Cool and slice meat. Place in 2-quart (12 x 7) glass baking dish. Pour sauce over top. Cover with plastic wrap.

4. Microwave on SIMMER for 10 to 12 minutes or until hot. Let stand, covered, 5 minutes.

5. Sauce: Combine all ingredients in a 4-cup measure.

4 to 6 Servings

TIP • Tongue may be cooked ahead, skinned and refrigerated until ready to slice. Add sauce and heat as directed in recipe. Increase cooking time 5 to 7 minutes if tongue and sauce are heated from refrigerated temperature.

VENISON AND RABBIT KEY: Venison roasts, steaks and chops microwave on ROAST to juicy tenderness.

Venison stew cooks with the typical microwave stew technique — first HIGH, then SIMMER. See the Stew Key on page 92.

Domestic rabbit is a light tender fine-textured meat much like chicken and it can be cooked quickly on Microwave HIGH.

All meat should be completely thawed or it will take longer to cook. See defrosting chart at beginning of chapter.

Large venison cuts roast well on a microwave roasting rack in an open flat glass dish. Turn larger cuts to assure even cooking. See roasting chart on page 51.

Smaller venison cuts and rabbit are cooked in glass casseroles or baking dishes covered tightly with glass lids, plastic wrap or wax paper. Pierce plastic wrap before removing it to prevent steam burns.

Venison is often marinated and/or cooked in sauce because it sometimes has a strong flavor. These methods are particularly suited to microwave cooking and produce especially good results — quickly.

Drain meat when called for to remove excess moisture and fat.

Meat continues to cook and heat after it is removed from the oven. Standing time allows cooking to finish gently.

Draining removes excess fat and moisture.

SAVORY VENISON CHOPS

    6 venison chops (1½ to 2 lbs.),
      trim off fat
    1 medium onion, finely chopped
    ¼ cup chopped celery
    ¼ cup chopped green pepper
    ¼ cup chili sauce
    ¼ cup dry sherry or water
    1 teaspoon salt
    ¼ teaspoon pepper

1. Place chops, onion, celery and green pepper in 2-quart (12 x 7) glass baking dish. Cover with plastic wrap.

2. Microwave on ROAST for 10 minutes. Drain and turn meat over. Combine remaining ingredients in 4-cup measure. Pour over chops. Recover and continue cooking on ROAST for 10 to 15 minutes. Let stand, covered, 5 minutes before serving.

3 to 4 Servings

TIP • Serve with zucchini and tossed green salad.

VENISON STEW *

    1½ lbs. venison stew meat, cubed
    2 tablespoons all-purpose flour
    2 tablespoons butter or margarine
    1 cup finely chopped carrots
    1 medium onion, chopped
    1 tablespoon dried parsley flakes
    1 teaspoon salt
    ½ teaspoon garlic salt
    ½ teaspoon Italian seasoning
    ¼ teaspoon pepper
    1 cup water
    1 can (8 oz.) tomato sauce
    1 can (10¾ oz.) condensed cream of
      mushroom soup

1. Coat meat with flour. Place butter and meat in 2-quart glass casserole. Cover with glass lid or plastic wrap.

2. Microwave on HIGH for about 10 minutes or until meat is no longer pink. Stir in remaining ingredients; recover.

3. Microwave on SIMMER for 30 minutes. Stir and continue cooking on SIMMER for 15 to 20 minutes or until meat is fork tender. Let stand, covered, 5 minutes before serving.   4 to 6 Servings

TIP • Serve atop wild rice.

RABBIT HASENPFEFFER

    1 cup cold water
    1 cup vinegar
    1 teaspoon sugar
    1 teaspoon salt
    ½ teaspoon whole cloves
    ⅛ teaspoon pepper
    ⅛ teaspoon allspice
    1 medium onion, sliced
    2 to 2½-lb. frozen cut up rabbit,
      thawed
    ¼ cup butter or margarine
    ⅓ cup dry bread crumbs
    1 teaspoon dried parsley flakes

1. Combine water, vinegar, sugar, seasonings and onion in medium mixing bowl. Add rabbit and marinate at room temperature 4 to 6 hours. Drain and reserve marinade.

2. Place butter in 2-quart (12 x 7) glass baking dish.

3. Microwave on ROAST for about 1½ minutes or until melted. Coat drained rabbit pieces in butter, then in bread crumbs. Place pieces, thick edges toward outside, in 2-quart (12 x 7) glass baking dish.

4. Microwave on HIGH for 10 minutes. Turn pieces over; add ¼ cup marinade. Sprinkle with parsley. Continue cooking on HIGH for 10 to 12 minutes or until meat is fork tender. Let stand, covered, 5 minutes before serving.   About 5 Servings

A hot meal in a single dish is a busy homemaker's secret weapon. Add microwave speed and that main dish lunch or supper turns into an unmatched time saver. Even when work calls for overtime or the bridge game lasts too long, family and guests can savor sauced meat in combination with vegetables, rice, pastas or beans.

Read the "grey box" keys in this chapter carefully; then use the recipes. Microwave oven techniques for cooked and uncooked ingredient combinations will become so familiar that new main dish creations will be as close as the refrigerator and cupboard shelf. Assemble ingredients at meal time or the day before — make some dishes a week or more ahead and store in the freezer. Use the reheating chart, too, and discover how fast and easy it is to warm leftovers.

Pictured top to bottom: Nutty Beef Casserole, page 77; Sweet Beef, page 74.

MAIN DISHES

MAIN DISH CHAPTER CONTENTS

HOW TO HEAT PRECOOKED REFRIGERATED MAIN DISHES

● Reheat main dishes in glass casseroles filled about ⅔ full.

● Cover with glass lid or plastic wrap.

● Microwave on REHEAT until hot.

● Stir once halfway through cooking.

● Let stand, covered, 5 minutes before serving.

GLASS CASSEROLE	SETTING	APPROXIMATE MINUTES
1-qt.	REHEAT	6 to 8
1½-qt.	REHEAT	10 to 12
2-qt.	REHEAT	12 to 15
3-qt.	REHEAT	14 to 17

HOW TO HEAT CANNED MAIN DISHES

● Spoon content into 1 or 1½-quart glass casserole.

● Cover with glass lid or plastic wrap.

● Microwave on REHEAT until hot.

● Let stand, covered, 5 minutes before serving.

MAIN DISH	CAN SIZE	SETTING	MINUTES
MEAT AND VEGETABLES IN SAUCE OR PORK BEANS Any kind	15-oz. to 16-oz.	REHEAT	4 to 6
	31-oz. to 42-oz.	REHEAT	6 to 8

MAIN DISHES MADE WITH UNCOOKED MEAT KEY: Beef and chicken main dishes begin cooking on Microwave HIGH for fast heat penetration, finish up on SIMMER slower heat that tenderizes both uncooked meat and vegetables.

Pork, lamb and veal are tender meats that respond best to ROAST cooking. Uncooked vegetables tenderize nicely at this setting, too.

Cook main dishes in glass casseroles or baking dishes. Cover tightly with glass lids, plastic wrap or wax paper. Pierce plastic wrap before removing it to prevent steam burns.

Drain, when called for in a recipe, to remove excess fat and moisture.

Stir mixtures so they cook evenly when specified in a recipe.

These meat and vegetable casseroles are ready to eat when meat is fork tender, vegetables tender-crisp.

Standing time lets mixture set for easy serving. A cover helps hold heat.

Most main dishes may be mixed ahead, then refrigerated until just before meal time. Add 5 to 8 minutes to final cooking period when main dish is cold.

Stir to cook all ingredients evenly.

SWEET BEEF

　2　**to 2¼-lb. beef round steak, cut into 1-inch cubes**
　1　**teaspoon salt**
　¼　**teaspoon pepper**
　2　**tablespoons packed brown sugar**
　1　**tablespoon lemon juice**
　1　**can (10½ oz.) condensed onion soup**
　1　**cup pitted whole prunes**
　1　**can (18 oz.) vacuum packed sweet potatoes**
　1　**envelope (¾ oz.) brown gravy mix**

1. Place beef cubes in 2-quart glass casserole. Cover with glass lid or plastic wrap.

2. Microwave on HIGH for 6 minutes. Drain and stir in salt, pepper, brown sugar, lemon juice and onion soup; recover.

3. Microwave on SIMMER for 15 minutes. Stir in prunes. Top with potatoes. Recover and continue cooking on SIMMER for 10 to 12 minutes or until beef is fork tender. Let stand, covered, 5 minutes before serving. Remove meat mixture to serving platter. Add gravy mix; stir well; recover.

4. Microwave on HIGH for 2 to 4 minutes until thickened and hot. Return meat to hot gravy; mix well. Let stand, covered, 5 minutes before serving.

4 to 6 Servings

CREAMY HORSERADISH BEEF

- 2 to 2¼-lb. beef round steak, cubed
- 1 large onion, thinly sliced
- 1 teaspoon salt
- 1 teaspoon curry powder
- ½ teaspoon pepper
- ¼ teaspoon ground ginger
- 1 tablespoon Worcestershire sauce
- 1 cup sour cream
- 2 tablespoons dried parsley flakes
- 2 teaspoons prepared horseradish

1. Combine meat and onion in 2-quart glass casserole. Cover with glass lid or plastic wrap.

2. Microwave on HIGH for 6 minutes. Drain and stir in remaining ingredients, except sour cream, parsley and horseradish; recover.

3. Microwave on SIMMER for 18 to 20 minutes or until fork tender. Stir in sour cream, parsley and horseradish. Let stand, covered, 5 minutes before serving. 4 to 6 Servings

Cover tenderizes mixture, aids even cooking.

ITALIAN-STYLE BRAZZOLI

- 2 to 2¼-lb. beef round steak, cut in ½-inch cubes
- 1 tablespoon dried parsley flakes
- 1 teaspoon salt
- 1 teaspoon leaf basil
- ¼ teaspoon pepper
- 1 clove garlic, finely chopped
- 1 cup water
- ¼ cup grated Parmesan cheese
- 1 can (8 oz.) tomato sauce
- 1 can (6 oz.) tomato paste
- 1 cup raisins
- Hot cooked spaghetti

1. Place meat in 1½-quart glass casserole. Cover with glass lid or plastic wrap.

2. Microwave on HIGH for 6 minutes. Drain; stir in parsley, salt, basil, pepper, garlic and water; recover.

3. Microwave on SIMMER for 20 minutes. Stir in remaining ingredients, except spaghetti. Recover and continue cooking on SIMMER for 15 to 20 minutes or until meat is fork tender. Let stand, covered, 5 minutes before serving. Serve over spaghetti. 4 to 6 Servings

TIP ● Substitute noodles for spaghetti.

BUSY DAY CASSEROLE

- 2 to 2¼-lb. beef round steak, cut into 1-inch cubes
- 1 envelope (1⅜ oz.) dehydrated onion soup mix
- 1 can (10½ oz.) condensed beef broth
- 1 can (10½ oz.) condensed cream of celery soup
- 1 cup sour cream

1. Place meat in 2-quart glass casserole. Cover with glass lid or plastic wrap.

2. Microwave on HIGH for 6 minutes. Drain and stir in remaining ingredients, except sour cream; recover.

3. Microwave on SIMMER for 25 to 30 minutes or until meat is fork tender. Blend in sour cream. Let stand, covered, 5 minutes before serving. About 4 Servings

Tender pork cooks best on ROAST.

CUBED PORK 'N BEANS

- 1 lb. lean fresh pork, cut in 1-inch cubes
- ½ cup chopped onion
- 2 tablespoons packed brown sugar
- 2 tablespoons prepared mustard
- ¼ cup molasses
- 1 can (31 oz.) pork and beans

1. Place meat and onion in 2-quart glass casserole. Cover with glass lid or plastic wrap.

2. Microwave on ROAST for 15 minutes. Drain and stir in remaining ingredients. Recover and continue cooking on ROAST for 8 to 10 minutes or until meat is fork tender. Let stand, covered, 5 minutes before serving. About 4 Servings

PORK IN A HURRY

- 1 to 1¼-lbs. lean fresh pork, cut into 1-inch cubes
- 1 medium onion, finely sliced
- 1 teaspoon salt
- ¼ teaspoon pepper
- 1 tablespoon dried parsley flakes
- 1 teaspoon Worcestershire sauce
- 1 can (8½ oz.) peas, undrained
- 1 can (16 oz.) whole potatoes, drained
- 1 can (10¾ oz.) condensed cream of mushroom soup

1. Place pork in 1½-quart glass casserole. Cover with glass lid or plastic wrap.

2. Microwave on ROAST for 8 to 10 minutes. Drain and stir in remaining ingredients. Recover and continue cooking on ROAST for 8 to 10 minutes or until meat is fork tender. Let stand, covered, 5 minutes before serving. 4 Servings

PORK "JAMBO"

    2 cups cubed lean fresh pork
    1 tablespoon cooking oil
    ½ cup chopped onion
    2 cups cubed cooked ham
    ¾ teaspoon salt
    ¾ teaspoon garlic salt
    1 teaspoon dry mustard
    ¾ teaspoon celery salt
    ½ teaspoon leaf thyme
    ¼ teaspoon pepper
    1 can (16 oz.) whole tomatoes,
      undrained
    ½ cup quick-cooking rice

1. Combine pork, oil and onion in 2-quart glass casserole. Cover with glass lid or plastic wrap.

2. Microwave on ROAST for 15 minutes. Drain and stir in remaining ingredients. Recover and continue cooking on ROAST for 8 to 10 minutes or until meat is fork tender. Let stand, covered, 5 minutes before serving.   4 to 6 Servings

TIP ● Garnish with tomato wedges and parsley.

CHICKEN 'N DUMPLINGS

    3 to 3¼-lb. stewing chicken, cut up
    3½ cups water
    ½ cup diced celery
    1 medium onion, sliced
    1 bay leaf
    4 peppercorns
    1 tablespoon salt
    4 carrots, sliced
    ⅓ cup unsifted all-purpose flour
    ½ cup water

Dumplings:
    1½ cups unsifted all-purpose flour
    2 teaspoons baking powder
    ½ teaspoon salt
    1 teaspoon dried parsley flakes
    ⅔ cup milk
    1 egg
    2 tablespoons cooking oil

1. Combine all ingredients, except flour, ½ cup water and Dumpling ingredients, in 3-quart glass casserole. Cover with glass lid or plastic wrap.

2. Microwave on HIGH for 15 minutes. Stir in a mixture of flour and ½ cup water.

3. Microwave on SIMMER for 50 to 60 minutes or until chicken is fork tender. Spoon Dumplings over hot chicken mixture. Recover and continue cooking on SIMMER for 10 to 12 minutes or until dumplings are no longer doughy. Let stand, covered, 5 minutes before serving.

4. Dumplings: Combine dry ingredients in medium mixing bowl. Blend milk, egg and oil in 2-cup measure. Pour into flour mixture. Stir until moistened.
                        5 to 6 Servings

Tender veal plus cooked vegetables cook well on ROAST.

BRAISED VEAL DELIGHT

    1 lb. fresh veal, cubed
    1 can (16 oz.) sliced carrots, drained
    1 tablespoon instant beef bouillon
    1 teaspoon salt
    1 teaspoon dried parsley flakes
    ¼ teaspoon celery seed
    ¼ teaspoon leaf thyme
    ¼ teaspoon pepper
    1 jar (16 oz.) whole onions, undrained
    1 tablespoon cornstarch

1. Place meat in 1½-quart glass casserole. Cover with glass lid or plastic wrap.

2. Microwave on ROAST for 10 minutes. Drain and stir in remaining ingredients, except onion juice and cornstarch. Blend onion juice and cornstarch in small mixing bowl. Pour over meat and vegetables. Recover and continue cooking on ROAST for 8 to 10 minutes or until meat is fork tender. Let stand, covered, 5 minutes before serving.
                        About 4 Servings

ROAST cooks gently – retains lamb's delicate flavor and texture.

MUSHROOM LAMB CURRY

    1 lb. lamb, cut into 1-inch cubes
    1 can (4 oz.) mushroom stems and pieces,
      drained
    1 can (10¾ oz.) condensed cream of
      mushroom soup
    1 teaspoon dried parsley flakes
    1 teaspoon instant chicken bouillon
    1 teaspoon curry powder
    ¼ teaspoon salt
    ¼ teaspoon garlic salt
    1 package (10 oz.) frozen peas

1. Place lamb in 1½-quart glass casserole. Cover with glass lid or plastic wrap.

2. Microwave on ROAST for 10 minutes. Drain and stir in remaining ingredients. Recover and continue cooking on ROAST 10 to 12 minutes or until meat is fork tender. Let stand, covered, 5 minutes before serving.   4 to 6 Servings

MAIN DISHES MADE WITH UNCOOKED GROUND BEEF KEY:
Ground beef casseroles are favorite budget stretchers. Microwave these mixtures in two steps. Cook meat on Microwave HIGH; then change setting depending on other ingredients added.

Dense raw vegetables microwave on HIGH.

Cooked vegetables simply need heating — use REHEAT.

"Critical" ingredients cook on ROAST to prevent curdling and burning. When cheese is added after dish is taken from the oven, a main dish can usually be cooked at the higher settings specified above. Cheese will melt during standing time.

Uncooked noodle dishes microwave on DEFROST to assure tenderness.

Use glass casseroles or baking dishes. Cover tightly with glass lids, plastic wrap or wax paper. Pierce plastic wrap before removing it to prevent steam burns.

Drain off excess fat and liquid when recipe specifies.

Stir mixtures to assure even cooking.

Mixture is done when meat and vegetables are tender.

Casserole dishes need standing time to absorb moisture and set for easiest serving. Cover helps hold heat.

Most main dishes may be mixed ahead, then refrigerated until just before meal time. Add 5 to 8 minutes to final cooking period when food is cold.

Final cooking period is on ROAST because of kidney beans.

BEANS EL RANCHO

- 1 lb. ground beef
- 1 cup chopped onion
- 1 teaspoon salt
- 2 tablespoons prepared mustard
- 1 tablespoon packed brown sugar
- 1 tablespoon vinegar
- ½ cup catsup
- 1 can (15½ oz.) pork and beans in tomato sauce
- 1 can (16 oz.) kidney beans, drained
- 1 can (17 oz.) lima beans, drained

1. Crumble ground beef in 2-quart glass casserole. Stir in onion. Cover with glass lid or plastic wrap.

2. Microwave on HIGH for 5 minutes. Drain and stir in remaining ingredients; recover.

3. Microwave on ROAST for 12 to 14 minutes or until hot. Let stand, covered, 5 minutes before serving.　　　　　　　　　　4 to 6 Servings

Canned cheese soup has a stabilizer so can cook on REHEAT during final cooking period of this main dish.

NUTTY BEEF CASSEROLE

- 1½ lbs. ground beef
- 1 large onion, chopped
- 1 teaspoon salt
- ¼ teaspoon pepper
- ½ teaspoon leaf basil
- ½ cup chopped green pepper
- ½ cup pimento stuffed olives
- 1 can (4 oz.) mushroom stems and pieces, drained
- 1 can (11 oz.) condensed Cheddar cheese soup
- ½ cup salted Spanish peanuts, if desired

1. Crumble ground beef in 2-quart glass casserole. Stir in onion. Cover with glass lid or plastic wrap.

2. Microwave on HIGH for 6 minutes. Drain and stir in remaining ingredients except salted nuts; recover.

3. Microwave on REHEAT for 10 to 12 minutes or until hot. Let stand, covered, 5 minutes. Sprinkle nuts on top and serve.　　　　　4 to 6 Servings

TIP ● Serve with parsley-buttered noodles.

Fresh vegetables, quick-cooking rice and ground beef cook well on HIGH.

STUFFED CABBAGE ROLLS*

- 1 large head cabbage, cored
- ½ cup water
- 1½ lbs. ground beef
- ½ cup finely chopped onion
- ½ cup quick-cooking rice
- 1 egg
- 1 teaspoon Worcestershire sauce
- ½ teaspoon leaf basil
- 1 teaspoon salt
- ¼ teaspoon pepper
- 1 can (8 oz.) tomato sauce

1. Place cabbage in 2-quart glass casserole. Pour water in bottom of dish. Cover with plastic wrap.

2. Microwave on HIGH for 8 to 10 minutes or until cabbage is partly cooked; set aside. Crumble ground beef in medium mixing bowl. Stir in remaining ingredients, except tomato sauce. Remove 12 cabbage leaves from partly cooked cabbage. Place an equal amount of meat mixture in each leaf. Roll up and secure with toothpick. Place in 2-quart (12 x 7) glass baking dish. Cover with plastic wrap.

3. Microwave on HIGH for 13 to 15 minutes. Pour tomato sauce over cabbage rolls. Recover and continue cooking on HIGH for 2 to 3 minutes or until hot. Let stand, covered, 5 minutes before serving.　　　　　　　About 6 Servings

BEEF AND BEANS MEXICAN STYLE

    1 lb. ground beef
    ¼ cup chopped onion
    ¼ teaspoon salt
    ½ teaspoon chili powder
    1 can (15½ oz.) kidney beans, drained
    1 can (10 oz.) enchilada sauce
    1 cup shredded Cheddar cheese

1. Crumble ground beef in 2-quart glass casserole. Stir in onions. Cover with glass lid or plastic wrap.

2. Microwave on HIGH for 5 minutes. Drain and stir in remaining ingredients, except cheese; recover.

3. Microwave on ROAST for 12 to 14 minutes or until hot. Sprinkle with cheese. Let stand, covered, 5 minutes or until cheese melts.   About 4 Servings

This layered casserole does not need stirring.

LAYERED BEEF CASSEROLE

    1 lb. ground beef
    1 teaspoon salt
    ¼ teaspoon pepper
    2 medium potatoes, thinly sliced
    ¼ cup finely chopped green pepper
    1 medium onion, thinly sliced
    1 can (10½ oz.) condensed tomato soup
    ½ teaspoon leaf chervil, if desired

1. Crumble ground beef in 2-quart glass casserole. Cover with glass lid or plastic wrap.

2. Microwave on HIGH for 5 minutes. Drain; stir, and season with salt and pepper. Layer 1 sliced potato on top of beef, then green pepper, onion and second potato. Pour on soup. Sprinkle with chervil. Recover and continue cooking on HIGH for 15 or 20 minutes or until potatoes are tender. Let stand, covered, 5 minutes before serving.

                                4 to 6 Servings

Kidney beans is a "critical" ingredient.

CHILI

    1 lb. ground beef
    1 medium onion, finely chopped
    2 teaspoons chili powder
    1½ teaspoons salt
    1 teaspoon prepared mustard
    1 clove garlic, finely chopped
    1 can (15½ oz.) kidney beans, drained
    1 can (16 oz.) tomatoes

1. Crumble ground beef in 2-quart glass casserole. Stir in onion, Cover with glass lid or plastic wrap.

2. Microwave on HIGH for 5 minutes. Drain and stir in remaining ingredients; recover.

3. Microwave on ROAST for 12 to 14 minutes or until hot. Let stand, covered, 5 minutes before serving.   4 to 6 Servings

Do not stir this casserole during cooking.

LASAGNA

    1 lb. ground beef
    1 teaspoon salt
    1 package (1 oz.) spaghetti sauce mix
    1 can (16 oz.) tomato sauce
    1 can (4 oz.) mushroom stems and pieces, drained
    1 package (8 oz.) lasagna noodles, cooked
    1 carton (12 oz.) creamed cottage cheese
    1 package (6 oz.) sliced Mozzarella cheese
    ½ cup grated Parmesan cheese

1. Crumble ground beef in 2-quart (12 x 7) glass baking dish. Cover with glass lid or plastic wrap.

2. Microwave on HIGH for 5 minutes. Drain and stir in salt, spaghetti sauce mix, tomato sauce and mushrooms; mix well. Assemble in 2-quart (12 x 7) glass baking dish by layers: ⅓ cooked noodles, ⅓ meat mixture, ½ cottage cheese and ½ Mozzarella cheese. Repeat layers. On third layer of noodles, spread last ⅓ of meat mixture and sprinkle with Parmesan cheese. Cover with plastic wrap.

3. Microwave on ROAST for 15 to 18 minutes or until hot in center. Let stand, covered, 5 minutes before serving.   6 to 8 Servings

Noodles must cook on DEFROST to tenderize.

ONE DISH MACARONI BEEF

    ½ lb. ground beef
    1 small onion, finely chopped
    1 cup uncooked macaroni
    1 can (8 oz.) tomato sauce
    1½ cups water
    ⅓ cup catsup
    1 can (7 oz.) whole kernel corn, undrained
    1 tablespoon packed brown sugar
    ½ teaspoon salt
    ¼ teaspoon pepper
    ¼ teaspoon chili powder

1. Crumble ground beef in 2-quart glass casserole. Stir in onion. Cover with glass lid or plastic wrap.

2. Microwave on HIGH for 3 minutes. Drain and stir in remaining ingredients; recover.

3. Microwave on DEFROST for 30 to 35 minutes or until macaroni is tender. Let stand, covered, 5 minutes before serving.   4 to 6 Servings

HAMBURGER VEGETABLE MEDLEY

- **1 lb. ground beef**
- **½ cup thinly sliced carrots**
- **1 cup finely chopped celery**
- **½ cup finely chopped green pepper**
- **1 teaspoon salt**
- **½ teaspoon leaf thyme**
- **¼ teaspoon pepper**
- **¼ teaspoon garlic salt**
- **1 can (16 oz.) tomatoes**
- **1 tablespoon dried parsley flakes**
- **2 cups cooked noodles**

1. Crumble ground beef in 2-quart glass casserole. Stir in carrots, celery and green pepper. Cover with glass lid or plastic wrap.

2. Microwave on HIGH for 5 minutes. Drain and stir in remaining ingredients; mix well; recover.

3. Microwave on REHEAT for 14 to 16 minutes or until hot. Let stand, covered, 5 minutes before serving. 4 to 6 Servings

Pictured: One Dish Macaroni Beef, page 78; basket of hot rolls, page 137.

Sour cream and cottage cheese need lower ROAST setting to prevent curdling and separating.

DAIRY BURGER DISH

- **1 lb. ground beef**
- **5 green onions, chopped**
- **1 teaspoon salt**
- **¼ teaspoon pepper**
- **¼ teaspoon garlic salt**
- **1 tablespoon dried parsley flakes**
- **1 can (4 oz.) tomato sauce**
- **1 cup cottage cheese**
- **½ cup sour cream**
- **2 cups cooked noodles**
- **½ cup shredded Cheddar cheese**

1. Crumble ground beef in 2-quart glass casserole. Stir in onions. Cover with glass lid or plastic wrap.

2. Microwave on HIGH for 5 minutes. Drain and stir in remaining ingredients, except Cheddar cheese; recover.

3. Microwave on ROAST for 15 to 16 minutes or until hot. Sprinkle Cheddar cheese on top. Let stand, covered, 5 minutes or until cheese melts.
4 to 6 Servings

TIP ● Cook noodles as directed in chart page 108.

MAIN DISHES MADE WITH COOKED MEAT
KEY: Generally all cooked meat and vegetable hot dish mixtures microwave on REHEAT because heating, not cooking, is the requirement. The small amounts of finely cut uncooked vegetables in these recipes will cook tender-crisp at this setting.

When cheese, sour cream or eggs are included in the cooked ingredients, however, the oven setting is lowered to ROAST to prevent curdling and drying. Sometimes shredded cheese can be added after food comes from the oven so mixture can microwave at the faster REHEAT setting.

Uncooked noodles in a casserole mixture require cooking at DEFROST.

Cook these main dishes in glass casseroles or cooking dishes. Cover tightly with glass lids, plastic wrap or wax paper. Pierce plastic wrap before removing it to prevent steam burns.

Cover during standing time to hold heat while mixture sets.

Most main dishes may be mixed ahead, then refrigerated until just before meal time. Add 5 to 8 minutes to final cooking period if food is cold.

Cook noodles as directed on page 108.

BEEF DIVINE*

　¼ **cup butter or margarine**
　⅓ **cup unsifted all-purpose flour**
　2 **cups milk**
　1 **jar (2½ oz.) dried beef, cut up**
　1 **can (4 oz.) mushroom stems and pieces, drained**
　2 **cups cooked noodles**
　½ **cup packaged seasoned croutons**

1. Place butter in 2-quart glass casserole.

2. Microwave on ROAST for about 1½ minutes or until melted. Blend in flour and milk.

3. Microwave on HIGH for 3 minutes. Stir and continue cooking on HIGH for 2 to 3 minutes or until thickened. Beat well with rotary beater. Mix in remaining ingredients except croutons. Cover with glass lid or plastic wrap.

4. Microwave on REHEAT for 8 to 10 minutes or until hot. Sprinkle with croutons. Let stand, covered, 5 minutes before serving.　4 to 6 Servings

TIPS ● Substitue green noodles if desired.
● Top with ½ cup shredded Cheddar cheese after dish comes from oven. Let stand, covered, 5 minutes before serving.

This layered casserole does not need stirring.

MUSHROOM BEEF RICE

　3 **cups cooked rice**
　8 **slices cooked beef roast**
　1 **can (10¾ oz.) condensed cream of mushroom soup**
　¼ **cup milk**
　1 **teaspoon leaf basil**
　½ **teaspoon salt**
　½ **teaspoon dried parsley flakes**

1. Place rice in 2-quart (8 x 8) glass baking dish. Top with beef slices. Combine soup, milk and seasonings in 4-cup measure. Pour over meat and rice. Cover with plastic wrap.

2. Microwave on REHEAT for 10 to 12 minutes. Let stand, covered, 5 minutes before serving.
　3 to 4 Servings

TIP ● Cook rice as directed on page 106.

Use HIGH to cook raw onion; lower setting to ROAST for cheese.

CHEESY CORNED BEEF

　⅓ **cup chopped onions**
　1 **can (10¾ oz.) condensed cream of chicken soup**
　½ **cup milk**
　1 **cup cubed process American cheese**
　1 **can (12 oz.) corned beef**
　2 **cups cooked green noodles**
　½ **cup packaged seasoned croutons**

1. Place onions in 1½-quart glass casserole. Cover with glass lid or plastic wrap.

2. Microwave on HIGH for 3 minutes. Stir in remaining ingredients, except croutons; recover.

3. Microwave on ROAST for 10 to 12 minutes or until hot and cheese melts. Let stand, covered, 5 minutes. Sprinkle croutons on top before serving.
　4 to 6 Servings

SOUPER CUBED PORK

　2 **cups cubed cooked pork**
　1 **can (10¾ oz.) condensed cream of celery soup**
　1 **can (8½ oz.) peas, undrained**
　½ **teaspoon dill weed**
　½ **teaspoon salt**
　¼ **teaspoon ground sage**
　⅛ **teaspoon pepper**

1. Combine all ingredients in 1½-quart glass casserole. Cover with glass lid or plastic wrap.

2. Microwave on REHEAT for 10 to 12 minutes. Let stand, covered, 5 minutes before serving.
　3 to 4 Servings

See the Pasta Key for details on noodle technique used at the beginning of this recipe.

HAM NOODLE BAKE

  1½ cups water
   1 cup uncooked noodles
   ¼ teaspoon dry mustard
   ⅛ teaspoon pepper
   1 cup cubed cooked ham
   1 can (10½ oz.) condensed cream of
     celery soup
   ⅓ cup milk
   1 can (3¼ oz.) French-fried onion rings

1. Pour water in 2-quart glass casserole. Cover with glass lid or plastic wrap.

2. Microwave on HIGH for 5 minutes or until water bubbles. Add noodles; recover.

3. Microwave on DEFROST for 10 to 12 minutes or until noodles are tender. Drain and stir in remaining ingredients, except onion rings; recover.

4. Microwave on REHEAT for 8 to 10 minutes or until hot. Place onion rings on top. Let stand, covered, 5 minutes before serving.
About 4 Servings

Cook on ROAST because of eggs.

HAM 'N EGG SPECIAL*

   3 tablespoons butter or margarine
   ¼ cup unsifted all-purpose flour
   2 cups milk
   ½ teaspoon salt
   ¼ teaspoon leaf oregano
   ¼ teaspoon pepper
   6 hard cooked eggs, sliced
   1 cup cubed cooked ham
   1 can (4 oz.) mushroom stems and pieces, drained
   ½ cup dry bread crumbs, if desired

1. Place butter in 2-quart glass casserole.

2. Microwave on ROAST for about 1½ minutes or until melted. Blend in flour and milk until smooth.

3. Microwave on HIGH for 3 minutes. Beat with rotary beater until smooth. Continue cooking on HIGH for 2 to 3 minutes until thickened. Beat with rotary beater. Stir in remaining ingredients, except bread crumbs. Cover with glass lid or plastic wrap.

4. Microwave on ROAST for 6 to 8 minutes or until hot. Sprinkle with bread crumbs. Recover and continue cooking on ROAST for 2 to 3 minutes or until piping hot. Let stand, covered, 5 minutes before serving.
4 to 6 Servings

ORIENTAL HAM

   2 tablespoons butter or margarine
   4 green onions, finely chopped
   ½ cup chopped green pepper
   2 cups cubed cooked ham
   2 cups cooked rice
   1 can (4 oz.) mushroom stems and pieces, drained
   1 can (16 oz.) bean sprouts, drained
   2 tablespoons soy sauce
   1 teaspoon salt
   ¼ teaspoon pepper

1. Place butter, onions and green pepper in 2-quart glass casserole. Cover with glass lid or plastic wrap.

2. Microwave on ROAST for 3 to 4 minutes or until vegetables are partly cooked. Stir in remaining ingredients. Cover with glass lid or plastic wrap.

3. Microwave on REHEAT for 10 to 12 minutes or until hot. Let stand, covered, 5 minutes before serving.
6 to 8 Servings

HAM SUPPER CASSEROLE

   1 can (10¾ oz.) condensed cream of chicken soup
   ½ cup sour cream
   1 can (16 oz.) cut green beans, drained
   2 cups cubed cooked ham
   ½ cup diced process American cheese

1. Combine soup and sour cream in 1½-quart glass casserole; mix well. Stir in green beans and ham. Cover with glass lid or plastic wrap.

2. Microwave on ROAST for 12 to 14 minutes or until hot. Sprinkle cheese on top. Let stand, covered, 5 minutes or until cheese melts.
4 to 6 Servings

HUNTER'S HAM DELIGHT

   3 slices bacon, cut up
   ½ cup finely chopped onion
   2 cups cubed cooked ham
   2 cups cooked noodles
   1 can (10¾ oz.) condensed tomato soup
   1 can (16 oz.) tomatoes
   1 can (16 oz.) whole kernel corn, drained
   1 can (17 oz.) lima beans, drained
   1 cup shredded process American cheese

1. Place bacon and onions in 3-quart glass casserole. Cover with glass lid or plastic wrap.

2. Microwave on HIGH for 5 minutes. Stir in remaining ingredients except cheese; mix well.

3. Microwave on REHEAT for 14 to 16 minutes or until hot in center. Sprinkle cheese on top. Let stand, covered, 5 minutes or until cheese melts.
8 to 10 Servings

TIP • Substitute 1 can (16 oz.) cut green beans for lima beans.

VEAL WITH NOODLES

> 2 cups cubed cooked veal
> 1 can (10¾ oz.) condensed cream of mushroom soup
> ¼ cup milk
> 1 cup cooked noodles
> 1 teaspoon salt
> 2 teaspoons dried parsley flakes
> ½ teaspoon garlic salt
> ½ teaspoon paprika
> ¼ teaspoon marjoram
> ¼ teaspoon pepper

1. Combine all ingredients in 1½-quart glass casserole; mix well. Cover with glass lid or plastic wrap.

2. Microwave on REHEAT for 10 to 12 minutes or until heated through. Let stand, covered, 5 minutes before serving. About 4 Servings

Cover helps food heat faster.

BEANS 'N KRAUT

> 1 lb. weiners (10)
> 1 can (31 oz.) pork and beans
> ¼ cup chili sauce
> 1 can (16 oz.) sauerkraut, drained
> 1 teaspoon caraway seeds

1. Cut half of weiners into ¼-inch slices. Combine with pork and beans and chili sauce in 2-quart glass casserole. Spread sauerkraut on top. Sprinkle with caraway seeds. Cover with glass lid or plastic wrap.

2. Microwave on REHEAT for 10 minutes. Arrange remaining weiners on top, spoke fashion. Recover and continue cooking on REHEAT for 4 to 5 minutes or until heated through. 3 to 4 Servings

Pictured: Beans 'n Kraut, this page.

EASY CHICKEN RICE

> 1 can (10½ oz.) condensed chicken broth
> 1 teaspoon soy sauce
> ⅓ cup finely chopped onion
> 1 cup quick-cooking rice
> 1 cup cubed cooked chicken
> 1 can (7 oz.) cut green beans, drained
> 1 can (5 oz.) water chestnuts, drained and sliced

1. Combine all ingredients in 2-quart glass casserole. Cover with glass lid or plastic wrap.

2. Microwave on HIGH for 8 to 10 minutes or until hot. Let stand, covered, 5 minutes before serving. About 4 Servings

BAKED CHICKEN A LA KING*

> ½ cup butter or margarine
> ½ cup unsifted all-purpose flour
> 3 cups milk
> 6 cups cubed cooked chicken
> 1 can (4 oz.) mushroom stems and pieces, undrained
> 2 tablespoons chopped pimento
> 1 teaspoon salt
> ¼ teaspoon pepper
> 1 cup packaged seasoned croutons

1. Place butter in 3-quart glass casserole.

2. Microwave on ROAST for 2 to 2½ minutes or until melted. Blend in flour. Gradually stir in milk; mix well.

3. Microwave on HIGH for 4 minutes. Beat with rotary beater and continue cooking on HIGH for about 4 minutes or until thickened. Beat with rotary beater until smooth. Stir in remaining ingredients, except croutons. Cover with glass lid or plastic wrap.

4. Microwave on REHEAT for 10 to 12 minutes or until hot. Let stand, covered, 5 minutes. Sprinkle croutons on top and serve. 6 to 8 Servings

CREAMY CHINESE CHICKEN

> 1 can (10¾ oz.) condensed cream of chicken soup
> ½ cup milk
> 1½ cups cubed cooked chicken
> 1 can (16 oz.) mixed Chinese vegetables, drained
> 1 can (5 oz.) chow mein noodles

1. Combine soup and milk in 2-quart glass casserole; mix well. Stir in chicken and Chinese vegetables. Cover with glass lid or plastic wrap.

2. Microwave on REHEAT for 10 to 12 minutes or until hot. Let stand, covered, 5 minutes. Serve over chow mein noodles. 4 to 6 Servings

TURKEY AND WILD RICE CASSEROLE

>   3 cups cubed cooked turkey
>   1 cup finely chopped celery
>   1 cup finely chopped onion
> 1½ cups cooked wild rice *(1/2 cup raw)*
>   1 can (10¾ oz.) condensed cream of
>   chicken soup
>   1 can (6 oz.) water chestnuts, drained
>   and sliced
>   1 can (4 oz.) mushroom stems and pieces,
>   undrained
>   3 tablespoons soy sauce
>   ¼ teaspoon pepper
>   2 tablespoons butter or margarine
>   ½ cup dry bread crumbs

1. Combine all ingredients, except butter and bread crumbs, in 2-quart glass casserole; mix well; set aside. Place butter in small glass mixing bowl.

2. Microwave on ROAST for about 1 minute or until melted. Stir in bread crumbs. Sprinkle buttered crumbs over turkey mixture. Cover with glass lid or plastic wrap.

3. Microwave on REHEAT for 24 to 26 minutes or until hot. Let stand, covered, 5 minutes before serving.   4 to 6 Servings

TURKEY 'N DRESSING*

>   1 package (8 oz.) herb-seasoned
>   dressing mix
>   3 cups cubed cooked turkey
>   ½ cup butter or margarine
>   ½ cup unsifted all-purpose flour
>   ¼ teaspoon salt
>   ⅛ teaspoon pepper
>   1 can (10¾ oz.) condensed chicken broth
>   1 soup can water
>   6 eggs, beaten

1. Prepare dressing mix as directed on package. Spread in 3-quart (13 x 9) glass baking dish. Arrange turkey on dressing; set aside. Place butter in medium glass mixing bowl.

2. Microwave on ROAST for about 2 minutes or until melted. Blend in flour, seasonings, chicken broth and water.

3. Microwave on HIGH for 2 minutes. Stir and continue cooking on HIGH for 3 to 4 minutes or until thickened. Blend some cream mixture into eggs; mix well. Pour over turkey and dressing.

4. Microwave on DEFROST for 25 to 30 minutes or until almost set in center. Let stand 5 minutes before serving.   6 to 8 Servings

TURKEY ORIENTAL

>   2 tablespoons cooking oil
>   1 cup finely chopped onion
>   1 cup finely chopped celery
>   2 cups cubed cooked turkey
>   1 can (6 oz.) water chestnuts, drained
>   and sliced
>   1 can (10¾ oz.) condensed chicken
>   broth
>   2 tablespoons cornstarch
>   1 tablespoon soy sauce
>   Hot cooked rice

1. Combine oil, onion and celery in 2-quart glass casserole.

2. Microwave on HIGH for 4 to 5 minutes or until onions are partly cooked. Stir in remaining ingredients, except rice; mix well. Cover with glass lid or plastic wrap.

3. Microwave on REHEAT for 10 to 12 minutes or until heated through and thickened. Let stand, covered, 5 minutes. Serve with hot cooked rice.
                          4 to 6 Servings

TURKEY NOODLE BAKE

>   1 can (10¾ oz.) condensed cream of
>   chicken soup
>   ¼ cup water
>   2 cups cubed cooked turkey
>   1 cup chopped celery
>   ½ cup coarsely chopped nuts
>   ¼ cup chopped onion
>   1 tablespoon chopped pimento
>   1 can (3 oz.) chow mein noodles

1. Combine all ingredients, including 1 cup chow mein noodles, in 2-quart glass casserole. Mix well. Cover with glass lid or plastic wrap.

2. Microwave on REHEAT for 8 to 10 minutes or until hot. Let stand, covered, 5 minutes. Sprinkle top with remaining noodles and serve.
                          About 4 Servings

TURKEY DIVAN*

>   2 packages (10 oz. each) frozen broccoli
>   spears
>   6 to 8 slices cooked turkey
> 1½ cups shredded process American cheese
>   1 can (10¾ oz.) condensed cream of
>   chicken soup
>   1 can (3½ oz.) French-fried onion rings

1. Place frozen broccoli in 2-quart (12 x 7) glass baking dish. Cover with plastic wrap.

2. Microwave on HIGH for about 10 minutes or until partly cooked; arrange in dish. Top with turkey slices and cheese. Spoon soup over all; recover.

3. Microwave on ROAST for 10 minutes. Place onion rings on top and continue cooking on ROAST for 1 to 2 minutes or until onions are hot.
                          4 to 6 Servings

MAIN DISHES MADE WITH UNCOOKED OR COOKED SEAFOOD KEY: Uncooked shrimp or lobster main dishes cook on HIGH unless, as with those in this collection, cheese or eggs are added. These mixtures finish cooking on ROAST to prevent curdling or burning.

Cooked seafood casseroles microwave on REHEAT. Food is already cooked and only needs heating. When cheese or eggs are included, microwave on ROAST to prevent curdling and burning.

Cook a main dish in a glass casserole or baking dish. Cover tightly with glass lid, plastic wrap or wax paper to heat mixtures through evenly and quickly. Pierce plastic wrap before removing it to prevent steam burns.

Cover during standing time so mixture stays hot while it sets.

Most main dishes may be mixed ahead, then refrigerated until just before meal time. Add 5 to 8 minutes to final cooking period because food is cold.

Use lower ROAST setting because of eggs in Hollandaise Sauce and mayonnaise.

SHRIMP WITH PEA PODS

    1 package (16 oz.) uncooked frozen shrimp
    1 package (6 oz.) frozen pea pods
    1 cup mayonnaise or salad dressing
    2 jars (6 oz. each) Hollandaise sauce
    2 cans (8½ oz. each) water chestnuts, drained and sliced
    2 teaspoons curry powder
    Chopped walnuts, if desired

1. Place shrimp and pea pods in 2-quart glass casserole. Cover with glass lid or plastic wrap.

2. Microwave on HIGH for 8 to 10 minutes or until shrimp is pink and pea pods partly cooked. Drain well and stir in remaining ingredients, except walnuts.

3. Microwave on ROAST for 10 to 12 minutes or until hot. Let stand, covered, 5 minutes. Sprinkle with walnuts and serve.   6 to 8 Servings

TIPS • Garnish with shrimps and parsley.

    • Substitute 1 can (10¾ oz.) condensed cream of shrimp soup for Hollandaise sauce.

Use ROAST setting because of eggs.

TUNA AND EGG CASSEROLE

    1 can (10¾ oz.) condensed cream of
       mushroom soup
    1 can (6½ oz.) chunk tuna, drained
    2 hard cooked eggs, chopped
    1 can (4 oz.) mushroom stems and pieces,
       drained
    ¼ cup finely chopped onion
    1 tablespoon chopped pimento
    1 package (10 oz.) potato chips, crumbled

1. Combine all ingredients, except potato chips, in 1½-quart glass casserole; mix well. Cover with glass lid or plastic wrap.

2. Microwave on ROAST for 10 to 12 minutes or until hot. Let stand, covered, 5 minutes. Sprinkle potato chips on top and serve.   About 4 Servings

TIP • Substitute 1 can (10¾ oz.) cream of chicken soup for mushroom soup.

Cheese requires lower ROAST setting.

FISHERMAN'S SPECIAL

    1 package (16 oz.) uncooked frozen shrimp
    2 cups cooked rice
    ¼ cup butter or margarine
    ½ cup chopped green pepper
    ½ cup chopped celery
    1 can (10¾ oz.) condensed cream of
       mushroom soup
    2 cups shredded Cheddar cheese
    1 teaspoon salt
    ¼ teaspoon pepper
       Paprika

1. Slit shrimp pouch. Place in 2-quart (8 x 8) glass baking dish.

2. Microwave on HIGH for 8 to 10 minutes. Take pouch out of dish; drain shrimp; set aside. Place cooked rice in bottom of baking dish; set aside. Combine butter, green pepper and celery in medium glass bowl. Cover with plastic wrap.

3. Microwave on ROAST for 5 minutes. Stir in shrimp and remaining ingredients, except paprika; mix well. Spoon over rice. Sprinkle with paprika. Cover with plastic wrap.

4. Microwave on ROAST for 10 to 12 minutes or until hot. Let stand, covered, 5 minutes before serving.   About 4 Servings

Pictured left to right: Shrimp with Pea Pods garnished with cooked shrimp and parsley, page 84; Pork "Jambo" garnished with tomato wedges and parsley, page 76.

Standing time allows mixture to set.

SEAFOOD CREOLE

    3 tablespoons butter or margarine
    1 cup finely chopped onion
    ½ cup finely chopped green pepper
    ½ cup finely chopped celery
    1 clove garlic, finely chopped
  1½ tablespoons all-purpose flour
    1 can (28 oz.) whole tomatoes, undrained
    1 can (6½ oz.) chunk tuna, drained
    1 can (6½ oz.) crabmeat, drained
    1 can (4½ oz.) shrimp, drained
    1 teaspoon salt
    2 bay leaves
    ½ teaspoon leaf thyme
    ¼ teaspoon allspice
    1 tablespoon Worcestershire sauce
    ¼ teaspoon Tabasco
    2 tablespoons dried parsley flakes

1. Combine butter, onion, green pepper, celery and garlic in 2-quart glass casserole. Cover with glass lid or plastic wrap.

2. Microwave on ROAST for about 5 minutes or until vegetables are partly cooked. Blend in flour. Stir in remaining ingredients; recover.

3. Microwave on REHEAT for 10 to 12 minutes or until hot. Let stand, covered, 5 minutes before serving.   6 to 8 Servings

TIP • Serve over hot rice.

Always microwave noodles on DEFROST. Heat canned fish on REHEAT.

TUNA NOODLE CASSEROLE

    1 cup water
  1½ cups uncooked noodles
    1 can (6½ oz.) flaked tuna, drained
    1 can (10¾ oz.) condensed cream of
       mushroom soup
    1 can (4 oz.) mushroom stems and pieces,
       drained
    1 can (17 oz.) green beans, drained
    ½ cup coarsely crushed potato chips

1. Pour water into 2-quart casserole. Cover with glass lid or plastic wrap.

2. Microwave on HIGH for 3 to 5 minutes or until water comes to a boil. Stir in noodles. Recover and cook on DEFROST for 11 to 12 minutes or until noodles are tender. Drain and stir in remaining ingredients except potato chips; recover.

3. Microwave on REHEAT for 8 to 10 minutes or until hot. Let stand, covered, 5 minutes. Sprinkle potato chips on top and serve.   6 to 8 Servings

Slow-simmering soups, bubbling stews and aromatic hot sandwiches have always drawn families toward the kitchen with delighted "oh-h-hs" and "ah-h-hs." Now microwave cooking takes the "slow" out of simmering, bubbling and heating to produce mouth-watering soups, stews and hot sandwiches that even the busiest cook can make — fast.

All three microwave cooking techniques are consistent and easy to learn. Ingredients determine specific settings. **"Grey box" keys** and charts spell out the basic instructions needed for easy use of these recipes and other favorites.

Pictured top to bottom: Creamy Chicken Stew garnished with snipped parsley, page 94; Shrimp Ham Creamy Soup garnished with whole green onion, page 92; Sliced Meat Sandwich garnished with green pepper slice and cherry tomato, page 96.

SOUP/STEW/SANDWICH CHAPTER CONTENTS

SOUPS, STEWS & SANDWICHES

HOW TO COOK DEHYDRATED SOUP MIX

● Pour water into glass casserole or 8-ounce mugs. Add soup mix if directed on package and heat. Heat water, only, if package directs.

● Cover containers with glass lids, saucers or plastic wrap.

● Microwave on HIGH until liquid is hot and bubbly.

● Stir in dry mix and continue cooking if package specified that mix is added after water boils.

● Microwave most soups on HIGH until hot.

● Microwave soups with dehydrated rice or noodles on DEFROST until rice or noodles are tender.

● Let stand, covered, 5 minutes before serving.

SOUP	AMOUNT	GLASS CONTAINER	WATER	SETTING	MINUTES
CUP O' SOUP					
any kind	1 envelope	1 (8-oz.) mug	⅔ cup	HIGH	2 to 2½
1½-oz. pkg. with	2 envelopes	2 (8-oz.) mugs	⅔ cup ea.	HIGH	3 to 3½
4 envelopes	4 envelopes	4 (8-oz.) mugs	⅔ cup ea.	HIGH	6 to 7
SOUP MIX					
without rice or noodles	1 envelope	2-qt. casserole	4 cups	HIGH ; add mix;	8 to 10
2¾-oz. pkg. with 2 envelopes				HIGH	4 to 5
with rice or noodles	1 envelope	2-qt. casserole	3 cups	HIGH ; add mix;	7 to 8
3½-oz. pkg. with 2 envelopes				DEFROST	5 to 6
5-oz. pkg.		2-qt. casserole	5 cups	HIGH ; add mix;	9 to 10
				DEFROST	10 to 12

HOW TO HEAT CANNED SOUP

● Pour soup into 1½-quart glass casserole.

● Add milk or water as directed on can.

● Cover with glass lid or plastic wrap.

● Microwave on REHEAT until hot — except mushroom soup which heats on ROAST to prevent "popping."

● Stir when taken from oven.

● Let stand, covered, 3 minutes before serving.

SOUP	SETTING	MINUTES
DILUTED		
Broth 10¾-oz.	REHEAT	3 to 4
Tomato, Cream Noodle or Vegetable		
10¾-oz.	REHEAT	5 to 6
26-oz.	REHEAT	8 to 9
Mushroom 10¾-oz.	ROAST	7 to 8
UNDILUTED		
Chunky Vegetable, Noodle or Split Pea and Ham		
10¾-oz.	REHEAT	2½ to 3½
19-oz.	REHEAT	5 to 7

SOUP KEY: Ingredients are the key to cooking soup in a microwave oven.

Soups made of raw vegetables plus fish and seafood (except clams and oysters that toughen) cook quickly on HIGH.

Soup made with uncooked meat or chicken starts cooking on HIGH for fast heating, finishes on SIMMER to blend flavors into broth and tenderize meat.

Soup made of cooked meat and/or vegetables heats on REHEAT so food holds its shape and texture.

Soup with ingredients that need gentle cooking — things such as clams, buttermilk or cream — microwaves on ROAST to prevent "popping," overcooking or curdling.

Broth is made by drawing all possible flavor and nutrients from meat and/or vegetables which are otherwise unusable. Microwave on ROAST which allows the longer cooking time needed.

Raw vegetables sauté in butter on ROAST, in the usual manner, before being added to a soup made of precooked ingredients.

Use the charts opposite for heating or cooking canned and dehydrated soup.

Trim fat from meat so soup is not greasy.

Microwave soups in glass containers at least twice the size of ingredient volume so mixture does not boil over. Pretty glass or pottery serving bowls without silver or other metal trim may be used.

Most soups are cooked covered with fitted glass lids, plastic wrap or wax paper. Pierce plastic wrap covering before removing to avoid steam burns.

Stir soup when specified to distribute ingredients through liquid for even cooking.

Standing times assure thorough heating and cooking.

Use ROAST to keep buttermilk from curdling.

TOMATO BREW

        1 can (10¾ oz.) condensed tomato soup
        1 can (16 oz.) tomatoes, undrained
        1 cup buttermilk
        2 tablespoons finely chopped onion
        ¼ teaspoon Worcestershire sauce
        ⅛ teaspoon dill weed

1. Combine all ingredients in 2-quart glass casserole. Break up whole tomatoes with other ingredients; mix until buttermilk is completely blended into other liquid. Cover with glass lid or plastic wrap.

2. Microwave on ROAST for 10 to 12 minutes or until hot.   4 to 6 Servings

TIP ● Garnish with parsley, seasoned croutons and/or Parmesan cheese.

Cook Chicken Soup on SIMMER to blend flavors into broth and tenderize meat.

CHICKEN SOUP COUNTRY STYLE*

    2½ to 3-lb. whole frying chicken,
        cut up
      4 cups water
      ½ cup finely chopped onion
      ½ cup finely chopped celery
      2 cups thinly sliced carrots
      1 tablespoon salt
      ½ teaspoon pepper
      ¼ teaspoon leaf thyme
      ¼ teaspoon ground sage
      ⅓ cup dried parsley flakes

1. Combine all ingredients in 3-quart glass casserole. Cover with glass lid or plastic wrap.

2. Microwave on HIGH for 15 minutes.

3. Microwave on SIMMER for 25 to 30 minutes or until chicken is fork tender. Remove chicken from seasoned broth; cool. Remove meat from bones and cut into small pieces. Return meat to casserole; mix well and recover.

4. Microwave on REHEAT for about 5 minutes or until hot. Let stand, covered, 5 minutes before serving.   6 to 8 Servings

TIP ● Add ½ cup quick-cooking rice during last cooking period.

HIGH cooks vegetables and flour thickening.

ONE POT MEAT SOUP*

      3 carrots, bias cut
      1 medium onion, sliced
      1 cup sliced unpeeled cucumber
      ½ cup unsifted all-purpose flour
      1 cup milk
      2 cups cubed cooked turkey
      1 can (10¾ oz.) condensed chicken
        broth
      2 cups water
      ¾ teaspoon salt
      ½ teaspoon celery seed
      ¼ teaspoon leaf thyme
      ⅛ teaspoon pepper

1. Combine carrots, onion and cucumber in 2½-quart glass casserole. Cover with glass lid or plastic wrap.

2. Microwave on HIGH for 5 minutes. Blend flour with milk in small mixing bowl. Stir into vegetables along with remaining ingredients. Recover and continue cooking on HIGH for 8 minutes. Stir; recover, and continue cooking on HIGH for 7 to 8 minutes or until vegetables are tender-crisp.

                    4 to 5 Servings

TIP ● Substitute homemade turkey or chicken broth for condensed chicken broth and water.

Raw vegetables microwave on HIGH.

Cooked on HIGH – even with clams – because the clams do not toughen when in a large amount of liquid and not overcooked.

BEEF VEGETABLE SOUP IN A HURRY

  2 cans (10½ oz. each) condensed beef broth
  1 cup water
  1 package (10 oz.) frozen mixed vegetables
  1 bay leaf
  1 teaspoon salt
  1 teaspoon celery salt
  ¼ teaspoon pepper
  1 tablespoon dry sherry, if desired

1. Combine all ingredients in 2-quart glass casserole. Cover with glass lid or plastic wrap.

2. Microwave on HIGH for 12 to 15 minutes or until vegetables are tender-crisp. Let stand, covered, 5 minutes before serving.   4 to 6 Servings

TIP ● Serve with toasted rounds of French bread.

POTATO SOUP

  3 cups cubed potatoes
  ¼ cup finely chopped onion
  ½ teaspoon salt
  1½ cups water
  2 tablespoons all-purpose flour
  ½ cup milk
  1½ cups milk

1. Combine potatoes, onion, salt and water in 2-quart glass casserole. Cover with glass lid or plastic wrap.

2. Microwave on HIGH for 12 to 15 minutes or until potatoes are tender. Blend flour with ½ cup milk to make smooth paste. Stir in 1½ cups milk. Stir into potato mixture and continue cooking on HIGH for 4 to 5 minutes or until thickened.

About 4 Servings

ROAST cooks meat flavors into broth.

TURKEY BROTH

  Turkey gizzard, heart, liver and neck
  3 cups water
  ½ teaspoon salt
  ⅛ teaspoon pepper
  1 bay leaf

1. Combine all ingredients in 2-quart glass casserole. Cover with glass lid or plastic wrap.

2. Microwave on ROAST for about 30 minutes. Remove meat and bay leaf from broth. Use broth for soup or gravy.   About 3 Cups Broth

TIP ● Grind cooked giblets and add to broth for more flavorful gravy.

BOUILLABAISSE*

  4 cups water
  1 can (8 oz.) tomato sauce
  ½ cup finely chopped onion
  1 clove garlic, finely chopped
  2 tablespoons dried parsley flakes
  2½ teaspoons salt
  1 teaspoon lemon juice
  ¼ teaspoon curry powder
  ¼ teaspoon pepper
  1 lb. fish fillets, cut into 2 inch pieces
  1 package (12 oz.) frozen shrimp, thawed
  6 ounces frozen crab or lobster meat, thawed
  1 pint oysters or clams

1. Pour water into 4-quart glass casserole. Cover with glass lid or plastic wrap.

2. Microwave on HIGH for 10 to 12 minutes or until bubbly. Stir in remaining ingredients in order given. Recover and continue cooking on HIGH for about 12 minutes. Stir and continue cooking on HIGH for 8 to 10 minutes or until seafood is done. Let stand, covered, 5 minutes before serving.

10 to 12 Servings

TIP ● Top with seasoned croutons.

Pictured: Bouillabaisse, page 90.

SHRIMP HAM CREAMY SOUP

>   ½ cup finely chopped celery
>   4 green onions, finely chopped
>   ¼ cup finely chopped green pepper
>   2 tablespoons butter or margarine
>   1 can (10½ oz.) condensed cream of
>   shrimp soup
>   2 cups milk
>   1 can (4½ oz.) shrimp pieces, drained
>   1 cup cubed cooked ham

1. Combine celery, green onion, green pepper and butter in 2-quart glass casserole. Cover with glass lid or plastic wrap.

2. Microwave on ROAST for 4 minutes. Stir in remaining ingredients; recover.

3. Microwave on REHEAT for 10 to 12 minutes or until hot.   4 to 6 Servings

CHEESY CLAM CHOWDER*

>   1 package (10 oz.) frozen mixed vegetables
>   1 can (10¾ oz.) condensed clam chowder
>   1 soup can milk
>   1 cup shredded Cheddar cheese

1. Combine all ingredients in 2-quart glass casserole. Cover with glass lid or plastic wrap.

2. Microwave on ROAST for 12 minutes. Stir; recover, and continue cooking on ROAST for 10 to 12 minutes or until piping hot.   4 to 6 Servings

CLAM CHOWDER*

>   2 slices bacon
>   2 cans (6½ oz. each) minced clams,
>   undrained
>   1 large potato, finely chopped
>   ¼ cup chopped onion
>   1 medium carrot, thinly sliced
>   2 tablespoons all-purpose flour
>   ⅓ cup milk
>   1 cup milk
>   1 teaspoon salt
>   Dash pepper
>   Parsley

1. Place bacon slices in 2-quart glass casserole.

2. Microwave on HIGH for 2 to 2½ minutes or until crisp. Remove bacon; crumble, and set aside. Add clam liquid, potato, onion and carrot to bacon drippings. Cover with plastic wrap and continue cooking on HIGH for 8 to 10 minutes or until vegetables are partly cooked. Blend flour with ⅓ cup milk. Stir into cooked vegetable mixture. Mix in 1 cup milk, salt, pepper and clams; recover.

3. Microwave on ROAST for 5 minutes. Stir and continue cooking on ROAST for 3 to 4 minutes or until mixture comes to a boil. Let stand, covered, 3 minutes. Garnish with crumbled bacon and parsley and serve.   3 to 4 Servings

STEW KEY: Stew cooked in the microwave oven is a simple 2-setting procedure. Ingredients dictate the first setting. Beef (except ground beef) and chicken stews start on HIGH. Pork, lamb, veal and all ground meat mixtures start on ROAST. The second stew setting is always SIMMER. This slower cooking blends meat, vegetable and seasoning flavors.

Canned stew or stews made of cooked ingredients, including cooked and seasoned gravies, heat on REHEAT. Meats in these mixtures have been tenderized during prior cooking and processing.

Trim fat from meat so pan juices are not greasy.

Microwave stews in glass or pottery containers with no silver, gold or other metal trim.

Cover stews to speed cooking, blend flavors and keep meat moist. Use glass lids, plastic wrap or wax paper. Pierce plastic wrap before removing it to prevent steam burns.

Stir when specified to distribute heat and ingredients for even cooking.

Stews made of meat coated with flour usually are not drained during cooking. Uncoated meat often produces fatty drippings which should be drained away.

Stews stand, covered, after coming from the oven to finish cooking and thicken gravies. Stir well before serving for thorough thickening.

Note that little liquid is added to stews cooked in a microwave oven. When adapting a conventional recipe, find a "model" in this chapter to help figure liquid needed.

TOMATO BEEF STEW

>   1½ lbs. beef stew meat
>   2 teaspoons salt
>   ½ teaspoon pepper
>   ½ teaspoon leaf tarragon
>   1 package (24 oz.) frozen vegetables
>   for stew
>   1 package (10 oz.) frozen peas
>   2 cans (10¾ oz. each) condensed
>   tomato soup
>   1 can (4 oz.) whole mushrooms, drained
>   1 whole fresh tomato, sliced

1. Place meat in 3-quart glass casserole. Cover with glass lid or plastic wrap.

2. Microwave on HIGH for 8 minutes. Drain and stir in remaining ingredients, except tomato; recover.

3. Microwave on SIMMER for 55 to 60 minutes or until meat is fork tender. Let stand, covered, 5 minutes before serving. Garnish with sliced fresh tomato.   About 4 Servings

SAVORY BEEF STEW

> **3** tablespoons all-purpose flour
> **1** teaspoon salt
> ½ teaspoon pepper
> 1½ lbs. beef stew meat
> **3** tablespoons butter or margarine
> **3** cups water
> **1** tablespoon soy sauce
> **1** tablespoon Worcestershire sauce
> ¼ teaspoon garlic salt
> **1** bay leaf
> ½ teaspoon leaf thyme
> **2** cups cubed peeled potatoes
> 1½ cups sliced carrots

1. Combine flour, salt and pepper in flat dish. Coat meat in seasoned flour. Place butter in 3-quart glass casserole with coated meat. Cover with glass lid or plastic wrap.

2. Microwave on HIGH for 8 minutes. Stir in remaining ingredients; recover.

3. Microwave on SIMMER for 45 to 50 minutes or until meat is fork tender.   4 to 6 Servings

TIP ● Thicken meat juices by blending ¼ cup unsifted all-purpose flour with ½ cup water. Stir into hot stew; recover. Microwave on SIMMER for 5 to 6 minutes or until thickened. Let stand, covered, 5 minutes. Stir well before serving.

BEEF STEW ITALIANO

> **2** lbs. beef stew meat
> **1** teaspoon Italian seasoning
> ½ teaspoon leaf oregano
> **2** teaspoons salt
> ¼ teaspoon garlic salt
> ¼ teaspoon pepper
> **3** large carrots, cut into chunks
> **2** medium onions, sliced ½ inch thick
> **2** tablespoons cornstarch
> **2** tablespoons water
> **2** cans (4 oz. each) whole mushrooms, drained
> **1** can (28 oz.) Italian pear-shaped tomatoes
> **1** carton (8 oz.) sour cream

1. Place meat in 3-quart glass casserole. Cover with glass lid or plastic wrap.

2. Microwave on HIGH for 10 minutes. Drain and stir in seasonings. Layer carrots and onions on top.

3. Microwave on SIMMER for 20 minutes. Blend cornstarch with water. Stir into meat mixture with mushrooms and tomatoes; mix well. Recover and continue cooking on SIMMER for 35 to 40 minutes or until meat is fork tender. Fold in sour cream. Let stand, covered, 5 minutes before serving.
          4 to 6 Servings

TIP ● Substitute ½ lb. fresh mushrooms for canned.

CANNED BEEF STEW

1. Spoon 1 can (24 oz.) beef stew (any kind) into 1-quart glass casserole. Cover with glass lid or plastic wrap.

2. Microwave on REHEAT for 4 to 6 minutes or until hot. Let stand, covered, 5 minutes before serving.   2 to 3 Servings

PAPRIKA PORK STEW

> 1½ lbs. boneless pork, cubed
> **1** large onion, chopped
> **1** clove garlic, finely chopped
> **1** tablespoon paprika
> **2** teaspoons salt
> ¼ teaspoon pepper
> **1** teaspoon caraway seed
> **1** cup water
> **1** carton (8 oz.) plain yogurt
> **1** fresh tomato, chopped

1. Place pork in 2-quart glass casserole. Cover with glass lid or plastic wrap.

2. Microwave on ROAST for 12 minutes. Drain and stir in remaining ingredients, except yogurt and tomato; recover.

3. Microwave on SIMMER for 20 to 25 minutes or until meat is fork tender. Stir in yogurt and tomato. Let stand, covered, 5 minutes before serving.
          4 to 6 Servings

Pork cooks best on ROAST.

PORK STEW WITH SAUERKRAUT

> **2** lbs. boneless pork, cubed
> **1** can (16 oz.) sauerkraut, drained
> **1** teaspoon salt
> ¼ teaspoon pepper
> **1** large onion, finely chopped
> **1** teaspoon garlic salt
> **2** teaspoons paprika
> **2** teaspoons dill weed
> **1** can (10¾ oz.) condensed chicken broth
> ½ cup sour cream

1. Place pork in 2-quart glass casserole. Cover with glass lid or plastic wrap.

2. Microwave on ROAST for 15 minutes. Drain and stir in remaining ingredients, except sour cream; recover.

3. Microwave on SIMMER for 25 to 30 minutes or until meat is fork tender. Blend in sour cream. Let stand, covered, 5 minutes before serving.
          4 to 6 Servings

Veal stays tender on ROAST.

VEAL ARTICHOKE STEW

     2 tablespoons all-purpose flour
    ½ teaspoon salt
    ¼ teaspoon pepper
    1½ lbs. boneless veal, cubed
     2 tablespoons butter or margarine
    ½ teaspoon leaf basil
     1 teaspoon paprika
     1 clove garlic, finely chopped
     1 tablespoon dried parsley flakes
    ¼ lb. fresh mushrooms, halved
     1 jar (2 oz.) chopped pimento, drained
     1 package (9 oz.) frozen artichokes
     2 tablespoons cornstarch
     1 can (10¾ oz.) chicken broth

1. Combine flour, salt and pepper in flat dish. Coat veal cubes in seasoned flour. Place butter in 2-quart glass casserole with coated meat. Cover with glass lid or plastic wrap.

2. Microwave on ROAST for 10 minutes. Stir in remaining ingredients, except cornstarch and broth. Blend cornstarch and broth in small mixing bowl. Mix into meat and vegetables; recover.

3. Microwave on SIMMER for 26 to 28 minutes or until meat is fork tender. Let stand, covered, 5 minutes. Stir well before serving.   4 to 6 Servings

Microwave tender lamb on ROAST.

IRISH STEW

     2 tablespoons all-purpose flour
     2 teaspoons salt
    ¼ teaspoon pepper
     2 lbs. lamb stew meat, trim off fat
     2 tablespoons butter or margarine
     1 cup finely sliced carrots
     1 cup finely sliced celery
     1 cup finely sliced turnips
     1 medium onion, chopped
     2 cups cubed raw potatoes
     1 bay leaf
     2 teaspoons rosemary
     2 tablespoons dried parsley flakes
     2 tablespoons cornstarch
     2 cups water

1. Combine flour, salt and pepper in flat dish. Coat meat in seasoned flour. Place butter in 2-quart glass casserole with coated meat. Cover with glass lid or plastic wrap.

2. Microwave on ROAST for 10 minutes. Stir in remaining ingredients, except cornstarch and water. Blend cornstarch with water in small mixing bowl. Mix into meat and vegetables; recover.

3. Microwave on SIMMER for 35 to 40 minutes or until meat is fork tender. Let stand, covered, 5 minutes. Stir well before serving.   4 to 6 Servings

CREAMY CHICKEN STEW

     2 medium potatoes, cut into 16 pieces
     1 cup coarsely sliced celery
     2 cups coarsely sliced carrots
     1 large onion, cut in eighths
     2 teaspoons salt
    ¼ teaspoon pepper
     1 teaspoon ground sage
    2½ to 3-lb. whole frying chicken, cut up
     2 cans (10¾ oz. each) condensed cream of chicken soup
    Parsley

1. Layer vegetables in 4-quart glass Dutch oven. Season with salt, pepper and sage. Place chicken, skin side down and thick edges toward outside of dish, on top of vegetables. Cover with glass lid or plastic wrap.

2. Microwave on HIGH for 15 minutes. Drain and turn chicken over. Pour soup over chicken; recover.

3. Microwave on SIMMER for 25 to 30 minutes or until fork tender. Let stand, covered, 5 minutes before serving. Garnish with snipped parsley.
                              4 to 6 Servings

Simmer chicken stews to blend flavors.

CHICKEN 'N NUTS STEW

     2 lbs. chicken drumsticks and thighs
    ½ cup coarsely sliced celery
    ½ medium green pepper, sliced
     8 whole small onions
    ½ teaspoon crushed dried red chili pepper
     1 can (10¾ oz.) condensed chicken broth
    ¾ cup peanut butter
    ½ cup salted peanuts

1. Place chicken, skin side down and thick edges toward outside of dish, in 3-quart glass casserole. Cover with glass lid or plastic wrap.

2. Microwave on HIGH for 10 minutes; turn chicken over; drain. Layer vegetables over chicken. Sprinkle with chili pepper. Pour broth over all; recover.

3. Microwave on SIMMER for 15 to 20 minutes or until chicken is fork tender and vegetables are tender-crisp. Remove chicken to platter; set aside. Blend peanut butter into pan juices. Return chicken and vegetables to casserole; recover, and continue cooking on SIMMER for 3 to 4 minutes or until piping hot. Let stand, covered, 5 minutes. Sprinkle nuts on top and serve.   About 4 Servings

SANDWICH KEY: Microwave oven settings for sandwiches depend on filling mixture.

Uncooked ground beef needs Microwave HIGH for fast heat penetration.

Most fillings are made of cooked ingredients so microwave on REHEAT.

Cheese fillings need the lower ROAST setting to melt smoothly and prevent overcooking.

Grilled cheese sandwiches brown and melt beautifully when a microwave browning grill is used in the oven. The manufacturer's instruction booklet which comes with this accessory gives complete directions.

Toasted bread makes a firmer base for hot sandwiches.

Paper absorbs moisture so most sandwiches microwave on a paper towel or napkin set on the oven floor. Wrap thick sandwiches, such as hot dogs and hamburgers, loosely in a paper towel or napkin.

SANDWICH	SETTING	MINUTES
1	HIGH	1 to 1½
2	HIGH	2 to 2½

HAMBURGERS

1. Prepare Ground Beef Patties as directed on page 59. Place cooked patties in split buns and wrap each one loosely in paper napkin or paper towel.

2. Microwave on REHEAT until heated through:
   1 hamburger — 15 to 20 seconds
   2 hamburgers — 25 to 30 seconds
   4 hamburgers — 45 to 50 seconds
   6 hamburgers — 1 to 1½ minutes

Wieners and buns are cooked – just heat through.

HOT DOGS

1. Place wieners in split hot dog buns and wrap each one loosely in paper napkin or paper towel in oven.

2. Microwave on REHEAT until heated through:
   1 hot dog — 30 to 35 seconds
   2 hot dogs — 45 to 50 seconds
   4 hot dogs — 1 to 1½ minutes
   6 hot dogs — 1½ to 2 minutes

TIP ● Heat wieners without buns on glass plate. Microwave on REHEAT until warm: 1 wiener 25 to 30 seconds; 2 wieners 35 to 40 seconds; 4 wieners 50 to 55 seconds; 6 wieners 1 to 1¼ minutes.

Taco shells can be heated on REHEAT for 15 to 20 seconds before filling.

HOW TO GRILL CHEESE SANDWICHES ON A MICROWAVE BROWNING GRILL

● Place sliced process American cheese between 2 slices of bread.

● Butter outside of bread.

● Preheat browning grill in oven on HIGH as directed in manufacturer's instruction booklet.

● Place sandwich(es) on grill; turn over once halfway through cooking.

● Grill until cheese melts and bread is toasted.

Pictured: Tacos, this page.

TACOS

    1 lb. ground beef
1½ teaspoons chili powder
  ½ teaspoon salt
  ½ teaspoon garlic powder
  ¼ teaspoon pepper
  ⅛ teaspoon cayenne pepper
  ¼ cup water
  Taco shells
  Cheddar cheese, shredded
  Lettuce, shredded
  Onion, finely chopped
  Tomato, chopped

1. Crumble ground beef in 1-quart glass casserole.

2. Microwave on HIGH for 6 minutes; drain. Stir in seasonings and water.

3. Microwave on HIGH for 3 to 4 minutes or until meat is well done.

4. Fill each taco shell with about 2 heaping tablespoons of meat filling. Top with remaining ingredients.   **10 to 12 Tacos**

SLOPPY JOE SANDWICHES

    1 lb. ground beef
    ½ cup chopped onion
    ½ cup chopped green pepper
    1 tablespoon packed brown sugar
    1 teaspoon salt
    ½ teaspoon paprika
    ¼ teaspoon pepper
    1 cup (8 oz.) tomato sauce
    6 hamburger buns

1. Crumble ground beef into 2-quart glass casserole. Stir in onion and green pepper. Cover with glass lid or plastic wrap.

2. Microwave on HIGH for 5 minutes; drain. Stir in remaining ingredients, except buns; recover, and continue cooking on REHEAT for 12 to 14 minutes or until hot. Let stand, covered, 5 minutes before serving. Spoon into warm hamburger buns.

                           About 6 Servings

TIP • Warm 6 buns 25 to 30 seconds on REHEAT.

TOMATO CHEESE SANDWICH

    1 slice of bread, toasted
    Mayonnaise or salad dressing
    2 slices tomato, ½ inch thick
    1 slice process American cheese,
      ¼ inch thick

1. Spread toasted bread slice with mayonnaise. Top with tomato slices, then cheese. Arrange sandwich on paper napkin or towel in oven.

2. Microwave on ROAST for 45 to 60 seconds or until cheese bubbles and is melted.   1 Sandwich

TIP • If natural cheese is used, cook a few seconds longer.

Pictured: Tomato Cheese Sandwich garnished with sweet pickle slices, this page; Canned Soup, page 88.

FISHWICHES

    1 package (8 oz.) frozen precooked
      breaded fish sticks
    4 hot dog buns, split and buttered
    Tartar sauce

1. Place fish sticks on glass plate in spoke fashion.

2. Microwave on DEFROST for 3 minutes. Spread buns with tartar sauce. Place 2 fish sticks on each bun. Arrange on paper towel in oven.

3. Microwave on REHEAT until heated through:
    1 fishwich — 45 to 60 seconds
    2 fishwiches — 1 to 1½ minutes
    4 fishwiches — 2½ to 3 minutes

TIP • Garnish with sliced dill pickle or pickle relish.

Make ahead for quick reheating.

REUBEN SALAD BUNS

    1 can (12 oz.) corned beef
    ¾ cup sauerkraut, drained
    1 small apple, cored and shredded
    1 cup shredded Swiss cheese
    2 tablespoons Thousand Island Dressing
    1 teaspoon dill weed
    2 teaspoons prepared mustard
    8 pumpernickel buns

1. Break up corned beef in medium mixing bowl. Stir in remaining ingredients, except buns; mix well. Spoon ½ cup corned beef mixture between each split roll. Wrap loosely in paper towel or napkin.

2. Microwave on REHEAT until hot through:
    1 bun — 1 to 1½ minutes
    2 buns — 1½ to 2 minutes
    4 buns — 3 to 3½ minutes
    8 buns — 3½ to 4 minutes
                    8 Reuben Salad Buns

TIP • Substitute 8 ounces corned beef, finely cut, for canned corn beef.

Paper towel or napkin keeps sandwich from getting soggy.

SLICED MEAT SANDWICHES

    Butter or margarine
    Mayonnaise or salad dressing
    Buns
    Sliced cooked meat

1. Spread butter and mayonnaise on buns. Place meat slices between split buns. Wrap loosely in paper towel or napkin.

2. Microwave on REHEAT until heated through:
    1 sandwich — 1 to 1½ minutes
    2 sandwiches — 1½ to 2 minutes
    4 sandwiches — 2½ to 3 minutes

TIP • Thinly-sliced meat heats more evenly than thick meat slices.

Paper wrapping absorbs excess moisture while assuring that loaf heats through.

HOT TUNA SANDWICH LOAF

   3 **hard cooked eggs, chopped**
   1 **can (6½ oz.) flaked tuna fish, drained**
   ¼ **cup chopped onion**
   1 **teaspoon salt**
   ¼ **teaspoon pepper**
   ½ **teaspoon prepared mustard**
   ½ **cup mayonnaise or salad dressing**
   1 **loaf (1 lb.) French bread, 15 inches long**
   3 **slices (¾ oz. each) process American cheese, cut in half**

1. Combine all ingredients, except bread and cheese, in medium mixing bowl; mix well; set aside. Slice off top ⅓ of bread horizontally. Hollow out bottom of loaf. Fill hollow with tuna mixture. Place cheese slices over filling. Place top crust of bread over cheese. Wrap loosely in paper towel or napkin.

2. Microwave on REHEAT for 4 to 5 minutes or until hot. Slice to serve.   About 6 Servings

TIP • Cut loaf of bread to fit oven if it is too long. Dry unused bread to make crumbs or dressing.

BARBECUE WRAP-UPS

   4 **hamburger buns, split and toasted**
   ½ **lb. cooked roast beef, thinly sliced**
   ¼ **cup bottled barbecue sauce**
   4 **slices (¾ oz. each) process American cheese**

1. Place bottom half of buns on paper towel. Top each half with 1 or 2 slices of meat. Spread 1 tablespoon barbecue sauce over meat. Top with slice of cheese. Wrap loosely in paper towel or napkin.

2. Microwave on ROAST for 3 to 5 minutes or until meat is hot and cheese is melted.   4 Sandwiches

Cheese requires gentle cooking.

HOT TURKEY SANDWICHES

   1 **cup chopped cooked turkey**
   ¼ **cup chopped onion**
   ⅓ **cup mayonnaise or salad dressing**
   2 **teaspoons prepared mustard**
   6 **slices bread, toasted**
   6 **slices (¾ oz. each) process American cheese**

1. Combine turkey, onion, mayonnaise and mustard in medium mixing bowl; mix well. Spread equal amounts of turkey mixture on each toasted bread slice. Top with cheese. Arrange on paper towel in oven.

2. Microwave on ROAST for 1½ to 2 minutes or until cheese is melted.   6 Sandwiches

HOT TURKEY SALAD BUNS

   2 **cups chopped cooked turkey**
   1 **cup shredded Cheddar cheese**
   ¼ **cup finely chopped celery**
   ¼ **cup finely chopped almonds**
   ½ **cup mayonnaise or salad dressing**
   ¼ **teaspoon salt**
   2 **tablespoons pickle relish**
   6 **hamburger buns, split and toasted**

1. Combine all ingredients, except buns, in medium mixing bowl; mix well. Spread turkey mixture between split toasted buns. Wrap loosely in paper towel or napkin.

2. Microwave on ROAST for 3½ to 4 minutes or until hot.   6 Sandwiches

TUNA SALAD SANDWICHES

   1 **can (6½ oz.) flaked tuna, drained**
   1 **cup cubed process American cheese**
   2 **tablespoons chopped onion**
   2 **tablespoons chopped green pepper**
   2 **tablespoons pickle relish**
   ¼ **cup sliced pimento stuffed olives**
   ⅓ **cup mayonnaise or salad dressing**
   6 **hot dog buns, split and toasted**

1. Combine all ingredients, except buns, in medium mixing bowl; mix well. Spread equal amounts of tuna mixture on bottom half of toasted buns. Place other half of bun on top. Wrap loosely in paper towel or napkin.

2. Microwave on ROAST for 3 to 5 minutes or until hot and cheese is melted.   6 Sandwiches

MUFFIN PIZZA

   1 **package (14 oz.) English muffins**
   1¼ **cups chili sauce**
       Italian seasoning

Pizza Garnishes:
   Green pepper, sliced
   Pepperoni, sliced
   Green onion, bias cut
   Mushrooms, sliced
   Olives, sliced
   Mozzarella cheese, shredded

1. Split English muffins in half. Top each muffin half with 1½ tablespoons chili sauce, a sprinkle of Italian seasoning and some Pizza Garnishes. Arrange 2 pizzas on paper towel in oven.

2. Microwave on ROAST for 2½ to 3 minutes or until cheese is melted.   12 Pizzas

TIPS • Pizza may be cooked on preheated microwave browning grill.

   • English muffins may be toasted, if desired.

Lively classics since ancient times — eggs and cheese take on new drama in microwave cooking.

Secret to light tender egg or cheese dishes has always been gentle heat. This is still true in a microwave oven.

Eggs are a particular delight because "just right" individual servings microwave right in their own glass or pottery dishes. Do remember not to use dishes with silver, gold or other metal trim.

Softening and melting cheese right from the refrigerator is miraculously simple, too.

Since both eggs and cheese microwave at the same ROAST setting, combination dishes are delicious.

Use the "grey box" keys and detailed cooking charts for top-notch results.

Pictured top to bottom: Scrambled Eggs sprinkled with paprika, page 101; Cheesy Eggs and Noodles garnished with sliced hard cooked eggs, page 102.

EGG/CHEESE CHAPTER
CONTENTS

EGG KEY: Beaten egg mixtures, hard cooked eggs and whole raw eggs all microwave on ROAST — but for different reasons.

Omelets, scrambled eggs and other dishes with egg white and yolk mixed are easiest to microwave. ROAST cooks the mixture's center without overcooking outside edges.

Most dishes calling for hard cooked eggs microwave on ROAST to preserve tender texture throughout.

Whole raw eggs need ROAST to keep yolks from cooking before the whites.

Carefully follow recipe directions for covering and standing times because egg yolk contains fat which cooks first and can toughen or even "pop." The cover keeps yolks tender while steam cooks the white. Use a fitted glass lid, saucer without metal trim or plastic wrap.

These recipes have been tested with large eggs taken directly from the refrigerator.

However, egg size and age varies — even within a single carton — so cooking time varies. Microwave eggs in individual glass or pottery dishes (without silver or other metal trim) so eggs may be taken from the oven as they reach desired doneness.

DO NOT microwave eggs in the shell. Rapid microwave cooking causes eggs in the shell to explode because yolks cook faster than the whites and tend to cause pressure.

HOW TO BAKE EGGS

• Break each egg into a buttered 10-ounce glass custard cup.

• Cover with plastic wrap.

• Microwave on ROAST.

• Let stand, covered, 1 minute before serving.

NO. OF EGGS	SETTING	MINUTES
1	ROAST	35 to 40 sec.
2	ROAST	1 to 1¼
4	ROAST	2 to 2¼

HOW TO FRY EGGS ON A MICROWAVE BROWN-ING GRILL·

• Preheat microwave browning grill as directed in browner's instruction booklet on HIGH.

• Melt 1 teaspoon butter on microwave browning grill.

• Break egg(s) on browning grill.

• Microwave on ROAST.

NO. OF EGGS	SETTING	MINUTES
1	ROAST	45 to 55 sec.
2	ROAST	1½ to 2
4	ROAST	2 to 2½

BRUNCH SPECIAL

  1 **package (12 oz.) frozen hash brown potatoes**
  ⅓ **cup sour cream**
  ⅓ **cup milk**
  ½ **teaspoon salt**
  1 **tablespoon snipped chives**
  4 **slices Canadian style bacon**
  4 **eggs**

1. Place potatoes in 2-quart (8 x 8) glass baking dish. Cover with plastic wrap.

2. Microwave on HIGH for 6 to 7 minutes or until partly cooked. Blend in sour cream, milk, salt and chives. Place bacon slices down center of dish. Make two hollows in potatoes on each side of bacon. Break 1 egg into each indentation; recover.

3. Microwave on ROAST for 6 to 8 minutes or until eggs are cooked to desired doneness. Let stand, covered, 2 minutes before serving. About 4 Servings

HOW TO SCRAMBLE EGGS

● Break eggs into soup bowl or 20-ounce glass casserole (1-quart size for 4, 5 or 6 eggs). Do not use dishes with silver, gold or other metal trim.

● Add milk and beat together with a fork.

● Add butter and other seasonings to taste.

● Cover with glass lid or plastic wrap.

● Microwave on ROAST. Stir 6 or more eggs once during cooking period.

● Stir gently with a fork before serving.

● If cooking scrambled eggs a while before serving, undercook slightly and warm on ROAST when served.

● Soak cooking dish immediately after emptying for easiest clean-up.

NO. OF EGGS	BUTTER OR MARGARINE	MILK	SETTING	MINUTES
1	1 tsp.	1 tbsp.	ROAST	1 to 1½
2	2 tsps.	3 tbsps.	ROAST	2 to 2½
4	4 tsps.	4 tbsps.	ROAST	4½ to 5
6	2 tbsps.	6 tbsps.	ROAST	4 stir 2½ to 3½

HOW TO POACH EGGS

● When poaching 1 to 3 eggs, use individual 6-ounce glass custard cups. Poach 4 eggs in a 1-quart glass casserole.

● Bring water and ¼ teaspoon vinegar to boil on HIGH.

● Break eggs carefully into hot water.

● Cover tightly with glass lid or plastic wrap.

● Microwave eggs in boiling water on ROAST .

● Let stand, covered, 1 minute before serving.

● To poach eggs in bouillon, omit vinegar; use ½ cup water per egg plus 1 cube or teaspoon chicken bouillon. Stir after first heating to dissolve bouillon.

WATER	GLASS CONTAINER	WATER SETTING AND TIME	EGGS	EGG SETTING AND TIME
¼ CUP	6-oz. custard cup	HIGH 1½ to 2 min.	1	ROAST 30 to 45 sec.
¼ CUP EA.	6-oz. custard cups	HIGH 2 to 2½ min.	2	ROAST 1 to 1½ min.
1 CUP	1-qt. casserole	HIGH 2½ to 3 min.	4	ROAST 2½ to 3 min.

*Pictured top to bottom: Brunch Special, page 100;
Denver Brunch Sandwich, page 102.*

Precooked ingredients in recipe microwave quickly.

CHEESY EGGS AND NOODLES

    4 cups cooked green noodles
    1 jar (8 oz.) process cheese spread
    6 hard cooked eggs, shelled and sliced
    1 teaspoon salt
    ⅛ teaspoon pepper
    2 teaspoons tarragon
    2 tablespoons butter or margarine

1. Combine all ingredients in 2-quart glass casserole; mix well. Cover with glass lid or plastic wrap.

2. Microwave on ROAST for 12 to 14 minutes or until hot. Let stand, covered, 5 minutes before serving. 4 to 6 Servings

TIPS ● Substitute plain cooked noodles for green noodles.

  ● Add ¼ cup chopped cooked ham when combining ingredients in Step 1.

CREAMED EGGS WITH CHIPPED BEEF

    6 hard cooked eggs, shelled and quartered
    1 can (10¾ oz.) condensed cream of mushroom soup
    1 package (3 oz.) corned beef, cut into pieces
    ¼ teaspoon dried parsley flakes

1. Combine all ingredients in 1½-quart glass casserole. Cover with glass lid or plastic wrap.

2. Microwave on ROAST for 8 to 10 minutes or until hot. 3 to 4 Servings

Dishes with scrambled eggs microwave well.

DENVER BRUNCH SANDWICH

    8 slices bacon
    6 eggs
    ⅓ cup milk
    ½ cup mayonnaise or salad dressing
    ¼ cup chopped pimento
    ¼ cup chopped green pepper
    ¼ teaspoon salt
    Tomato slices

1. Place bacon slices between paper napkin or paper towels in 1½-quart (10 x 6) glass baking dish.

2. Microwave on HIGH for 7 to 9 minutes or until bacon is crisp. Remove bacon; drain drippings; crumble bacon; set aside. Combine eggs, milk and mayonnaise in medium mixing bowl; beat well with rotary beater. Stir in bacon and remaining ingredients. Pour into baking dish. Cover with plastic wrap.

3. Microwave on ROAST for 6 to 7 minutes or until center is almost set. Garnish with tomato slices. Let stand, covered, 5 minutes before serving. 4 to 6 Servings

HERB OMELET*

    1 tablespoon butter or margarine
    3 eggs
    3 tablespoons water
    ¼ teaspoon salt
    ⅛ teaspoon pepper
    ¼ teaspoon leaf basil

1. Place butter in 9-inch glass pie plate.

2. Microwave on ROAST for about ½ minute or until melted. Beat remaining ingredients into melted butter. Cover with plastic wrap.

3. Microwave on ROAST for 2 minutes. Stir lightly; recover, and continue cooking on ROAST for 1 to 1½ minutes or until almost set in center. Let stand, covered, 2 minutes before serving. 1 to 2 Servings

CHEESE KEY: Cheese dishes are smooth and creamy when cooked on Microwave ROAST. Fondue seems to be an exception — taking the gentle SIMMER setting because of the large proportion of cheese in the recipe.

  Remember that cheese should be cooked below the boiling point and as quickly as possible to avoid separation and toughening.

  Cheeses can be interchanged in microwave recipes, but only within their own categories: soft, semi-soft, hard or processed.

  Since both cheese and eggs microwave superbly at ROAST, dishes combining these two nutritious foods are very successful.

  Follow recipe directions carefully as to covering and standing times.

  When a cover is called for, use a fitted glass lid or tightly-tucked plastic wrap.

CHEESE AND EGG PUFF*

    1 tablespoon butter or margarine
    4 eggs, well beaten
    ¼ cup unsifted all-purpose flour
    1 cup milk
    1 cup shredded Swiss cheese
    ¼ teaspoon salt
    ¼ teaspoon pepper
    2 tablespoons snipped chives

1. Place butter in 9-inch glass pie plate.

2. Microwave on ROAST for about ½ minute or until melted. Beat eggs in medium mixing bowl; then gradually beat in flour until smooth. Stir in remaining ingredients; mix well. Pour into buttered pie plate. Cover with plastic wrap.

3. Microwave on ROAST for 5 minutes. Gently fold over omelet; recover, and continue cooking on ROAST for 3 to 4 minutes. Let stand, covered, 5 minutes before serving. 3 to 4 Servings

Gentle cooking makes a smoother mixture.

CREAMY SMOOTH CHEESE FONDUE*

1½ cups dry sherry
5 cups shredded process American Cheese
2 tablespoons cornstarch
¼ teaspoon dry mustard
⅛ teaspoon garlic salt
1 loaf French bread

1. Pour sherry into 2-cup glass measure.

2. Microwave on HIGH for 4 to 5 minutes or until very hot but not boiling. Toss remaining ingredients together, except bread, in 3-quart glass mixing bowl. Pour hot sherry over cheese mixture; stir to blend well.

3. Microwave on SIMMER for 3 minutes. Stir and continue cooking on SIMMER for 3 to 4 minutes or until hot. Beat mixture until smooth. Serve hot with chunks of French bread.   About 4 Cups Fondue

Cover keeps both cheese and macaroni tender and moist.

TRADITIONAL MACARONI WITH CHEESE*

2 tablespoons butter or margarine
¼ cup finely chopped onion
2 cups shredded process American cheese
¾ cup milk
1 teaspoon salt
⅛ teaspoon pepper
4 cups cooked elbow macaroni

1. Place butter and onion in 2-quart glass casserole.

2. Microwave on ROAST for about 3 minutes or until onion is partly cooked. Stir in remaining ingredients. Cover with glass lid or plastic wrap.

3. Microwave on ROAST for 4 minutes. Stir lightly; recover, and continue cooking on ROAST for 4 to 5 minutes or until piping hot. Let stand, covered, 5 minutes before serving.

About 6 Servings

HOW TO SOFTEN CREAM CHEESE AND SPREADS

● Remove foil wrapper from cream cheese and place in glass bowl or dish to be used in recipe.

● Cheese spreads may be warmed in their original containers after the cap is removed — or in a glass or pottery serving dish which has no silver or other metal trim.

● Microwave on WARM until cheese is soft.

Quiche is a cream custard, so use gentle DEFROST setting to prevent edges from overcooking before the center is done.

QUICHE LORRAINE

1 (9-inch) Baked Pastry Shell, Page 147
½ lb. bacon
1 cup shredded Cheddar cheese
⅓ cup finely chopped onion
1 cup light cream
3 eggs
¾ teaspoon salt
¼ teaspoon sugar
⅛ teaspoon cayenne pepper

1. Place bacon slices between layers of paper towel in 2-quart (12 x 7) glass baking dish.

2. Microwave on HIGH for 8 to 9 minutes or until crisp; cool. Crumble into bottom of 9-inch Baked Pastry Shell in glass pie plate. Sprinkle cheese and onion on top; set aside. Pour cream into 1-cup glass measure.

3. Microwave on HIGH for 1 to 1½ minutes or until cream is hot. In small bowl beat eggs and seasonings; slowly blend in heated cream. Pour over bacon, cheese and onion in pie shell.

4. Microwave on DEFROST for 30 to 35 minutes or until knife inserted near center comes out clean. Let stand 5 minutes before serving.

5 to 6 Servings

ITEM	SIZE	SETTING	MINUTES
CREAM CHEESE	3-oz. pkg.	WARM	1 to 2½
	8-oz. pkg.	WARM	3 to 5
CHEESE SPREAD	8-oz. container	WARM	1½ to 2½

Great, Great Grandma's convenience foods — rice, pastas and cereals! All three are easy to store and prepare. There's no peeling, scraping — or waste.

Charts throughout this chapter are the guides to successful microwave cooking for all three.

Quick-cooking cereals are especially convenient for breakfast because single servings cook right in individual bowls.

Wild rice lovers know that this favorite is a grass seed not a cereal grain. Cooking directions for it, however, are included in this chapter.

Reheating rice and pasta dishes is a cinch. Homemakers can fix supper dishes well ahead of time — heat them fast just before a meal.

Become familiar with "grey key" techniques for preparing rice, pastas and cereals — they're basic to microwave main dish cooking.

Pictured clockwise from the top: Oh! So Good Spaghetti, page 108; Cooked Cereal garnished with brown sugar and dried apricot half, page 109; Rice Supper Dish garnished with parsley, page 107.

RICE KEY: Bring water, butter and seasonings to a full rolling boil, covered, on Microwave HIGH before stirring in rice. Hot tap water comes to a boil the fastest.

Microwave raw rice on DEFROST. Slow cooking gives light fluffy texture.

Rice expands two to three times its dry volume so use a glass bowl that's big enough to hold both rice and water.

Cover rice with a fitted glass lid or plastic wrap when cooking.

Let rice stand 5 minutes, covered, before serving so it absorbs all moisture and fluffs.

Toss cooked rice as little as possible so it does not mush.

Converted white rice can be substituted for long grain white rice, but add 5 minutes to the cooking time.

Rehydrate quick-cooking rice right in a glass serving casserole. Bring water to a rolling boil on Microwave HIGH. Stir in quick-cooking rice, cover and let stand as directed on package.

Wild rice is more tender when presoaked as directed in chart.

Reheat rice, covered, on REHEAT until steaming hot. If rice has been refrigerated, stir once during heating.

Cook rice ahead and use in casserole dishes calling for rice.

RICE YIELDS

1 cup raw white rice = 3 cups cooked rice
1 cup raw brown rice = 4 cups cooked rice
1 cup raw wild rice = 3½ cups cooked rice
1 cup quick-cooking rice = 2 cups cooked rice

HOW TO COOK RICE

• Choose a glass cooking dish two to three times as large as the amount of dry rice to be cooked — rice expands during cooking.

• Add 1 teaspoon salt and 1 tablespoon butter to water.

• Bring water and seasonings to a full rolling boil on Microwave HIGH.

• Stir in raw rice and microwave on DEFROST.

• Always cook rice covered. Use a fitted glass lid or tautly-stretched plastic wrap.

• Let cooked rice stand, covered, 5 minutes after being removed from the oven.

• Cook quick-cooking rice in a glass or pottery serving casserole without silver, gold or other metal trim. Boil water on Microwave HIGH. Stir in quick-cooking rice; cover, and let stand as directed on package.

• Wild rice is most tender if washed, drained, covered with tap water and soaked 2 to 3 hours.

RICE	COVERED GLASS CASSEROLE	WATER	FIRST SETTING AND TIME	RICE	SECOND SETTING AND TIME
SHORT GRAIN WHITE	2-qt.	2 cups	HIGH 4 to 5 min.	1 cup	DEFROST 15 to 16 min.
LONG GRAIN WHITE	2-qt.	2 cups	HIGH 4 to 5 min.	1 cup	DEFROST 15 to 18 min.
WHITE AND WILD MIX	2-qt.	2½ cups	HIGH 5 to 6 min.	6-oz. pkg.	DEFROST 30 to 35 min.
BROWN	3-qt.	3 cups	HIGH 6 to 7 min.	1 cup	DEFROST 25 to 30 min.
WILD RICE soaked in water 3 hours	3-qt.	3 cups	HIGH 6 to 7 min.	1 cup raw or 2 cups soaked	DEFROST 50 to 60 min.
QUICK-COOKING	1-qt.	1 cup	HIGH 3 to 4 min.	1 cup	Rest, covered, 5 min. or until all water absorbs

Cook rice right in serving casserole – see rice cooking chart.

RICE SUPPER DISH *

　¼ **cup butter or margarine**
　⅓ **cup chopped onion**
　½ **cup chopped celery**
　3 **cups cooked rice**
4 to 5 **smokie breakfast sausage links, sliced**
　2 **medium tomatoes**

1. Combine butter, onion and celery in 2-quart glass casserole.

2. Microwave on ROAST for 4 to 5 minutes or until vegetables are partly cooked. Stir in rice and sausage. Cover with glass lid or plastic wrap.

3. Microwave on REHEAT for 3 minutes. Stir gently; recover, and continue cooking on REHEAT for 2 to 3 minutes or until hot. Garnish with tomato slices.　　　　　　　　　　4 to 6 Servings

Cover keeps rice dishes tender.

SPANISH RICE *

　2 **tablespoons butter or margarine**
　1 **medium onion, finely chopped**
　¼ **cup chopped green pepper**
　2 **cups cooked rice**
　1 **can (16 oz.) tomatoes**
　1 **envelope (2 oz.) dry tomato-vegetable soup mix**
　2 **teaspoons sugar**
　½ **teaspoon leaf basil**

1. Place butter, onion and green pepper in 2-quart glass casserole.

2. Microwave on ROAST for 4 to 5 minutes or until vegetables are partly cooked. Stir in remaining ingredients. Cover with glass lid or plastic wrap.

3. Microwave on REHEAT for 3 minutes. Stir well, breaking up tomatoes by cutting through with a spoon. Recover and continue cooking on REHEAT for 2 to 3 minutes or until hot. Let stand, covered, 5 minutes so rice absorbs juices.　4 to 6 Servings

Bring water to rolling boil before adding rice.

RICE PILAF

　¼ **cup butter or margarine**
　¾ **cup finely chopped onion**
　1 **cup chopped celery**
　1 **envelope (1¾ oz.) dry chicken noodle soup mix**
2½ **cups water**
　1 **teaspoon salt**
　¼ **teaspoon pepper**
　¼ **teaspoon ground sage**
　¼ **teaspoon ground thyme**
　1 **cup long grain white rice**

1. Combine butter, onion and celery in 2-quart glass casserole.

2. Microwave on ROAST for about 5 minutes or until onions and celery are partly cooked. Stir in remaining ingredients, except rice; mix well. Cover with glass lid or plastic wrap.

3. Microwave on HIGH for 5 to 6 minutes or until boiling. Stir in rice; recover.

4. Microwave on DEFROST for 18 to 20 minutes or until rice is tender. Let stand, covered, 5 minutes before serving.　　　　　　5 to 6 Servings

---

PASTA KEY: Bring water, oil and salt to a full, rolling boil, covered, on Microwave HIGH. Hot tap water boils fastest.

　Small amount of fat in water prevents mixture from bubbling over.

　Stir in pasta and microwave on DEFROST.

　Macaroni (basically flour and water) and noodles (flour, water and eggs) should be cooked covered with water so they tenderize completely. Use a large glass casserole so water will be deep enough to cover pasta.

　Cover pasta during cooking with a fitted glass lid or plastic wrap.

　Cooking chart in this chapter gives pasta cooking times. Test to see if pasta is tender before draining.

　Rinse drained pasta with hot water and serve.

　Reheat pasta dishes, covered, on REHEAT until steaming hot. If pasta has been refrigerated, stir once during heating.

PASTA YIELDS:
1 package (7 oz.) spaghetti = 4 cups cooked
1 package (7 oz.) macaroni = 4 cups cooked
4 cups egg noodles = 4 cups cooked

HOW TO COOK PASTAS

● Bring water, 1 tablespoon cooking oil and 1 teaspoon salt to a full rolling boil in a 3-quart covered glass casserole on Microwave HIGH. Hot tap water boils fastest.

● Stir in pasta and recover with fitted glass lid or plastic wrap.

● Microwave on DEFROST.

● Taste for tenderness.

● Drain, rinse with hot water and serve.

PASTA	COVERED GLASS CONTAINER	WATER	FIRST SETTING AND TIME	PASTA	SECOND SETTING AND TIME
SPAGHETTI	3-qt. casserole	4 cups	HIGH 8 to 10 min.	7-oz. pkg.	DEFROST 10 to 12 min.
MACARONI	3-qt. casserole	3 cups	HIGH 6 to 8 min.	2 cups	DEFROST 10 to 12 min.
EGG NOODLES	3-qt. casserole	6 cups	HIGH 10 to 12 min.	4 cups	DEFROST 12 to 14 min.
LASAGNA NOODLES	3-qt. (13 x 9) baking dish	6 cups	HIGH 10 to 12 min.	8-oz. pkg.	DEFROST 12 to 14 min.

Make sure pastas are cooked covered with water.

OH! SO GOOD SPAGHETTI

     2 lbs. ground beef
    ¼ cup finely chopped onion
     1 can (16 oz.) whole tomatoes
     1 can (6 oz.) tomato paste
     1 can (8 oz.) tomato sauce
     1 tablespoon dried parsley flakes
    ½ teaspoon Worcestershire sauce
    ¼ teaspoon garlic salt
    ¼ teaspoon leaf oregano
     Salt
     Pepper
     Grated Parmesan cheese

1. Crumble ground beef into 4-quart glass casserole. Stir in onion.

2. Microwave on HIGH for 7 minutes; drain. Stir in remaining ingredients, except cheese. Cover with glass lid or plastic wrap.

3. Microwave on REHEAT for 9 to 10 minutes or until meat absorbs juices. Serve with hot cooked spaghetti. Sprinkle Parmesan cheese on top of each serving.   6 to 8 Servings

HOW TO PREPARE PASTA OR RICE MIXES

● When preparing pasta or rice box dinner mixes, pour water in glass casserole; cover, and microwave on HIGH until water boils.

● Stir in pasta or rice and seasonings.

● Cover with fitted glass lid or plastic wrap.

● Microwave on DEFROST.

● Serve foods directly from the oven.

MACARONI BAKE*

     2 tablespoons butter or margarine
     4 cups cooked shell macaroni
    ½ cup sour cream
     1 package (4 oz.) sliced ham, cut into pieces
    ¼ teaspoon dried parsley flakes
     Salt
     Pepper

1. Combine all ingredients in 2-quart glass casserole. Cover with glass lid or plastic wrap.

2. Microwave on ROAST for 4 minutes. Stir; recover, and continue cooking on ROAST for 4 to 6 minutes or until hot.   4 to 6 Servings

TIP ● Substitute leftover cooked ham for package ham slices.

DEHYDRATED PASTA MIXES	COVERED GLASS CASSEROLE	WATER	FIRST SETTING AND TIME	PASTA AND SEASONING MIX	SECOND SETTING AND TIME
MACARONI AND CHEESE	2-qt.	2 cups	HIGH 4 to 5 min.	7¼-oz. pkg.	DEFROST 16 to 18 min.
SPAGHETTI BOX DINNER: Spaghetti Sauce	3-qt. 1-qt.	4 cups	HIGH 7 to 8 min.	8-oz. pkg.	DEFROST 12 to 14 min. DEFROST 3 to 4 min.
SEASONED RICE MIX	2-qt.	2 cups	HIGH 4 to 5 min.	8-oz. pkg.	DEFROST 20 to 22 min.

HOW TO PREPARE CANNED PASTA

- Remove all processed food from cans and place in glass casserole.

- Cover with fitted glass lid or plastic wrap.

- Microwave on REHEAT. Stir once during cooking.

CANNED PASTA	SIZE	COVERED GLASS CASSEROLE	SETTING AND TIME
SPAGHETTI	15-oz.	1-qt.	REHEAT 4 to 5 min.
MACARONI AND CHEESE	14¾-oz.	1-qt.	REHEAT 4 to 5 min.
MEAT AND NOODLES IN SAUCE	15 to 16-oz.	1-qt.	REHEAT 4 to 6 min.

CEREAL KEY: Microwave individual bowls of quick-cooking cereal on ROAST setting — enjoy a breakfast miracle!
Use the chart for complete directions.

HOW TO MICROWAVE QUICK-COOKING CEREALS

- Measure water, salt and cereal into individual serving bowls; mix well.

- Microwave on ROAST as directed in chart.

- Stir after cooking.

- Let stand 1 to 2 minutes before serving.

FRUITED CEREALS

When water is boiling rapidly in cereal bowl, stir in 2 tablespoons of one of the following: raisins, cut-up dry apricots, cut-up dates, cut-up pitted prunes. Add cereal and cook as directed in cereal chart.

CEREAL TOPPINGS

Garnish and flavor each bowl of cooked cereal with 2 tablespoons of one of the following: applesauce, brown sugar, jam, marmalade, honey, maple syrup.

SERVINGS	WATER	SALT	CEREAL	SETTING AND TIME
1	¾ cup	¼ tsp.	⅓ cup	ROAST _high_ 1 to 1½ min.
2	¾ cup ea.	¼ tsp. ea.	⅓ cup ea.	ROAST 1½ to 2 min.
4	¾ cup ea.	¼ tsp. ea.	⅓ cup ea.	ROAST 4 to 5 min.

VEGETABLES

Tender-crisp, chock-full of vitamins — that's what makes cooked fresh or frozen vegetables as special as early garden peas and carrots.

Because microwave cooking requires little or no liquid, vegetable flavors are fresh and young — colors bright and natural.

Will canned vegetables microwave? They're delicious — piping hot in seconds. It seems like magic!

There's a "knack" to cooking vegetables in a microwave oven — but it's a cinch to understand.

"Grey boxes" throughout the chapter are important keys to cooking-style changes for frozen, fresh, canned or creamy vegetables, vegetable combinations — and lentils. For example, pierce or prick whole fresh vegetables with "tough" skins — potatoes, yams, squash — to prevent food bursts.

The Fresh and Frozen Vegetable Cooking Chart on page 112 and the Canned Vegetable Heating Chart on page 121 are complete accurate reference guides for easy, everyday vegetable microwave cooking.

Pictured: Tangy Mustard Cauliflower, page 117, shown with fresh, frozen and canned vegetables.

VEGETABLE CHAPTER CONTENTS

HOW TO MICROWAVE FRESH AND FROZEN VEGETABLES

- Microwave all fresh and frozen vegetables on HIGH setting.

- Average cooking time for a 2-lb. package of frozen vegetables is 10 to 12 minutes.

- Microwave all frozen vegetables icy side up.

- Slit all frozen vegetable pouches before cooking so steam can escape.

- Add ¼ cup water when cooking fresh vegetables except for Baked Potatoes and Squash.

- For softer cooked vegetables, add more water and increase total cooking time.

- Arrange spear vegetables with the stalk end which takes longest to cook toward the outside of the cooking dish.

- IMPORTANT! Pierce or prick whole fresh vegetables, such as squash, white or sweet potatoes, before placing in the microwave.

- Microwave vegetables in a covered glass baking dish or casserole.

- Rearrange or stir vegetables half way through cooking.

- Microwave cooking continues after food is taken from the oven — especially with vegetables like squash or potatoes. This additional standing time varies from 2 to 5 minutes, depending on the amount and density of food being cooked.

FRESH AND FROZEN VEGETABLE COOKING CHART

VEGETABLES	AMOUNT	MINUTES	SAUCES AND SEASONINGS	
ARTICHOKES Fresh 3½ inches in diameter	1 2 3 4	5 to 6 7 to 8 9 to 10 11 to 12	Sauces:	Cream, Hollandaise, Mornay
			Seasonings:	Butter, Lemon Juice, Nutmeg
Frozen Hearts	10-oz. pkg.	5 to 6		
ASPARAGUS: SPEARS, CUT Fresh	¾ lb. 1½ lbs.	5 to 6 9 to 10	Sauces:	Béchamel, Cheese, Creamed Egg, Creamy Dill, Hollandaise, Sour Cream, Creamed
Frozen	9-oz. pouch 10-oz. pkg.	6 to 7 8 to 9		
			Seasonings:	Butter, Lemon Butter, Toasted Almonds
BEANS: GREEN AND WAX Fresh	1 lb. 2 lbs.	12 to 14 16 to 18	Sauces:	Creamed, Creamy Mustard,
Frozen French Style or Cut	10-oz. pkg. 10-oz. pouch	8 to 9 8 to 9	Seasonings:	Butter, Cheese, Chives, Crumbled Bacon, Mushrooms, Nutmeg, Toasted Almonds, Water Chestnuts
BEANS: LIMA Fresh	1 lb. 2 lbs.	10 to 12 14 to 16	Sauces:	Cheese, Sour Cream
Frozen	10-oz. pkg. 10-oz. pouch	10 to 11 8 to 9	Seasonings:	Butter, Chopped Ham, Crumbled Bacon

Microwave all fresh and frozen vegetables on HIGH setting.

FRESH AND FROZEN VEGETABLE COOKING CHART

VEGETABLES	AMOUNT	MINUTES	SAUCES AND SEASONINGS	
BEETS Fresh Whole	4 medium	16 to 18	Seasonings:	Butter, Orange Juice Concentrate, Orange Marmalade
BROCCOLI Fresh	1½ lbs.	10 to 12	Sauces:	Cheese, Creamed Egg, Creamy Mustard, Hollandaise, Mornay, Sour Cream
Frozen	10-oz. pkg. 10-oz. pouch	8 to 9 8 to 9		
BRUSSELS SPROUTS Fresh	½ lb. 1 lb.	5 to 7 7 to 8	Sauces:	Cream, Cream Cheese, Creamy Mustard, Hollandaise
Frozen	8-oz. pkg. 10-oz. pouch	8 to 9 6 to 7	Seasonings:	Butter
CABBAGE Fresh Shredded	½ medium 1 medium	5 to 6 8 to 9	Sauces: Seasonings:	Cheese, Cream Cheese, Creamed, Creamy, Mustard, Butter, Crumbled Bacon, Nutmeg
CARROTS Fresh Sliced, Diced, Slivered	2 medium 4 medium 6 medium	5 to 6 8 to 10 10 to 12	Sauces: Seasonings:	Cream Cheese, Creamed Butter, Cinnamon, Cloves,
Frozen Diced or Whole	10-oz. pkg. 10-oz. pouch	8 to 10 8 to 9		Crumbled Bacon, Ginger, Glazed, Nutmeg, Parsley
CAULIFLOWER Fresh Broken into Flowerets Whole Whole	1 medium 1 medium 1 large	7 to 8 8 to 9 12 to 14	Sauces: Seasonings:	Cheese, Cream, Hollandaise Butter, Chives, Nutmeg, Thousand Island Dressing
Frozen	10-oz. pkg. 10-oz. pouch	8 to 9 8 to 9		
CELERY Fresh	6 stalks	10 to 12	Sauces: Seasonings:	Cheese, Cream Bouillon, Brown Gravy Mix, Butter

(Continued, next page)

Microwave all fresh and frozen vegetables on HIGH setting.

FRESH AND FROZEN VEGETABLE COOKING CHART

VEGETABLES	AMOUNT	MINUTES	SAUCES AND SEASONINGS
CORN Fresh Cut from Cob	1½ cups 3 cups	6 to 7 7 to 8	Sauces: Cream Cheese, Creamed
Frozen	10-oz. pkg. 10-oz. pouch	6 to 7 5 to 6	Seasonings: Butter, Chive Butter, Cream Cheese, Crumbled Bacon, Green Pepper and Pimento, Onion Dip, Parmesan Cheese
CORN ON THE COB Fresh	2 4 6	4 to 5 7 to 8 9 to 10	Seasonings: Butter, Chive Butter, Onion Butter
Frozen	2 4	6 to 8 10 to 12	
ONIONS Fresh Quartered	8 small or 2 large 4 large	6 to 7 8 to 9	Sauces: Sour Cream, Creamed, Cream Cheese
Frozen In Cream Sauce	10-oz. pkg. 10-oz. pouch	6 to 7 6 to 7	Seasonings: Butter, Currant Jelly, Nutmeg
PARSNIPS Fresh Quartered	4	8 to 9	Sauces: Béchamel Seasonings: Bacon Drippings, Brown Sugar Glaze, Butter
PEAS, GREEN Fresh	2 lbs. 3 lbs.	8 to 9 10 to 11	Sauces: Creamed, Cream Cheese
Frozen	10-oz. pkg. 10-oz. pouch	6 to 7 6 to 7	Seasonings: Butter, Chives, Cream, Green Onions, Mint,
Frozen Pods	6-oz. pouch	3 to 4	Mushrooms, Onion Dip, Orange Marmalade
PEAS AND CARROTS Frozen	10-oz. pkg.	7 to 8	Sauces: Cream, Creamed Seasonings: Butter, Chives, Crumbled Bacon
PEAS, BLACK-EYED Frozen	10-oz. pkg.	10 to 12	Sauces: Creamed Seasonings: Bacon Drippings, Butter, Ham

Microwave all fresh and frozen vegetables on HIGH setting.

FRESH AND FROZEN VEGETABLE COOKING CHART

VEGETABLES	AMOUNT	MINUTES	SAUCES AND SEASONINGS
POTATOES Fresh baking *(Do not overcook* *potatoes as extreme* *dehydration might* *cause smoke or fire.)*	1 medium 2 medium 4 medium 6 medium 8 medium	4 to 4½ 7 to 8 10 to 12 16 to 18 22 to 24	Seasonings: Butter, Cheese, Chives, Crumbled Bacon, Parsley, Green Onions, Onion Soup Dip, Paprika, Sour Cream, Toasted Almonds, Whipped Cream Cheese
Fresh boiling Quartered	2 4	10 to 11 18 to 20	Sauces: Cheese, Creamed Onions Seasonings: Bouillon, Butter, Chives, Green Onions, Onion Soup Mix, Paprika, Parsley
POTATOES, SWEET OR YAMS Fresh	1 medium 2 medium 4 medium 6 medium	4 to 4½ 6 to 7 8 to 9 10 to 11	Seasonings: Brown Sugar Glaze, Butter, Glaze, Crumbled Bacon, Maple Syrup Glaze, Mashed, Miniature Marshmallows, Pineapple Glaze
SPINACH Fresh	1 lb.	6 to 7	Sauces: Cheese, Cream Cheese, Egg, Mushroom Soup
Frozen Leaf or Chopped	10-oz. pkg. 10-oz. pouch	7 to 8 7 to 8	Seasonings: Butter, Crumbled Bacon, Lemon Juice, Nutmeg, Onion Dip, Sliced Raw Onion
SQUASH, ACORN OR BUTTERNUT Fresh Whole	1 medium 2 medium	8 to 9 14 to 16	Sauces: Cranberry Seasonings: Brown Sugar Glaze, Honey Glaze, Butter, Cinnamon, Nutmeg, Cooked Apples or Other Fruit, Maple Syrup, Sausage
SQUASH, HUBBARD Fresh	6" x 6" pc.	8 to 9	Seasonings: Brown Sugar Glaze, Butter, Maple Syrup, Mashed with Ginger or Nutmeg, Orange Marmalade, Pineapple
Frozen	10-oz. pkg.	6 to 7	

(Continued, next page)

Microwave all fresh and frozen vegetables on HIGH.

FRESH AND FROZEN VEGETABLE COOKING CHART

VEGETABLES	AMOUNT	MINUTES	SAUCES AND SEASONINGS	
SQUASH, ZUCCHINI Fresh Sliced	2 medium or 3 cups	7 to 8	Sauces:	Creamed, Creamed Egg
			Seasonings:	Butter, Chive Sour Cream, Parmesan Cheese
TURNIPS Fresh Cut in Eighths	4 medium	12 to 14	Sauces:	Creamed
			Seasonings:	Butter, Chives, Lemon Juice
VEGETABLES, MIXED Frozen	10-oz. pkg. 10-oz. pouch	6 to 7 6 to 7	Sauces:	Béchamel, Cheese, Creamed, Cream Cheese
			Seasonings:	Butter, Crumbled Bacon

MIX AND MATCH VEGETABLE CHART

It's fun to experiment with vegetable combinations. But remember, combine canned vegetables with canned, fresh with fresh or frozen with frozen.

Check the chart above for the vegetable in the mixture which has the longest cooking time and use that.

Cover the cooking dish tightly with plastic wrap or a fitted lid.

Watch the cooking process and stir the mixture to assure even cooking.

Try these combinations:

Cut Asparagus/Corn
Beans/Mushrooms
Beans/Onions
Brussel Sprouts/Carrots
Carrots/Cauliflower
Black-Eyed Peas/Carrots
Peas/Carrots
Peas/Mushrooms
Potatoes/Creamed Peas
Potatoes/Peas/Onions

Pictured top to bottom: Corn on the Cob, page 114 (Cooking times are the same whether corn is cooked in husks or casserole.); Baked Lentils, page 117; Double Onion Bake, page 119.

FRESH VEGETABLE KEY: Cook all fresh vegetables on Microwave HIGH setting to capture ultimate goodness, nutrition and tender-crispness.

Remember that fresh vegetables should be eaten soon after being picked or purchased to capture flavor and vitamins.

Important! Pierce or prick whole, unpeeled vegetables, such as squash, tiny red potatoes, white or sweet potatoes, before placing in the microwave. Piercing allows steam to escape during cooking, prevents "popping" and a messy oven. Do not be concerned if oven is steamy while vegetables-with-skin-on are cooking.

Arrange fresh spear vegetables, such as broccoli, in the cooking dish so the part that takes longer to cook (stalk) is toward the outside of the dish.

Salt brings out vegetable flavors. It is most convenient to add salt before cooking. But since salt tends to dehydrate food, it may be added at the end of the cooking period. Test and see which you prefer.

Always use a cover. A fitted glass lid or plastic wrap stretched tightly over the cooking casserole or dish helps trap steam and hasten cooking.

Pierce plastic wrap and allow steam to escape from dish before removing it from oven. Tip glass lids away from hand or arm when lifting.

Stir and rearrange vegetables halfway through the cooking period. This helps distribute moisture from the bottom of the dish and cooking is more even.

Microwave cooking continues after food is taken from the oven — especially unpeeled vegetables because skins hold heat. When a recipe calls for a "standing" period, follow directions carefully.

HONEY COATED CARROTS*

    4 medium carrots, sliced
    2 tablespoons butter or margarine
    2 tablespoons honey
    2 tablespoons water
    ¼ teaspoon salt

1. Combine all ingredients in 1-quart glass casserole. Cover with glass lid or plastic wrap.

2. Microwave on HIGH for 5 minutes. Stir and continue cooking on HIGH for 3 to 4 minutes or until carrots are tender-crisp. Let stand, covered, 3 minutes before serving.   2 to 3 Servings

SEASONED CABBAGE CASSEROLE*

    4 cups shredded cabbage
    ½ teaspoon salt
    ¼ cup milk
    ¼ cup chopped onion
    2 tablespoons butter or margarine
    ⅛ teaspoon ground nutmeg
    ½ cup shredded Cheddar cheese

1. Combine cabbage, salt, milk, onion, butter and nutmeg in 2-quart glass casserole. Cover with glass lid or plastic wrap.

2. Microwave on HIGH for 4 minutes. Stir and continue cooking on HIGH for 3 to 4 minutes or until cabbage is tender-crisp. Stir in cheese. Let stand, covered, 2 minutes.   4 Servings

TANGY MUSTARD CAULIFLOWER

    1 medium head cauliflower
    2 tablespoons water
    ½ cup mayonnaise or salad dressing
    1 teaspoon finely chopped onion
    1 teaspoon prepared mustard
    ½ cup shredded Cheddar cheese

1. Place cauliflower in 1½-quart glass casserole. Add water; cover with glass lid or plastic wrap.

2. Microwave on HIGH for 8 to 9 minutes or until tender-crisp. Combine mayonnaise, onion and mustard in small mixing bowl. Spoon mustard sauce on top of cauliflower. Sprinkle with cheese.

3. Microwave on ROAST for 1½ to 2 minutes to heat topping and melt cheese. Let stand 2 minutes before serving.   6 to 8 Servings

Cover and standing time is secret to tenderness.

BAKED LENTILS*

    1 cup (½ lb.) dry lentils, washed and sorted
    3 cups water
    2 slices bacon, cut into pieces
    ¼ cup packed brown sugar
    ¼ cup chopped onion
    ¼ cup chili sauce
    ¼ cup molasses
    1 teaspoon salt
    1 teaspoon prepared mustard

1. Combine all ingredients in 3-quart glass casserole. Cover with glass lid or plastic wrap.

2. Microwave on HIGH for 10 minutes. Stir and recover.

3. Microwave on SIMMER for 50 to 55 minutes or until tender. Let stand, covered, 5 minutes before serving.   5 to 6 Servings

TIP • Water should be added, if necessary, during cooking time.

Tangy taste – sunny appearance.

GLAZED CARROTS 'N APPLES*

4 to 5 medium carrots, sliced
   1 tart cooking apple, peeled, cored and chopped
   2 tablespoons packed brown sugar
   2 tablespoons butter or margarine
   2 tablespoons water
   ¼ teaspoon salt

1. Combine all ingredients in 1-quart glass casserole. Cover with glass lid or plastic wrap.

2. Microwave on HIGH for 5 minutes. Stir and continue cooking on HIGH for 3 to 4 minutes or until carrots are tender-crisp. Let stand, covered, 3 minutes before serving.   5 to 6 Servings

HONEYED ONIONS

   8 medium whole onions, peeled
   2 tablespoons butter or margarine
   ½ cup honey

1. Place onions in 1-quart glass casserole. Cover with glass lid or plastic wrap.

2. Microwave on HIGH for 7 to 8 minutes or until onions are tender-crisp. Drain. Stir in butter and honey; recover, and continue cooking on HIGH for 2 to 3 minutes or until onions are glazed. Let stand, covered, 3 minutes before serving.
     3 to 4 Servings

TIP • Substitute apple jelly for honey.

Piercing releases steam held by skins.

STUFFED BAKED POTATOES

   4 medium baking potatoes
   2 tablespoons butter or margarine
   ½ cup milk
   Salt and pepper
   ½ cup shredded process American cheese

1. Prick potatoes and place in oven.

2. Microwave on HIGH for 10 to 12 minutes or until fork-tender. Cut potatoes in half. Carefully scoop cooked potato out of shells and into mixing bowl. Add butter, milk, salt and pepper to taste; mash until lump-free. Fill potato shells; top with cheese and place on glass serving platter. Continue cooking on HIGH for 4 to 5 minutes or until hot. Let stand 3 minutes before serving.
     4 to 8 Servings

TIP • If made ahead and refrigerated, Microwave on HIGH for 6 to 7 minutes during final cooking period.

Fresh peas and potatoes excellent team-mates.

CREAMY PEAS AND POTATOES

   1 lb. small red potatoes
  1½ cups fresh shelled peas
   2 tablespoons water
   2 tablespoons butter or margarine
   1 tablespoon chopped onion
   2 tablespoons all-purpose flour
  1¼ teaspoon salt
   1 teaspoon dill weed
   ⅛ teaspoon pepper
  1½ cups milk

1. Prick potatoes before cooking. Place in oven.

2. Microwave on HIGH for 10 to 11 minutes or until potatoes are fork-tender. Set aside. Combine peas and water in 2-quart glass casserole. Cover with glass lid or plastic wrap.

3. Microwave on HIGH for 6 minutes or until peas are tender-crisp. Set aside. Combine butter and onion in 4-cup glass measure.

4. Microwave on ROAST for about 1 minute or until melted. Blend in flour, salt, dill and pepper. Stir in milk.

5. Microwave on HIGH for 4 to 5 minutes or until mixture thickens. Peel potatoes and add to peas in casserole. Pour hot cream sauce over vegetables; stir gently to thoroughly coat vegetables. Return to oven and continue cooking on HIGH for 2 to 3 minutes or until piping hot. Let stand 3 minutes before serving.   4 to 5 Servings

Corn, green pepper and tomatoes – perfect go-togethers.

CORN FILLED TOMATOES

   6 large tomatoes
   Salt
   2 tablespoons butter or margarine
   1 tablespoon chopped onion
   2 tablespoons chopped green pepper
   1 can (16 oz.) whole kernel corn, drained
   ¼ cup potato chips, crushed
   Grated Parmesan cheese

1. Cut tops off tomatoes; hollow out inside. Save tomato pulp for soup. Place tomatoes on glass serving platter. Sprinkle with salt. Combine butter, onion and green pepper in 4-cup glass measure.

2. Microwave on ROAST for 4 to 5 minutes or until butter is melted. Stir in corn and crushed potato chips. Spoon crumb mixture into tomatoes. Sprinkle with Parmesan cheese.

3. Microwave on HIGH for 6 to 7 minutes or until heated through. Let stand 3 minutes before serving.
     6 Servings

Microwave ahead and reheat.

GLAZED SWEET POTATOES*

    4 medium sweet potatoes
    ½ cup packed brown sugar
    ¼ cup butter or margarine

1. Pierce potatoes and place in oven.

2. Microwave on HIGH for 8 to 9 minutes or until fork tender. Peel and slice into 1½-quart glass casserole. Sprinkle with brown sugar; dot with butter. Cover with glass lid or plastic wrap. Continue cooking on HIGH for 4 minutes. Stir and continue cooking on HIGH for 3 to 4 minutes or until hot. Let stand, covered, 3 minutes before serving.

6 to 8 Servings

Piercing is important to prevent skins "popping."

ACORN SQUASH 'N APPLES

    2 acorn or butternut squash
    Salt
    2 medium apples, peeled, cored and sliced
    ½ cup packed brown sugar
    ¼ cup butter or margarine
    Cinnamon

1. Pierce whole squash and place in oven.

2. Microwave on HIGH for 10 to 12 minutes, or until squash feel soft to touch. Let stand 5 minutes. Cut in half; remove seeds. Place, cut side up, in 2-quart (12 x 7) glass baking dish. Fill centers of squash with apples. Top each with 2 tablespoons brown sugar, 1 tablespoon butter and dash of cinnamon. Cover with plastic wrap. Continue cooking on HIGH for 6 to 7 minutes or until apples are tender. Let stand, covered, 2 to 3 minutes before serving. 4 Servings

TIP ● Substitute prepared apple pie filling mix for fresh apples and butter. Reduce final cooking time about 4 minutes.

Pierce plastic wrap or remove lid carefully to prevent steam burns.

HONEY SWEETENED SQUASH*

    4 cups (2 lb.) 1-inch cubed Hubbard squash
    ⅓ cup butter or margarine
    ⅓ cup honey
    1 teaspoon salt
    1 tablespoon grated orange peel

1. Combine all ingredients in 2-quart glass casserole. Cover with glass lid or plastic wrap.

2. Microwave on HIGH for 5 minutes. Stir and continue cooking on HIGH for 4 to 5 minutes or until fork-tender. Let stand, covered, 3 minutes before serving. 4 to 5 Servings

---

FROZEN VEGETABLE KEY: Frozen vegetables are best cooked on Microwave HIGH setting. Faster cooking insures crisp, but tender, eating.

Arrange frozen broccoli and other spear vegetables so that the stalk, which takes longest to cook, is toward the outside of the cooking dish.

Salt enhances vegetable flavor. It is more convenient to add salt before cooking. But since salt tends to dehydrate food, it may be added at the end of the cooking period.

Always cover vegetables when cooking. Use fitted, glass lids or plastic wrap stretched tightly over the cooking casserole or dish. Covers trap steam and hasten cooking. Pierce plastic wrap and allow steam to escape before removing dish from the oven.

Stir or rearrange vegetables halfway through the cooking period to help distribute moisture from the bottom of the dish and cook food more evenly.

Microwave cooking continues after food is taken from the oven. When a recipe calls for a "standing" period, follow directions carefully.

Extra-quick way to fix onions.

DOUBLE ONION BAKE*

    1 teaspoon butter or margarine
    ¼ cup slivered almonds
    1 package (10 oz.) frozen creamed onions
    ¼ cup shredded Cheddar cheese
    1 tablespoon dried parsley flakes
    1 can (3½ oz.) French-fried onion rings

1. Combine butter and almonds in 1-quart glass casserole.

2. Microwave on ROAST for 2 minutes. Stir and continue cooking on ROAST for 1 to 2 minutes. Add onions, cheese and parsley. Cover with glass lid or plastic wrap.

3. Microwave on HIGH for 3 minutes. Stir and continue cooking on HIGH for 3 to 4 minutes or until onions are tender-crisp. Top with onion rings. Let stand, covered, 3 minutes before serving.

2 to 3 Servings

TIP ● When using frozen creamed onions in pouch, place pouch in oven. Microwave on HIGH for 3 to 4 minutes. Remove creamed onions from pouch; spoon into casserole with remaining ingredients and continue cooking on HIGH for 2 to 3 minutes or until hot.

Microwave speed prevents mushing.

ONION TOPPED BEANS

> 2 packages (10 oz. each) frozen French-cut green beans
> 1 can (5 oz.) water chestnuts, drained and sliced
> 2 cans (10 ¾ oz. each) condensed cream of celery soup
> 1 can (3½ oz.) French-fried onion rings

1. Place frozen beans in 2-quart (12 x 7) glass baking dish. Cover with plastic wrap.

2. Microwave on HIGH for 7 to 8 minutes or until beans are tender-crisp. Add water chestnuts. Spread soup over beans. Top with onion rings. Continue cooking on HIGH for about 5 minutes or until hot. Let stand 2 to 3 minutes before serving.

6 to 8 Servings

TIP • Substitute fresh beans or other green vegetables for beans. See chart for cooking instructions.

Cheese microwaves best on gentler setting.

BROCCOLI WITH LEMON SAUCE*

> ½ cup slivered almonds
> 1 tablespoon butter or margarine
> 2 packages (10 oz. each) frozen broccoli spears
> 2 packages (3 oz. each) cream cheese
> ⅓ cup milk
> 1 teaspoon grated lemon peel
> 1 tablespoon lemon juice
> ½ teaspoon ground ginger
> ¼ teaspoon salt

1. Combine almonds and butter in small glass bowl.

2. Microwave on ROAST for 3 minutes. Stir and continue cooking on ROAST for 2 to 3 minutes or until almonds are light brown. Set aside.

3. Place frozen broccoli in 2-quart glass casserole. Cover with glass lid or plastic wrap.

4. Microwave on HIGH for 4 to 5 minutes or until broccoli; cover, and continue cooking on HIGH for 6 to 7 minutes or until tender-crisp. Let stand, covered.

5. Place cream cheese in 2-cup glass measure, Microwave on WARM for about 4 minutes or until softened. Cream until smooth. Stir in remaining ingredients.

6. Microwave on ROAST for 3 to 4 minutes or until hot. Place broccoli spears on serving platter and pour sauce over. Sprinkle with almonds and serve.

6 to 8 Servings

Keep stalk ends toward outside of cooking dish where they will Microwave sooner.

NIPPY CHEESE BROCCOLI*

> 2 tablespoons butter or margarine
> 2 tablespoons all-purpose flour
> ½ teaspoon salt
> 1 cup milk
> 1 cup shredded Cheddar cheese
> 2 packages (10 oz. each) frozen broccoli spears
> 1 medium tomato, sliced

1. Place butter in 2-cup glass measure.

2. Microwave on ROAST for 2 minutes. Stir and until melted. Blend in flour, salt and milk.

3. Microwave on HIGH for 1 to 2 minutes or continue cooking on HIGH for about 1 minute or until mixture thickens. Stir in cheese until melted. Place broccoli, icy side up, on glass serving platter. Cover with plastic wrap.

4. Microwave on HIGH for 6 minutes. Rearrange spears and continue cooking on HIGH 6 to 8 minutes or until broccoli is tender-crisp. Drain well. Top with cheese sauce and garnish with tomato slices.

5. Microwave on HIGH for 2 to 3 minutes until hot.

6 to 8 Servings

TIP • Substitute fresh broccoli. See vegetable chart for cooking directions.

Pictured: Nippy Cheese Broccoli, this page.

A savory treat.

ORIENTAL ASPARAGUS*

- **2 tablespoons butter or margarine**
- **2 tablespoons slivered almonds**
- **1 package (10 oz.) frozen cut asparagus**
- **½ cup thinly sliced celery**
- **1 can (5 oz.) water chestnuts, drained and sliced**
- **1 tablespoon soy sauce**

1. Combine butter and almonds in 1-quart glass casserole.

2. Microwave on ROAST for 2 minutes. Stir and continue cooking on ROAST for 2 to 3 minutes or until golden brown. Remove almonds. Add asparagus, celery and water chestnuts to butter. Cover with glass lid or plastic wrap.

3. Microwave on HIGH for 5 minutes. Stir and continue cooking on HIGH for 3 to 4 minutes or until tender-crisp. Stir in soy sauce and almonds. Let stand, covered, 3 minutes before serving.
4 Servings

Stirring assures even cooking.

PEAS 'N ONIONS WITH MUSHROOMS*

- **2 tablespoons butter or margarine**
- **¼ cup chopped onion**
- **1 can (4 oz.) mushroom stems and pieces, drained**
- **1 package (10 oz.) frozen peas**
- **¼ teaspoon salt**
- **Dash pepper and allspice**

1. Combine butter and onion in 1-quart glass casserole. Cover with glass lid or plastic wrap.

2. Microwave on HIGH for 3 minutes or until onion is partly cooked. Add mushrooms, frozen peas, salt, pepper and allspice. Recover, and continue cooking on HIGH for 4 minutes. Stir and continue cooking on HIGH for 3 to 4 minutes or until peas are tender-crisp. Let stand, covered, 3 minutes before serving.
4 Servings

CANNED VEGETABLE KEY: Canned vegetables are already cooked — so heat them quickly on Microwave REHEAT to prevent mushiness.

Combine canned vegetables easily, too. Vegetables with similar density will heat well together — things like peas and carrots or peas and mushrooms.

See the chart, below, which tells exactly how to heat a can of vegetables.

HOW TO HEAT A CAN OF VEGETABLES

- Microwave canned vegetables either undrained or drained.
- Empty vegetables into 1-quart glass casserole and cover with glass lid or plastic wrap.
- Microwave on REHEAT.
- Let stand 2 to 3 minutes to heat through.

CANNED VEGETABLE	MINUTES UNDRAINED	MINUTES DRAINED
VEGETABLES all kinds		
8-oz.	2 to 2½	1½ to 2
15-oz.	3 to 4	2½ to 3
17-oz.	4 to 5	3 to 3½

Perfect for a buffet supper or picnic.

COMPOTE OF BEANS*

- **4 slices bacon**
- **⅓ cup sugar**
- **1 tablespoon cornstarch**
- **1 teaspoon salt**
- **⅛ teaspoon pepper**
- **½ cup vinegar**
- **1 medium onion, sliced**
- **1 can (16 oz.) cut green beans, drained**
- **1 can (16 oz.) cut wax beans, drained**

1. Arrange bacon slices in single layer in 2-quart glass casserole. Cover with paper towel.

2. Microwave on HIGH for 3 to 4 minutes or until bacon is crisp. Remove paper towel and bacon. Blend sugar, cornstarch, salt and pepper with bacon drippings. Stir in vinegar. Add remaining ingredients. Cover with glass lid or plastic wrap.

3. Microwave on REHEAT for 7 minutes. Stir and continue cooking on REHEAT for 6 to 8 minutes or until slightly thickened. Let stand, covered, 3 minutes before serving.
8 to 10 Servings

QUICKIE BAKED BEANS

  1 **can (16 oz.) beans and pork in tomato sauce**
  ¼ **cup chopped onion**
  ¼ **cup catsup**
  ½ **teaspoon prepared mustard**
  2 **tablespoons packed brown sugar**
  4 **slices bacon, cut into pieces**

1. Combine all ingredients except bacon in 1-quart glass casserole. Top with bacon pieces. Cover with glass lid or plastic wrap.

2. Microwave on REHEAT for 12 to 14 minutes or until mixture bubbles. Let stand, covered, 3 minutes before serving.   4 Servings

Excellent creamy blend of flavor.

HARVARD BEETS*

  ¼ **cup sugar**
  1 **tablespoon cornstarch**
  ½ **teaspoon salt**
  . **Dash pepper**
  ¼ **cup vinegar**
  1 **can (16 oz.) diced beets**
  1 **cup beet liquid plus water**

1. Combine sugar, cornstarch, salt and pepper in 1-quart glass casserole. Stir in vinegar and beet liquid. Add beets. Cover with glass lid or plastic wrap.

2. Microwave on REHEAT for 5 minutes. Stir and continue cooking on REHEAT for 4 to 5 minutes or until slightly thickened. Let stand, covered, 3 minutes before serving.   4 to 5 Servings

Peachy garnish for turkey, chicken or pork.

YAMS WITH PEACHES

  1 **can (28 oz.) peach halves, undrained**
  1 **can (17 oz.) vacuum packed yams or sweet potatoes, mashed**
  2 **tablespoons packed brown sugar**
  2 **tablespoons butter or margarine**
  2 **tablespoons brandy or brandy flavoring**
  ½ **tablespoon grated orange peel**
  ¼ **teaspoon salt**

1. Place peach halves, cut side up, on glass serving platter. Combine 4 tablespoons peach syrup and remaining ingredients in mixing bowl; mix well. Spoon mixture into peach halves.

2. Microwave on REHEAT for 6 to 7 minutes or until hot. Let stand for 3 minutes before serving.
          6 Servings

TIP ● Make ahead and reheat at serving time.

Also good with fresh cooked beets.

SPICY BEETS*

  1 **can (16 oz.) sliced beets, drain and reserve liquid**
  ⅓ **cup sugar**
  ⅓ **cup beet liquid**
  ⅓ **cup vinegar**
  1 **teaspoon pickling spice, tied in cheese cloth**

1. Combine beets, sugar, beet liquid and vinegar in glass serving dish. Add pickling spice. Cover with plastic wrap.

2. Microwave on REHEAT for 4 minutes. Stir and continue cooking on REHEAT for 3 to 4 minutes or until mixture bubbles. Cool and remove pickling spices before serving.   2 Cups Beets

TIP ● Substitute a mixture of 3 whole cloves, 2 whole allspice and ½ stick cinnamon for pickling spices.

A quick and easy special for busy days.

SAVORY POTATOES

  1½ **cups water**
  ½ **teaspoon salt**
  2 **tablespoons butter or margarine**
  ½ **cup milk**
  1½ **cups potato flakes**
  ½ **cup sour cream**
  ½ **teaspoon onion salt**
  1 **egg**
  Shredded cheese

1. Combine water, salt and butter in 1½-quart glass casserole. Cover with glass lid or plastic wrap.

2. Microwave on HIGH for 3 to 4 minutes or until mixture bubbles. Stir in milk and potato flakes. Blend in sour cream, onion salt and egg. Mix well. Sprinkle with cheese. Recover.

3. Microwave on ROAST for 6 to 8 minutes or until hot. Let stand, covered, 3 minutes before serving.
          4 to 5 Servings

TIPS ● To make ahead, prepare as directed in steps 1 and 2. Cover with plastic wrap and refrigerate. At serving time, Microwave on ROAST for 10 to 12 minutes or until hot.

 ● Substitute 3 cups fresh, mashed potatoes for potato flakes. Add sour cream, onion salt, egg and cheese as directed.

Cover traps steam, speeds heating.

SWEET POTATOES BRULEE

    1 can (17 oz.) vacuum packed sweet
      potatoes, mashed
    2 tablespoons butter or margarine
    3 tablespoons orange juice
    Salt
    ⅛ teaspoon cinnamon
    3 tablespoons chopped nuts
    ¼ cup packed brown sugar

1. Combine potatoes, butter, orange juice, salt and cinnamon in 1-quart glass casserole. Sprinkle top with nuts and brown sugar. Cover with glass lid or plastic wrap.

2. Microwave on REHEAT for 6 to 7 minutes or until hot. Let stand, covered, 3 minutes before serving.   4 to 5 Servings

---

CREAM OR EGG MIXTURE KEY: Vegetable recipes made with sour cream, eggs or cream should be cooked on Microwave ROAST. The slightly lower setting helps avoid separation and curdling of a cream or custard mixture.

Creamy canned soups and other saucy mixtures made with a flour or cornstarch base can be cooked on Microwave HIGH.

See the fresh, frozen or canned "grey key boxes" for general techniques covering the kind of vegetable you are using.

CORN PUDDING*

    2 tablespoons butter or margarine
    2 eggs, slightly beaten
    1 cup milk
    1 can (12 oz.) cream-style corn
    2 tablespoons all-purpose flour
    1 teaspoon salt
    ½ teaspoon pepper
    1 tbs onion
1. Place butter in 1-quart glass casserole.

2. Microwave on ROAST for 1 minute or until butter melts. Add remaining ingredients. Cover with glass lid or plastic wrap.

3. Microwave on ROAST for 9 minutes. Stir and continue cooking on ROAST for 7 to 8 minutes or until pudding is slightly soft in center. Let stand, covered, 5 minutes or until pudding is set in center.   4 to 6 Servings

Cover keeps souffle tender.

SPINACH SOUFFLE

    2 packages (10 oz. each) frozen, chopped
      spinach
    ¼ cup butter or margarine
    2 cups cooked rice
    2 cups shredded process American cheese
    ⅔ cup milk
    4 eggs
    ½ cup finely chopped onion
    2 tablespoons dried parsley flakes
    1 teaspoon salt
    ¼ teaspoon leaf thyme
    ½ teaspoon nutmeg

1. Place frozen spinach, icy side up, in 2-quart glass casserole. Cover with glass lid or plastic wrap.

2. Microwave on HIGH for 8 to 10 minutes. Drain well through sieve. Stir in butter until melted. Add rice and cheese. Combine milk and eggs in 4-cup glass measure. Blend in remaining ingredients. Stir into spinach mixture until well blended. Cover with glass lid or plastic wrap.

3. Microwave on ROAST for 25 minutes or until knife inserted near center comes out clean. Let stand, covered, 5 minutes before serving.
                                    6 to 8 Servings

CHEESE CREAM ONIONS

    2 jars (16 oz. each) onions, drained
    1 jar (8 oz.) process cheese spread
    1 tablespoon dried parsley flakes
    ¼ cup buttered dry bread crumbs

1. Combine onions, cheese and parsley flakes in 1½-quart glass casserole. Cover with glass lid or plastic wrap.

2. Microwave on ROAST for 4 minutes. Stir; sprinkle with buttered crumbs, and continue cooking on ROAST for 3 to 4 minutes or until hot. Let stand, covered, 3 minutes before serving.
                                    3 to 4 Servings

SPINACH DELISH*

    1 package (10 oz.) frozen chopped spinach
    ½ cup sour cream
    2 tablespoons dry onion soup mix

1. Place spinach, icy side up, in 1-quart glass casserole. Cover with glass lid or plastic wrap.

2. Microwave on HIGH for 4 minutes. Stir and continue cooking on HIGH for about 3 minutes or until tender-crisp. Stir in sour cream and onion soup mix. Recover.

3. Microwave on ROAST for 1 to 2 minutes or until hot. Let stand, covered, 2 minutes before serving.
                                    3 to 4 Servings

A salad expert likes to mix, measure and blend ingredients in her (his) own kitchen to create a flavorful original — and a microwave oven's speed makes the job much faster.

Raw vegetables cook tender-crisp and crunchy. Gelatin melts and mixes smoothly in no time. Dressing flavors become zesty or mellow blends as they heat.

Read the "grey box" keys to discover which salads and dressings can be cooked really fast — which need lower heat because of critical ingredients. Adapt new recipes, too, using these as a guide.

Pictured: Hot Apple Slaw with sliced ham rolls and Swiss cheese, page 126.

SALAD/DRESSING
CHAPTER CONTENTS

SALAD KEY: Hot salads made with raw vegetables microwave on HIGH to tender-crispness.

Gelatin mixtures for salads heat and melt fast on HIGH.

Salads made with cooked ingredients microwave on REHEAT.

Hot salad mixtures dressed with mayonnaise microwave on ROAST to prevent separation.

Cook or heat in glass containers. Cover with glass lids or plastic wrap, when specified, to hold moisture and heat quickly.

Standing time, when called for in a recipe, allows salad to heat through thoroughly.

HIGH melts gelatin.

PINEAPPLE CHEESE SALAD*

- 1 can (13 oz.) crushed pineapple, undrained
- 1 package (3 oz.) lime-flavored gelatin
- 1 cup cottage cheese
- 1 cup whipping cream, whipped

1. Pour pineapple juice into 4-cup glass measure. Add enough water to make 1½ cups liquid. Stir in gelatin; mix well.

2. Microwave on HIGH for 2 minutes. Stir and continue cooking on HIGH for 1 to 2 minutes or until mixture boils. Chill until consistency of unbeaten egg white. Beat until foamy with rotary beater. Fold in pineapple, cottage cheese and whipped cream. Pour into oiled 1½-quart mold. Chill until firm. Unmold to serve.   6 to 8 Servings

Cooked ingredients heat quickly without "mushing" on REHEAT.

HOT BEAN SALAD

- 6 slices bacon, cut into pieces
- 1 cup finely chopped onion
- 1 tablespoon all-purpose flour
- ½ cup wine vinegar
- 2 tablespoons sugar
- 1½ teaspoons salt
- ¼ teaspoon pepper
- 2 cans (15½ oz.) kidney beans, drained
- ½ cup finely chopped celery
- 1 tablespoon dried parsley flakes

1. Place bacon and onion in 2-quart glass casserole.

2. Microwave on HIGH for 5 to 7 minutes. Blend in flour. Stir in remaining ingredients, except celery and parsley. Cover with glass lid or plastic wrap.

3. Microwave on REHEAT for 4 to 5 minutes or until hot. Stir in celery and parsley. Let stand, covered, 3 minutes before serving.   4 to 6 Servings

HOT APPLE SLAW

- ⅓ cup vinegar
- ¼ cup water
- 2 tablespoons sugar
- 1 teaspoon celery seed
- 1 teaspoon salt
- 6 cups shredded cabbage
- 1 small apple, finely sliced
- 2 tablespoons butter or margarine

1. Combine vinegar, water, sugar, celery seed and salt in 2-quart glass casserole. Toss with cabbage and apple slices. Dot with butter. Cover with glass lid or plastic wrap.

2. Microwave on HIGH for 4 to 5 minutes or until heated through. Let stand, covered, 3 minutes. Toss and serve.   3 to 4 Servings

TIP ● Serve with cooked ham slices and Swiss cheese.

Heating mayonnaise in a salad requires the ROAST setting to prevent separation.

TURKEY SALAD BAKE

- 1 cup mayonnaise or salad dressing
- 1 tablespoon lemon juice
- 5 cups cubed cooked turkey
- 2 cups finely chopped celery
- ¼ cup slivered almonds
- 2 green onions, finely chopped

1. Combine all ingredients in 2-quart glass bowl or casserole. Cover with glass lid or plastic wrap.

2. Microwave on ROAST for 7 to 9 minutes or until hot; stir to blend. Let stand, covered, 3 minutes before serving.   About 4 Servings

HOT CHILI MEXICAN SALAD

- 1 lb. ground beef
- 1 medium onion, chopped
- 1 can (15½ oz.) kidney beans, drained
- ⅓ cup catsup
- ¼ cup mayonnaise or salad dressing
- ½ teaspoon salt
- 1 teaspoon chili powder
- 1 cup shredded Monterey Jack cheese
- 2 tomatoes, coarsely chopped
- 1 small avocado, peeled and sliced
- 1 head lettuce, shredded

1. Combine ground beef and onion in 2-quart glass casserole. Cover with glass lid or plastic wrap.

2. Microwave on HIGH for 5 minutes; drain. Stir in beans, catsup, mayonnaise, salt and chili powder; mix well; recover.

3. Microwave on ROAST for 5 to 6 minutes or until hot. Let stand, covered, 3 minutes before serving. Toss with cheese, tomatoes and avocado. Serve atop a bed of shredded lettuce.   4 to 6 Servings

WILTED SALAD

- **5 slices bacon**
- **¼ cup vinegar**
- **1 tablespoon sugar**
- **2 tablespoons water**
- **½ teaspoon salt**
- **¼ teaspoon pepper**
- **¼ teaspoon dry mustard**
- **1 head leaf lettuce, torn apart**
- **2 green onions, finely chopped**

1. Place bacon in 2-quart (12 x 7) glass baking dish. Cover with paper towel or napkin.

2. Microwave on HIGH for 5 to 6 minutes or until bacon is crisp. Remove bacon; crumble, and set aside. Combine remaining ingredients, except lettuce and onion, with 2 tablespoons bacon drippings in small glass mixing bowl; mix well.

3. Microwave on HIGH for about 2 minutes or until hot. Place lettuce and onion in salad bowl. Pour on hot dressing. Toss lightly to coat lettuce leaves. Garnish with cooked crumbled bacon. Serve immediately.   About 6 Servings

TIP ● Add two chopped hard cooked eggs when salad is tossed.

HOT CRAB SALAD

- **¾ cup mayonnaise or salad dressing**
- **2 tablespoons lemon juice**
- **1 can (6½ oz.) crab meat, drained**
- **1 can (6½ oz.) water-packed white tuna, drained**
- **1 can (6 oz.) water chestnuts, drained and sliced**
- **4 green onions, finely chopped**
- **½ teaspoon salt**
- **2 teaspoons dill weed**

1. Combine all ingredients in 1½-quart glass casserole; mix well. Cover with glass lid or plastic wrap.

2. Microwave on ROAST for 7 to 9 minutes or until hot; stir to blend. Let stand, covered, 3 minutes before serving.   About 4 Servings

SAUERKRAUT 'N FRANK SALAD

- **4 cups prepared potato salad**
- **1 can (8 oz.) sauerkraut, drained**
- **1 package (8 oz.) cocktail franks**
- **½ teaspoon salt**
- **½ teaspoon caraway seed**
- **Paprika**

1. Combine all ingredients, except paprika, in 2-quart glass casserole. Cover with glass lid or plastic wrap.

2. Microwave on REHEAT for 8 to 9 minutes or until hot. Let stand, covered, 3 minutes. Sprinkle paprika on top before serving.   About 6 Servings

---

DRESSING KEY: Simple dressings without critical ingredients such as cream or eggs microwave on HIGH. Microwave dressings on ROAST when cream or eggs are included.

Most dressings can be mixed and cooked right in a glass container.

Mix with salad as recipe specifies.

TART FRUIT DRESSING*

- **2 eggs, well beaten**
- **¼ cup sugar**
- **¼ cup orange juice**
- **¼ cup lemon juice**
- **¼ teaspoon salt**
- **½ cup whipping cream, whipped**

1. Beat eggs in 4-cup glass measure. Stir in sugar, orange juice, lemon juice and salt; mix well.

2. Microwave on ROAST for 3 minutes. Beat with rotary beater until smooth and continue cooking on ROAST for 1 to 2 minutes or until thickened. Beat well with rotary beater until smooth. Chill well. Fold whipped cream into thickened egg mixture. Serve over fresh fruit salad.   About ⅔ Cup Dressing

CLASSIC DRESSING*

- **1 cup milk**
- **1 tablespoon cornstarch**
- **2 teaspoons sugar**
- **1 teaspoon dry mustard**
- **1 teaspoon salt**
- **¼ teaspoon paprika**
- **¼ teaspoon pepper**
- **1 egg yolk, beaten**
- **2 tablespoons vinegar**
- **¼ cup cooking oil**

1. Pour milk into 4-cup glass measure. Blend in cornstarch, sugar, mustard, salt, paprika and pepper; mix well.

2. Microwave on HIGH for 3 minutes. Beat with rotary beater until smooth and continue cooking on HIGH for 1 to 1½ minutes or until thickened. Beat with rotary beater until smooth. Add a little warm mixture to beaten egg yolk. Stir and combine with remaining hot cream mixture.

3. Microwave on ROAST for 1 to 2 minutes or until slightly thickened. Stir in vinegar and oil. Beat with rotary beater until smooth.
                    About 1⅓ Cups Dressing

TIPS ● Stir in ⅓ cup finely chopped cucumber or zucchini and 1 tablespoon snipped chives.

● Stir in 2 chopped hard cooked eggs and 1 teaspoon dried parsley flakes.

● Stir in ¼ cup sour cream and 1 teaspoon dried parsley flakes.

"Saucery" is an art made simple through microwave cooking. How? The Microwaves cook from all directions and eliminate scorching — the saucemaker's devil.

Even though you've never "fussed" with sauces before, try sweet dessert sauces that turn plain cakes, puddings and ice creams into tempting gourmet treats. Then make savory sauces to highlight vegetables, meat, fish and poultry.

Two techniques apply to both sweet and savory sauces: Microwave HIGH cooks non-critical mixtures; ROAST carefully blends butter sauces that tend to spatter and cream or egg sauces that could curdle. **Read the "grey box" keys** for detailed cooking methods.

Microwave some of the family's favorite sauces, too. Use a similar recipe from this collection as a guide.

Pictured top to bottom: Heavenly Chocolate Fondue, page 131; Hot Mustard Sauce garnished with onion slice and parsley, page 130.

HOW TO COOK BASIC SAUCES

● Mix ingredients for basic savory and sweet sauces in 2 or 4-cup glass measure. Sauce should not fill measure more than half full.

● Microwave at setting directed in chart.

● Stir once during cooking.

● Stir well to assure a smooth sauce.

SAUCE	AMOUNT	SETTING	MINUTES
BASIC BROWN OR	1 cup	HIGH	3 to 3½
BASIC WHITE	2 cups	HIGH	5 to 5½
SWEET CORNSTARCH	1 cup	HIGH	3 to 3½
	2 cups	HIGH	5 to 6½

SAVORY SAUCE KEY: Use tart, spicy and sometimes creamy sauces with meat, fish, poultry and vegetables. Microwave on HIGH unless the recipe calls for eggs or quite a bit of butter. Microwave such sauces on ROAST to keep egg mixtures smooth or butter from spattering in the oven.

Plan to measure, mix and cook right in a glass measure that holds at least twice the volume of the sauce. A too-small cooking container allows the sauce to bubble over.

Flour and cornstarch mixtures must boil to cook and thicken. Starches tend to settle to the bottom. Stir such sauces once during the last half of the cooking period when recipe directs.

Spoons, whisks or scrapers of wood, plastic, rubber or metal may be left in the sauce during cooking. Do not use silver tableware in a microwave oven because it will tarnish.

If sauce overcooks and separates, "smooth" it with an electric mixer or blender.

Most sauces can be made ahead, refrigerated and reheated uncovered on REHEAT.

GRAVY *

   ⅓ **cup meat or poultry drippings**
   ⅓ **cup unsifted all-purpose flour**
   2 **cups warm broth or water**
   Salt
   Pepper

1. Combine drippings and flour in 4-cup glass measure. Stir in broth. Season to taste.

2. Microwave on HIGH for 2 minutes. Stir and continue cooking on HIGH for 1 to 2 minutes or until thickened. About 2 Cups Gravy

TIP ● Make gravy for beef, veal, pork roasts and turkey using this recipe.

BASIC BROWN SAUCE *

   2 **tablespoons butter or margarine**
   1 **small onion, thinly sliced**
   2 **tablespoons all-purpose flour**
   1 **cup beef broth**
   ¼ **teaspoon salt**
   ⅛ **teaspoon pepper**

1. Combine butter and onion in 2-cup glass measure.

2. Microwave on ROAST for about 2 minutes or until onion is partly cooked. Stir in remaining ingredients.

3. Microwave on HIGH for 2 minutes. Stir and continue cooking on HIGH for 1 to 1½ minutes or until thickened. About 1 Cup Sauce

TIPS ● Make beef broth by diluting a can of condensed beef broth or dissolving 1 beef bouillon cube in 1 cup boiling water.

   ● Substitute drippings from a meat cooking pan for beef broth.

Serve with ham and smoked chops.

HOT MUSTARD SAUCE *

   1 **egg, beaten**
   ½ **cup prepared mustard**
   ⅓ **cup sugar**
   ⅓ **cup vinegar**
   ½ **teaspoon salt**
   Pepper

1. Combine all ingredients in 2-cup glass measure.

2. Microwave on ROAST for 3 minutes. Stir and continue cooking on ROAST for 1 to 2 minutes or until thickened. Stir before serving.
About 1¼ Cups Sauce

BASIC WHITE SAUCE*

    1 cup milk
    2 tablespoons all-purpose flour
    ¼ teaspoon salt
    ⅛ teaspoon pepper
    2 tablespoons butter or margarine

1. Combine all ingredients in 2-cup glass measure; mix well.

2. Microwave on HIGH for 2 minutes. Stir and continue cooking on HIGH for 1 to 1½ minutes or until thickened.   About 1 Cup Sauce

TIPS ● Make EGG WHITE SAUCE by stirring 2 to 3 hard cooked eggs, finely chopped, into Basic White Sauce when sauce is stirred during Step 2.

     ● Make CHEESE SAUCE by stirring ¼ teaspoon dry mustard and ½ cup shredded American process cheese into Basic White Sauce when sauce is stirred in Step 2.

SWEET SAUCE KEY: dessert sauces microwave on HIGH unless the recipe calls for cream or condensed milk. Microwave these sweet creamy sauces on ROAST to prevent separation. See Dessert chapter for egg custard sauce technique.

Sauces are fast and fun to make because microwaves cook from all directions and eliminate scorching problems.

Usually you can measure, mix and cook right in a glass measure.

Allow for boiling. Make certain the cooking cup or bowl is at least twice the size of the sauce volume.

Stir sauce once during last half of cooking period to keep it smooth and creamy.

Stirring spoons, whisks, or scrapers of wood, plastic, rubber or metal (not silver) may be left in the sauce during cooking.

If a sauce curdles, it is overcooked. Use an electric mixer or blender to regain smoothness.

Store leftover sauces in glass jars in the refrigerator. Reheat without a cover on REHEAT. Heat sauce in its glass storage jar if jar is no more than half full. Stir sauce occasionally while it heats. Serve over ice cream, cake or pudding.

CARAMEL SAUCE*

    ½ cup light cream
    ⅔ cup white corn syrup
   1¼ cups packed brown sugar
    2 tablespoons butter or margarine

1. Combine all ingredients in 4-cup glass measure; mix well.

2. Microwave on ROAST for 8 minutes. Stir and continue cooking on ROAST for 4 to 6 minutes or until hot. Beat until smooth.
                        About 1½ Cups Sauce

HEAVENLY CHOCOLATE FONDUE

    1 can (14 oz.) sweetened condensed milk
    1 jar (10 oz.) marshmallow creme
    ½ cup milk
    1 teaspoon vanilla
    1 package (12 oz.) semi-sweet chocolate pieces

1. Combine all ingredients in medium glass mixing bowl.

2. Microwave on ROAST for 4 to 6 minutes. Beat until well blended and creamy.
                        About 4 Cups Fondue

TIPS ● Pineapple chunks, fresh apple slices, orange sections, banana chunks, marshmallows, angel food and other cake squares are good fondue dunkers.

     ● Keep fondue sauce warm while serving in a chafing dish over hot water or in a heavy pottery crock over very low heat.

FUDGE SAUCE*

    1 cup light cream
    2 cups sugar
    4 squares unsweetened chocolate
    2 tablespoons butter or margarine
    ½ teaspoon salt
    1 teaspoon vanilla

1. Combine all ingredients, except vanilla, in 4-cup glass measure.

2. Microwave on ROAST for 5 minutes. Stir and continue cooking on ROAST for 5 to 6 minutes or until thickened. Stir in vanilla. Beat sauce light and smooth by hand or for 10 seconds at "low" speed in a blender.   About 2 Cups Sauce

Glass measure or bowl should be at least twice as large as sauce volume.

ORANGE SAUCE*

       2 tablespoons butter or margarine
     1½ tablespoons cornstarch
       ¼ cup sugar
       ¼ cup packed brown sugar
       1 cup water
       1 tablespoon grated orange peel
       ⅓ cup orange juice
 1 to 2 tablespoons Grand Marnier or other orange flavored liqueur, if desired.

1. Combine all ingredients, except liqueur, in 4-cup glass measure; mix well.

2. Microwave on HIGH for 3 minutes. Stir and continue cooking on HIGH for 1 to 1½ minutes or until boiling. Stir in Grand Marnier.
                        About 1½ Cups Sauce

Yeast and quick breads are a whole new world when there's a microwave oven in the kitchen.

Freshly mixed yeast dough raises twice in less than an hour — bakes in under 15 minutes. Breads do not brown so will not have a hard crust. Kids think this is great — so does mom when she has to make fancy tea sandwiches. Bread baked in a microwave oven makes especially good toast, too.

Quick breads really are quick when cooked in a microwave oven. Make these from "scratch," biscuit mix, package mixes or canned refrigerated dough.

Major microwave techniques in this chapter revolve around the very gentle raising and cooking speeds needed to keep yeast alive for light bread and the speedier cook-and-set combination necessary to raise and bake quick breads.

Each recipe and chart in the collection is a model for adapting other recipes — do try them all. **Check "grey box" keys** for special tips.

Pictured top to bottom: Wheat Germ Bread, page 135;
Biscuit Mix Coffee Cake, page 136.

YEAST/QUICK BREAD CHAPTER
CONTENTS

HOW TO MICROWAVE QUICK BREAD MIXES AND YEAST BREAD

● Prepare quick bread mix as directed on package.

● Fill glass cooking dish only half full.

● Pour extra batter into paper lined individual glass custard cups.

● Microwave on SIMMER then HIGH when directed on chart; serve.

● Mix yeast bread as directed in a favorite recipe. Raise on WARM using microwave technique in English Muffin Bread, page 135.

● Bake 1 or 2 loaves of bread in well-greased glass loaf dish(es) on SIMMER as directed in chart.

● Allow bread to stand 5 minutes. Turn out on wire rack to cool before slicing.

BREADS AND QUICK BREADS	SIZE	GLASS CONTAINER	FIRST SETTING AND TIME	SECOND SETTING AND TIME
APPLE CINNAMON COFFEE CAKE MIX*	19-oz. pkg.	9-in. round dish	SIMMER 7 min.	HIGH 4 to 5 min.
DATE BREAD MIX*	17-oz. pkg.	1½-qt. casserole	SIMMER 10 min.	HIGH 2 to 3 min.
BANANA BREAD MIX*	15½-oz. pkg.	(8 x 4) loaf dish	SIMMER 10 min.	HIGH 2 to 3 min.
CORN MUFFIN MIX 6 Muffins	8½-oz. pkg.	Cupcake liners in individual custard cups	SIMMER 5 to 6 min.	
BLUEBERRY MUFFIN MIX 4 Muffins 6 Muffins	13½-oz. pkg.	Cupcake liners in individual custard cups	SIMMER 4 to 4½ min. 6 to 6½ min.	
HOMEMADE BREAD 1 Loaf 2 Loaves	1 lb. 1 lb. ea.	(8 x 4) loaf dish	SIMMER 10 to 11 min. 12 to 13 min.	

YEAST BREAD KEY: Raising yeast bread is a delicate process — but fast and successful in a microwave oven on WARM. This low speed keeps yeast alive and active. Steps 3, 4 and 5 in the following English Muffin Bread recipe outline the technique for raising most any freshly mixed yeast bread dough — and the whole process takes less than one hour.

Bake yeast bread dough quickly on Microwave SIMMER for even texture — and so edges stay tender while center cooks.

Though frozen bread dough takes longer to raise than freshly mixed dough, use WARM and follow steps in the How to Bake Frozen Bread Dough recipe — bake on SIMMER recipe directs.

Always use glass bowls and dishes when raising or baking bread. Make certain dishes are well greased.

Standing time is important to finish cooking process and so breads' bottom surface will set.

Cool, then wrap baked bread tightly to preserve softness.

Bread will not brown and so does not have a hard crust. It's great for tea sandwiches — makes especially good toast and French toast.

Heat baked bread and rolls in seconds on a paper plate, paper towel, paper or cloth napkin so moisture is absorbed. Use REHEAT.

Dry bread for crumbling on Microwave WARM. Then whirl it in an electric blender or crush with a rolling pin.

WARM raises bread fully; SIMMER cooks dough.

ENGLISH MUFFIN BREAD

   3 cups unsifted all-purpose flour
   2 packages active dry yeast
   1 tablespoon sugar
  ¼ teaspoon soda
   1 tablespoon salt
2½ cups milk
   2 cups unsifted all-purpose flour
     Melted butter

1. Combine 3 cups flour, yeast, sugar, soda and salt in large mixer bowl; set aside. Pour milk into 4-cup glass measure.

2. Microwave on HIGH for 2 to 2½ minutes or until warm. Stir milk into flour mixture. Beat at medium speed with electric mixer until smooth. Stir in remaining 2 cups flour. Knead on floured surface until smooth and elastic, 5 to 8 minutes.

3. Raising: Place dough in greased large glass bowl; brush with melted butter, and cover loosely with plastic wrap or wax paper. Place bowl of dough in 3-quart (13 x 9) glass baking dish containing 6 cups warm water.

4. Microwave on WARM for 15 minutes. Let stand for 10 minutes. Repeat these two steps until doubled in size. Punch down dough; divide in half. Shape each half into a loaf. Place in 2 greased (8 x 4) glass loaf dishes. Brush tops with melted butter. Place crosswise in 3-quart (13 x 9) glass baking dish containing 6 cups warm water. Cover loosely with plastic wrap or wax paper.

5. Microwave on WARM for 10 minutes. Let stand 10 minutes or until loaves are light and doubled in size. Remove dish of water and uncover bread.

6. Baking: Microwave on SIMMER for 18 to 20 minutes or until no longer doughy. Let stand 5 minutes. Turn out on rack to cool.

                            2 Loaves Bread

Follow raising steps carefully.

HOW TO BAKE FROZEN BREAD DOUGH*

1. Grease 1-pound loaf frozen bread dough; place in greased (8 x 4) glass loaf dish. Cover loosely with plastic wrap. Place dish of dough in 3-quart (13 x 9) glass baking dish. Pour 6 cups warm water into baking dish.

2. Microwave on WARM for 20 minutes.

3. Let stand in oven for 10 minutes. Repeat these two steps until dough is just above top of dish, about 2 times. Remove dish of water and plastic wrap.

4. Microwave on SIMMER for 10 to 11 minutes or until no longer doughy.   1 Loaf Bread

TIP ● Frozen bread dough must be fresh or it will not raise fully.

Bowls and baking dishes must be well greased.

WHEAT GERM BREAD

   1 cup warm water
   1 package active dry yeast
  ¼ cup packed brown sugar
1½ teaspoons salt
   2 tablespoons cooking oil
   1 egg
  ½ cup wheat germ
1½ cups unsifted all-purpose flour
   1 cup unsifted all-purpose flour
     Melted butter

1. Combine warm water and yeast in large glass mixer bowl. Stir in brown sugar, salt, oil, egg, wheat germ and 1½ cups flour. Beat abour 3 minutes at medium speed with electric mixer. Stir in remaining 1 cup flour to form a stiff dough. Knead on floured surface until smooth and elastic, 5 to 8 minutes.

2. Raising: Place dough in greased large glass bowl; brush with melted butter and cover loosely with plastic wrap or wax paper. Place bowl of dough in 3-quart (13 x 9) glass baking dish containing 6 cups warm water.

3. Microwave on WARM for 15 minutes. Let stand for 10 minutes. Repeat these two steps until doubled in size. Punch down dough. Shape into a loaf and place in greased (8 x 4) glass loaf dish. Brush top with melted butter. Cover loosely with plastic wrap or wax paper. Return to dish with warm water.

4. Microwave on WARM for 10 minutes. Let stand 10 minutes or until doubled in size. Remove dish of water and uncover bread.

5. Baking: Microwave on SIMMER for 10 to 11 minutes or until no longer doughy. Let stand 5 minutes. Turn out on rack to cool.   1 Loaf Bread

<table>
<tr><td>

QUICK BREAD KEY: Tender tasty quick breads from "scratch" or biscuit mix start cooking on SIMMER, finish up on HIGH to set the batter. It's technique similar to cake baking.

Coffee cake from canned refrigerated biscuits cooks very quickly on ROAST because this is a "shorter" dough.

Glass cooking dishes are a must. Since batter raises higher than usual in a microwave oven, do not fill dishes more than half full.

Coffee cakes are prettiest when recipe calls for fruit toppings or brown sugar glazes because a microwave oven does not brown bread dough.

Quick breads are cooked when a toothpick inserted near center of bread comes out clean.

Popovers CANNOT be baked in a microwave oven because they do not form a crust to hold dough in shape. Leftover popovers reheat nicely. See how in the bread reheating chart.

</td></tr>
</table>

Quick breads with toppings are prettiest.

PUMPKIN BREAD WITH PUMPKIN TOPPING*

  1½ **cups unsifted all-purpose flour**
  1½ **cups sugar**
   1 **teaspoon soda**
  ¾ **teaspoon salt**
  ½ **teaspoon nutmeg**
  ½ **teaspoon cinnamon**
   1 **cup mashed cooked pumpkin**
  ½ **cup cooking oil**
  ⅓ **cup water**
   2 **eggs**
  ½ **cup chopped walnuts**
  ½ **cup chopped pitted dates**

Pumpkin Topping:
   1 **cup whipping cream**
  ¼ **cup powdered sugar**
  ¼ **teaspoon nutmeg**
  ¼ **teaspoon cinnamon**
  ¾ **cup mashed cooked pumpkin**

1. Combine all bread ingredients, except walnuts and dates, in large mixer bowl. Beat at medium speed about 1 minute. Fold in walnuts and dates. Pour batter into 2-quart (9 x 5) glass loaf dish.

2. Microwave on SIMMER for 20 minutes.

3. Microwave on HIGH for 5 to 6 minutes or until toothpick inserted near center comes out clean. Let stand 2 minutes; unmold. Serve with Pumpkin Topping.

4. **Pumpkin Topping:** Whip cream with powdered sugar and spices. Fold in pumpkin. 1 Loaf Bread

TIP ● 1 can (16 oz.) pumpkin is enough for both bread and topping.

Quick bread microwave technique is similar to the one for baking cake.

BISCUIT MIX COFFEE CAKE*

   2 **cups biscuit mix**
   2 **tablespoons sugar**
  ⅔ **cup water**
   1 **egg**
Topping:
  ⅓ **cup biscuit mix**
  ⅓ **cup packed brown sugar**
  ½ **teaspoon cinnamon**
  ¼ **cup butter or margarine**

1. Combine 2 cups biscuit mix, sugar, water and egg in medium mixing bowl; mix well. Spread in 9-inch round glass baking dish. Sprinkle with Topping.

2. Microwave on SIMMER for 7 minutes.

3. Microwave on HIGH for 4 to 4½ minutes or until toothpick inserted near center comes out clean.

4. **Topping:** Combine ⅓ cup biscuit mix, brown sugar and cinnamon; cut in butter.
About 6 Servings

Super-fast no-think coffee cake will delight the family at breakfast.

CARAMEL BISCUIT RING-A-ROUND

  ⅓ **cup packed brown sugar**
   3 **tablespoons butter or margarine**
   1 **tablespoon water**
  ⅓ **cup chopped nuts**
   1 **can (8 oz.) refrigerated biscuits**

1. Combine brown sugar, butter and water in 1-quart glass casserole.

2. Microwave on ROAST for about 2 minutes or until butter is melted. Stir in nuts. Separate biscuits; cut each one into quarters. Add biscuits to sugar mixture; stir to coat each piece. Push biscuits and coating away from center of casserole and set a custard cup or glass, open end up, in center.

3. Microwave on ROAST for 5 to 5½ minutes or until biscuits are no longer doughy. Let stand 2 minutes; twist out custard cup and invert biscuit ring on serving plate. Serve warm with forks to pull sections apart into individual servings.
About 6 Servings

TIPS ● Use dark brown sugar instead of light brown for a richer, darker color.

● Use a sharp pointed knife to loosen custard cup if it sticks to caramel and will not twist out easily.

HOW TO WARM BREAD AND ROLLS

● Place rolls or muffins on paper plate, paper towel, cloth or paper napkin.

● Warm on REHEAT since all breads are precooked.

● Do not over heat or breads will toughen — surface should be "warm" rather than "hot."

BREAD	AMOUNT	SETTING	TIME FROM ROOM TEMPERATURE	TIME FROM FREEZER
BUNS AND ROLLS	1	REHEAT	10 to 15 sec.	15 to 20 sec.
Hamburger, Hot Dog,	2		15 to 20 sec.	20 to 25 sec.
Dinner, Bagel	4		20 to 25 sec.	25 to 30 sec.
	6		25 to 30 sec.	35 to 40 sec.
	8		35 to 40 sec.	50 to 55 sec.
ENGLISH MUFFINS	1	REHEAT	20 to 25 sec.	35 to 40 sec.
	2		30 to 35 sec.	50 to 60 sec.
	4		55 to 60 sec.	2 to 2½ min.
	6		1 to 1¼ min.	2¾ to 3 min.
FRENCH BREAD	1½ lb.	REHEAT	30 to 45 sec.	1½ to 2 min.
DOUGHNUTS	1	REHEAT	15 to 20 sec.	25 to 30 sec.
Regular, Raised,	2		25 to 30 sec.	35 to 40 sec.
SWEET ROLLS	4		40 to 45 sec.	50 to 60 sec.
COFFEE CAKE WEDGE	6		50 to 60 sec.	1¼ to 1½ min.
MUFFINS	1	REHEAT	10 to 15 sec.	20 to 25 sec.
Raisin, Fruit,	2		20 to 30 sec.	35 to 40 sec.
Date	4		30 to 35 sec.	55 to 60 sec.
	6		40 to 45 sec.	1¾ to 2 min.
NUT BREAD				
Canned	8 oz.	REHEAT	2 to 2½ min.	
PANCAKES, FRENCH	1	REHEAT	20 to 30 sec.	35 to 45 sec.
TOAST, WAFFLES	2		35 to 45 sec.	1 to 1½ min.
	4		1 to 1½ min.	1½ to 2 min.
POPOVERS	2 to 4	REHEAT	30 to 60 sec.	

Think "round" when you think cakes baked in a microwave oven. Other dish shapes can be used, of course, but round shapes bake most evenly. And — a tender wedge of richly frosted round cake automatically says "party" to sweet-loving kids — toddlers to grandpas.

Cake, frosting and filling techniques outlined in the chapter's **"grey box" keys are easy to follow.** Cake batters must raise, then set to hold shape. Frostings must thicken and hold shape when beaten and cooled. Fillings are essentially thick sweet sauces which cook quickly — how quickly is defined by the ingredients.

Nearly all cake mixes microwave delectably high and light — more so than in a conventional oven. "From scratch" cake techniques presented in these recipes are designed to help a cake cook adapt her own specialities.

Pictured: Cake Made from a Mix, page 140; Lemon Filling, page 143; Five-Minute Snowy White Frosting, page 143.

CAKE/FROSTING/FILLING
CHAPTER CONTENTS

CAKES, FROSTINGS & FILLINGS

CAKE KEY: Cakes microwave on SIMMER to raise, then on HIGH to set the batter. Cupcakes bake on SIMMER throughout cooking because of the small amount of batter in each one.

Fruit cake is a dense batter so cooks gently as it must in a conventional oven. Total cooking time on DEFROST is only about 40 minutes.

Cakes raise higher than usual in a microwave oven, so fill baking dishes no more than half full. Use extra batter for cupcakes. See chart on page 141.

Use glass dishes for cakes. Round shapes work especially well — try layer cake dishes and large mixing bowls.

Push a glass down in the center of the batter, open end up, when cake is baked in a bowl. This creates a tube-type baking dish that allows cake center to cook evenly and completely.

Line the bottom of any flat cake dish with wax paper if the cake is to be unmolded.

Bake layers one at a time. Use the same dish for the second layer, but replace the wax paper.

If the dish is still warm, cake may cook about 30 seconds faster.

Cakes can be cooked in rectangular dishes when recipe specifies but surface will be slightly uneven.

Do not grease or flour cake dishes; the mixture forms a layer on the bottom of the cake.

Cakes are done when a toothpick inserted near the center comes out clean.

Frosting spreads most easily and evenly if a cake has been standing long enough to dry the surface slightly or if it has been cooled in the refrigerator.

Cakes do not brown in a microwave oven, so white cakes are really white — and there are no dark crumbs in the frosting.

Moist-top cakes absorb toppings quickly and well.

Cake batter made from a mix may be refrigerated up to a week in a covered dish.

Want to adapt a favorite cake recipe to the microwave oven? Reduce leavening ¼ to ⅓ (experiment) and bake as outlined above.

HOW TO BAKE CAKE

● Prepare batter as directed in recipe or on cake mix package.

● Use glass dish specified in chart. It will not always be the same as suggested on the recipe or package.

● Do not fill dish more than half full.

● Use extra batter to make cupcakes as directed in chart.

● Line bottom of flat dishes with wax paper if cake is to be unmolded.

● Bake layers one at a time. Second layer may be baked in the same dish but replace wax paper. If dish is warm, decrease cooking time about 30 seconds.

● When cake batter is cooked in a large bowl, press a glass into the center of the batter, open end up.

● Cake is done when a toothpick inserted near center comes out clean.

● Let cake stand 5 minutes to set.

● Turn out on serving plate to cool or cool in dish on wire rack.

CAKE	GLASS CONTAINER	FIRST SETTING AND TIME	SECOND SETTING AND TIME
CAKE MIX* 17 to 18½-oz. pkg.	9-in. round dish	SIMMER 7 min.	HIGH 3 to 4 min.
	3-qt. (13 x 9) baking dish	SIMMER 9 min.	HIGH 6 to 7 min.
SNACKING CAKE MIX* 14.5-oz. pkg.	9-in. round dish	SIMMER 7 min.	HIGH 3 to 4 min.

CAKE	GLASS CONTAINER	FIRST SETTING AND TIME	SECOND SETTING AND TIME
CUPCAKES FROM MIX			
2	Paper cupcake liners in individual custard cups	SIMMER 2 to 2½ min.	
4		3 to 3½ min.	
6		4½ to 5 min.	
POUND CAKE MIX*			
14-oz. pkg.	1½-qt. casserole	SIMMER 10 min.	HIGH 2 to 3 min.
GINGERBREAD MIX*			
15-oz. pkg.	2-qt. (8 x 8) baking dish	SIMMER 7 min.	HIGH 3 to 4 min.
HOMEMADE CAKE*			
	9-in. round dish	SIMMER 7 min.	HIGH 3 to 4 min.

EASY COMPANY CAKE*

¼ cup butter or margarine
¾ cup sugar
2 eggs
¼ teaspoon vanilla
¾ cup unsifted all-purpose flour
½ teaspoon baking powder
½ teaspoon salt
¼ cup milk

Topping:
¼ cup butter or margarine
¼ cup sugar
1 tablespoon milk
1 tablespoon all-purpose flour
⅓ cup slivered almonds

1. Place butter in large mixing bowl.

2. Microwave on ROAST for about 30 seconds or until softened. Beat in sugar, eggs and vanilla until light and fluffy. Stir in dry ingredients alternately with milk; mix well after each addition. Beat until smooth. Pour into 9-inch round glass baking dish.

3. Microwave on SIMMER for 7 minutes.

4. Microwave on HIGH for 3 to 4 minutes or until toothpick inserted near center comes out clean. Pour Topping over warm cake. Serve warm or cold.

5. Topping: Combine butter, sugar and milk in 2-cup glass measure; stir until blended. Blend in flour. Stir in almonds.

6. Microwave on ROAST for 1 to 2 minutes or until slightly thickened; stir to blend.

6 to 8 Servings

Microwave oven bakes fruitcake quickly – but dense fruit batter requires gentle cooking.

FRUITCAKE

2 eggs
¾ cup packed brown sugar
2 tablespoons molasses
⅓ cup cooking oil
1½ cup unsifted all-purpose flour
1 teaspoon baking powder
½ teaspoon salt
¼ teaspoon allspice
¼ teaspoon nutmeg
¼ teaspoon ground cloves
½ cup orange juice
1 lb. mixed candied fruit
1 cup raisins
½ lb. pitted dates, cut up
1 cup chopped nuts

1. Combine eggs, brown sugar and molasses in large mixing bowl; beat well. Beat in oil. Stir in dry ingredients alternately with orange juice; mix well after each addition. Stir in fruit and nuts. Line 2-quart (9 x 5) glass loaf dish with wax paper. Paper should extend at least 2 to 3 inches above sides of dish. Pour cake batter into dish.

2. Microwave on DEFROST for 35 to 40 minutes or until toothpick inserted near center comes out free of batter. Let stand in dish 5 minutes. Turn out on rack to cool.   18 to 20 Slices

TIP • Fruit toughens if not stored properly. Wrap cake in several layers of clean linen. Soak with ¼ cup rum or brandy. Store in tightly sealed container to hold moisture.

Pictured: Birthday Cake Cones topped with ice cream, this page; Cupcakes from a Mix, page 141.

BIRTHDAY CAKE CONES

    1 package (9 oz.) cake mix
    8 flat bottom ice cream cones

1. Prepare cake mix as directed on package. Spoon about 2 tablespoons batter into each ice cream cone. Place in oven; allow about 1-inch space between each cone.

2. Microwave on SIMMER:
    1 cone — 45 seconds to 1 minute
    2 cones — 1½ to 2 minutes
    4 cones — 3 to 3½ minutes
    6 cones — 4½ to 4¾ minutes
    8 cones — 5 to 5½ minutes
Cake Cones are done when toothpick inserted near center of each cake comes out clean. Cake will be slightly soft around edges when cones come from oven. Cool on wire rack. Frost.   8 Cake Cones

TIP • Top each Cake Cone with a scoop of ice cream and use colored gum drops to make face on ice cream "head".

PARTY CAKE IN A BOWL*

1. Prepare 1 package (18½ oz.) cake mix as directed on package using a large glass mixer bowl; beat well. Push a water glass, open end up, into center of batter.

2. Microwave on SIMMER for 7 minutes.

3. Microwave on HIGH for 6 to 7 minutes or until toothpick inserted near center comes out clean. Let cool 1 minute. Remove glass with a twisting motion and invert cake on serving platter. Frost or sprinkle with powdered sugar.

                        About 12 Servings

PINEAPPLE UPSIDE DOWN CAKE*

    ¼ cup butter or margarine
    ½ cup packed brown sugar
    6 slices canned pineapple, drained
    6 maraschino cherries
    1 package (9 oz.) yellow cake mix

1. Place butter in 9-inch round glass baking dish.

2. Microwave on ROAST for about 2 minutes or until melted. Stir in brown sugar. Arrange pineapple on top. Place a cherry in center of each pineapple slice. Prepare cake mix as directed on package. Pour over pineapple.

3. Microwave on SIMMER for 7 minutes.

4. Microwave on HIGH for 3 to 4 minutes or until toothpick inserted near center comes out clean. Let stand 1 minute. Turn out onto platter and serve warm or cool.   4 to 6 Servings

FROSTING KEY: Frosting mixtures are of three basic kinds. The high-sugar frostings, much like candy, cook on ROAST into rich syrups that cool and hold shape when beaten.

Simple sweet sauce frostings, with less sugar and some thickening, cook on HIGH.

Custard sauce-type frostings, with critical ingredients such as eggs, condensed milk or cream, need the gentler cooking of ROAST.

Cook frostings in glass containers at least twice the volume of the ingredients. Most can be mixed and cooked right in a glass measure.

Stirring and beating, as directed in the recipe, are important to a finished frosting that is smooth, light and spreadable.

Stirring spoons, whisks or scrapers made of wood, plastic, rubber or metal (not silver) may be left in the dish during cooking.

CREAMY WHIPPED FROSTING*

    ¾ cup sugar
    ¼ cup unsifted all-purpose flour
    ¾ cup milk
    ½ cup butter or margarine
    1 teaspoon vanilla

1. Combine sugar and flour in small glass mixer bowl. Stir in milk.

2. Microwave on HIGH for 2 minutes. Beat well and continue cooking on HIGH for 1 to 2 minutes or until mixture boils and thickens. Add butter and beat until smooth. Refrigerate about 1 hour or until cool. Add vanilla and beat with electric mixer at high speed until light and fluffy.
        Frosts 13 x 9-Inch or Two 9-Inch Layers

FILLINGS **143**

FUDGE FROSTING*

- ⅔ cup milk
- 2 cups sugar
- ½ cup butter or margarine
- 3 squares (1 oz. each) unsweetened chocolate
- ½ teaspoon salt
- 2 teaspoons vanilla

1. Combine all ingredients, except vanilla, in small glass mixer bowl.

2. Microwave on ROAST for 6 minutes. Stir and continue cooking on ROAST for about 3 minutes or until mixture reaches a full rolling boil. Stir in vanilla. Cool.

3. Beat with electric mixer at high speed until frosting is spreading consistency.
Frosts 13 x 9-Inch or Two 9-Inch Layers

Custard sauce-type frostings need gentle cooking because these contain eggs, cream or condensed milk.

COCONUTTY FROSTING*

- 1 cup evaporated milk
- 3 eggs
- 1 cup sugar
- ½ cup butter or margarine
- 1 teaspoon vanilla
- 1⅓ cup flaked coconut
- 1 cup chopped nuts

1. Combine milk, eggs, sugar and butter in 4-cup glass measure. Beat well with rotary beater.

2. Microwave on ROAST for 5 minutes. Beat with rotary beater and continue cooking on ROAST for 2 to 3 minutes or until mixture boils. Stir in remaining ingredients; beat well.
Frost 13 x 9-Inch or Two 9-Inch Layers

Stirring and beating make frosting smooth.

FIVE-MINUTE SNOWY WHITE FROSTING

- 1 cup sugar
- ½ cup water
- ¼ teaspoon cream of tartar
- Dash salt
- 2 egg whites
- 1 teaspoon vanilla

1. Combine sugar, water, cream of tartar and salt in 2-cup glass measure.

2. Microwave on ROAST for 4 to 5 minutes or until mixture boils.

3. Beat egg whites in small mixer bowl until soft peaks form. Gradually pour in hot syrup; beat about 5 minutes or until thick and fluffy. Blend in vanilla.

Frosts 13 x 9-Inch or Two 9-Inch Layers

FILLING KEY: Cake fillings are essentially thick sweet sauces. Cook fillings with cornstarch or other thickening on Microwave HIGH; fillings with eggs, cream or condensed milk on ROAST.

Ingredients can usually be measured, mixed and cooked in a glass measure. Do use a measure large enough to hold twice the filling volume so mixture doesn't bubble over during cooking.

Stir a filling once during the last half of cooking to keep it smooth and satiny.

Stirring spoons, whisks or scrapers made of wood, plastic, rubber or metal (not silver) may be left in the dish during cooking.

If filling curdles, whirl in an electric blender to regain smoothness.

Cool filling before spreading on cake.

Fast cooking is possible because there are no critical ingredients – measure, mix and cook in a glass measure.

LEMON FILLING*

- ½ cup sugar
- 2 tablespoons cornstarch
- ⅛ teaspoon salt
- ⅔ cup water
- 1½ teaspoons grated lemon peel
- 2 tablespoons lemon juice
- 1 tablespoon butter or margarine

1. Combine all ingredients in 2-cup glass measure; mix well.

2. Microwave on HIGH for 2 minutes. Stir and continue cooking on HIGH for 2 to 2½ minutes or until thickened; beat well. Cool and spread on cake.
1 Cup Filling

TIP ● Yellow food coloring maybe added, if desired.

Eggs need gentle cooking – stirring keeps filling smooth.

VANILLA CREAM FILLING*

- 1½ cups milk
- ⅓ cup sugar
- 2 tablespoons cornstarch
- ¼ teaspoon salt
- 2 egg yolks
- 2 teaspoons vanilla

1. Combine all ingredients, except vanilla, in 2-cup glass measure. Beat well with rotary beater.

2. Microwave on ROAST for 4 minutes. Stir and continue cooking on ROAST for 3 to 3½ minutes or until thickened. Stir in vanilla; beat until smooth. Cool and spread on cake.

2 Cups Filling

Delicately light colored and tender — in the wink of an eye! That's pie baked in a microwave oven. Crumb crusts are a delicious short cut — especially with cooked custard and gelatin fillings. Remember that tender flaky pastry takes an airy touch — too much flour toughens, too much liquid makes it soggy, too much shortening turns it crumbly and greasy.

The "grey box" key describes microwave techniques for crumb crusts, pastry shells, custard pies and gelatin-base pie fillings. There's also an excellent microwave-conventional oven technique for fresh fruit pies. Try recipes and heating charts in this section. See the Freezer to Table chapter before baking or heating frozen pies. Then adapt recipes from other sources.

Pictured: Pecan Pie, page 146.

PIES (vertical)

PIE KEY: Microwave pie crust in a 9-inch glass pie plate in less than 9 minutes on ROAST — heat that cooks and sets a pastry mixture without burning it. Favorite pastry (mixed with water), pie crust mixes and crumb crust mixtures all microwave well. Prick pastry shells before cooking. Cool crusts before filling.

Custard pies cook in 9-inch baked shells on DEFROST. Custards are critical mixtures that need low heat to prevent curdling or separation. Cook these pies in glass pie plates.

Gelatin-base pie fillings heat and melt together quickly on HIGH. If eggs are used, cook gelatin mixtures on ROAST to prevent curdling or burning. Fill 9-inch baked pie shells. Chill before serving.

Fruit pies call for a microwave-conventional oven technique that's an outstanding success and bakes a 2-crust, 9-inch fruit pie made "from scratch" in less than 25 minutes. Assemble pie in a 9-inch glass pie plate. Microwave on HIGH to quickly heat and start cooking. Transfer pie to preheated conventional 450° F. oven to finish cooking and brown crust.

Heating charts in this chapter tell how to warm a whole pie or a single piece. Freezer to Table chapter outlines techniques for baking and heating frozen uncooked and cooked pies.

HOW TO HEAT PIES AND TARTS

• Heat prebaked pies in glass pie plate.

• Place prebaked tarts on glass or pottery dessert plates. Dishes should not have silver or other metal trim.

• Microwave as directed on chart or until filling is warmed through. Serve.

PIE	GLASS DISH	SETTING AND TIME
FRUIT 2 crust whole	9-in. pie plate	REHEAT 4½ to 5 min.
1 pc.	dessert plate	REHEAT 30 to 35 sec.
2 pcs.	dessert plate	REHEAT 65 to 70 sec.
CUSTARD 1 crust whole	9-in. pie plate	ROAST 4 to 4½ min.
1 pc.	dessert plate	ROAST 40 to 45 sec.
2 pcs.	dessert plate	ROAST 50 to 55 sec.
FRUIT TART 1	dessert plate	REHEAT 30 to 45 sec.
2	dessert plate	REHEAT 45 to 60 sec.

Two crust fruit pies do well when started in a microwave oven and finished in a conventional oven to gain a golden brown color.

FRESH FRUIT PIE

1. Preheat conventional oven to 450° F. Prepare favorite recipe for 2-crust 9-inch fresh fruit pie. Assemble in 9-inch glass pie plate.

2. Microwave on HIGH for 7 to 8 minutes or until juices start bubbling through slits in pie crust. Transfer to preheated conventional oven and bake 10 to 15 minutes or until golden brown.   9-Inch Pie

TIPS • Try cherry, rhubarb, peach, apple or combination fruit pies.

• Microwave an 8-inch 2-crust fruit pie 6 or 7 minutes; microwave a 10-inch pie 8 to 9 minutes.

• Freezer to Table chapter tells how to cook and/or heat frozen pies.

Low heat prevents burning.

PECAN PIE

   3 tablespoons butter or margarine
   3 eggs, slightly beaten
   1 cup dark corn syrup
   ¼ cup packed brown sugar
   1½ teaspoons all-purpose flour
   1 teaspoon vanilla
   1½ cups pecan halves
   1 (9-inch) Baked Pastry Shell in glass pie plate, page 147

1. Place butter in medium glass mixing bowl.

2. Microwave on ROAST for about 1 to 1½ minutes or until melted. Stir in remaining ingredients, except Baked Pastry Shell; mix well; pour filling in shell.

3. Microwave on DEFROST for 25 to 30 minutes or until knife inserted near center comes out clean. Cool.   9-Inch Pie

Beating helps keep filling smooth.

PUMPKIN PIE

    3 eggs
   ½ cup sugar
   ½ cup packed brown sugar
   1 tablespoon all-purpose flour
   ½ teaspoon salt
   2 teaspoons pumpkin pie spice
   1 can (16 oz.) mashed cooked pumpkin
   1 cup milk
   1 (9-inch) Baked Pastry Shell in glass
      pie plate, this page

1. Combine all ingredients, except Baked Pastry Shell; beat until smooth; pour in shell.

2. Microwave on DEFROST for 50 to 55 minutes or until knife inserted near center comes out clean. Cool.   9-Inch Pie

TIP • Extra filling can be cooked separately individual custard cups.

Gelatin mixed with eggs melts on ROAST.

KEY LIME PIE*

    2 eggs, separated
   ½ cup water
   ⅓ cup lime juice
   ¾ cup sugar
   1 envelope unflavored gelatin
4 to 5 drops green food coloring
   1 teaspoon grated lime peel
   2 tablespoons sugar
   1 cup whipping cream, whipped
   1 (9-inch) Baked Pastry Shell,
      this page

1. Beat egg yolks in large glass mixing bowl. Add water, lime juice, ¾ cup sugar and gelatin; mix well.

2. Microwave on ROAST for 3 minutes. Beat mixture smooth with spoon and continue cooking on ROAST for 2 to 3 minutes or until mixture begins to bubble. Stir in food coloring and lime peel. Cool until consistency of unbeaten egg whites. Beat egg whites in small mixer bowl until frothy. Gradually beat in 2 tablespoons sugar, beating until mixture holds stiff peaks. Fold egg whites and whipped cream into gelatin. Pour into Baked Pastry Shell. Refrigerate at least 4 hours before serving.
           9-Inch Pie

TIPS • If gelatin-egg mixture should curdle, beat well with rotary beater until smooth.

     • Substitute 1 package (4½ oz.) frozen whipped topping for whipping cream.

GRASSHOPPER PIE

    3 cups miniature marshmallows
   ½ cup milk
   2 tablespoons crème de cocoa
   2 tablespoons green crème de menthe
   1 cup whipping cream, whipped
   1 (9-inch) chocolate Cookie Crumb Crust,
      below

1. Combine marshmallows and milk in large glass mixing bowl.

2. Microwave on HIGH for about 2 minutes or until marshmallows begin to puff; stir to blend. Stir in crème de cocoa and crème de menthe; mix well. Cool about 30 minutes or until consistency of unbeaten egg white. Fold whipped cream into cream mixture. Pour into crust. Refrigerate at least 4 hours or until ready to serve.   9-Inch Pie

TIPS • Garnish with whipped cream and chocolate curls.

     • Substitute 1 package (4½ oz.) frozen whipped topping for whipped cream.

     • Stir 4 to 5 drops green food coloring in with liqueurs for a richer green color.

Always cool before filling.

COOKIE CRUMB CRUST

   ⅓ cup butter or margarine
   ¼ cup sugar
  1½ cups crushed cookies

1. Place butter in 9-inch glass pie plate.

2. Microwave on ROAST for 1½ to 2 minutes or until melted. Stir in sugar and cookie crumbs; mix well. Press in bottom and sides of 9-inch glass pie plate.

3. Microwave on ROAST for 2½ to 3½ minutes or until set. Cool before filling.   9-inch Crumb Crust

TIP • Make 1½ cups crumbs from about 18 graham crackers, 36 vanilla wafers, 30 gingersnaps or 24 chocolate wafers.

BAKED PASTRY SHELL

1. Prepare favorite pie crust recipe or pie crust mix as directed on package. Line 9-inch glass pie plate. Flute edge; prick bottom and sides of crust with fork.

2. Microwave on ROAST for 7 to 9 minutes or until brown spots just begin to appear in crust. Cool.   9-inch Pastry Shell

TIPS • Enhance crust color. Mix 1 or 2 drops of yellow food coloring into water before adding it to dry ingredients.

     • Bring a commercially-prepared frozen uncooked pie shell to room temperature or until easy to handle. Transfer to glass pie plate. Microwave on ROAST for 5 to 6 minutes or until cooked.

Light chilled soufflé to old-fashioned applesauce — a microwave oven is truly versatile when it comes to desserts.

Fruit and "touchy" milk custards won't scorch — and what a relief — because microwaves cook from all directions, not just the bottom.

"Grey box" keys outline the major microwave techniques used in this chapter: very gentle heat for baked egg custard; low heat-and-stir cooking for soft egg or cream custards; super-fast cooking for tender juicy fruit desserts. Special dessert concoctions combine several different microwave techniques — results are delicious.

A microwave oven is a special help with individual fruits, too. It rehydrates dried fruits quickly; makes a peach easier to peel; heats half a grapefruit in its serving dish — even makes a lime, lemon or orange juicier. Seem almost magical? Try it.

Pictured clockwise from the left: Chocolate Mousse garnished with whipped cream, page 154; Trifle, page 150; Hot Pink Pears, page 152.

DESSERT/FRUIT/PUDDING CHAPTER CONTENTS

ONE-OF-A-KIND DESSERT KEY: This is a one-of-a-kind dessert recipe collection for microwave cooks who like to experiment. Basic cooking methods from a variety of chapters are used — shortcake, for example, is a quick bread; trifle has a cake base.

Check these selections to see how different microwave cooking techniques can operate to create delectable sweet treats. Then develop and adapt other recipes which will bring raves from friends and family.

Cake and soft custard microwave techniques combine to create this old English treat.

TRIFLE

    1 layer yellow cake from mix, page 140
    Vanilla Custard Sauce for Ice Cream
      (through Step 2), page 154
    1 jar (12 oz.) strawberry preserves
    1 cup whipping cream, whipped
    Sliced almonds

1. Cut cake into 1-inch cubes. Place half of cubes in 2-quart serving bowl. Pour half of Custard Sauce over cake. Spread half of preserves over top; repeat once. Chill 1 hour.

2. Garnish with whipped cream and sliced almonds.　　　About 8 Servings

TIP ● Substitute raspberry preserves for strawberry preserves.

Quick bread technique yields a classic dessert.

LAST MINUTE SHORTCAKE*

    1 cup unsifted all-purpose flour
    3 tablespoons sugar
    1 teaspoon baking powder
    ¼ teaspoon salt
    ¼ cup butter or margarine
    ⅓ cup milk
    1 egg
    Sweetened fruit
    Whipped cream

1. Combine flour, sugar, baking powder and salt in large mixing bowl. Cut in butter until crumbly. Measure milk in small bowl and beat in egg. Blend into flour mixture. Spoon into 4 or 5 individual glass custard cups.

2. Microwave on SIMMER for 3 minutes.

3. Microwave on HIGH for 2 to 3 minutes or until cake is no longer doughy.

4. Serve warm topped with sweetened fruit and whipped cream.　　　4 to 5 Servings

Always soften ice cream on low WARM.

ICE CREAM DESSERT-DRINK

    1 quart vanilla ice cream
    3 tablespoons rum
    3 tablespoons sweet vermouth

1. Place ice cream in medium glass mixing bowl. Cover with plastic wrap.

2. Microwave on WARM for 3 to 6 minutes or until softened. Blend in rum and vermouth. Pour into chilled stem glasses. Freeze for about 30 minutes or until desired consistency.　　　5 to 6 Servings

TIPS ● Make Grasshoppers. Substitute Crème de Menthe and white Crème de Cocoa for rum and sweet vermouth.

● Make Brandy Alexanders. Substitute brandy and Crème de Cocoa for rum and sweet vermouth.

Eggnog cooks on ROAST to prevent curdling.

EGGNOG HOLIDAY DESSERT

    2 cups commercial eggnog
    2 tablespoons cornstarch
    1 cup diced candied mixed fruit
    2 tablespoons rum or rum flavoring
    Yellow or white cake

1. Combine eggnog and cornstarch in medium mixing bowl; mix well.

2. Microwave on ROAST for 4 minutes; beat until smooth. Stir in fruit and rum; continue cooking on ROAST for 3 to 4 minutes. Spoon over cake.　　　About 2¼ cups

TIP ● Sauce thickens on standing. Microwave on REHEAT to warm and soften.

Use microwave techniques for softening cream cheese and reheating cake.

LAYERED CREAM TORTE

    1 box (11¼ oz.) frozen baked pound cake, thawed
    2 packages (3 oz. each) cream cheese
    ½ cup strawberry preserves
    2 tablespoons sliced almonds

1. Split cake in thirds horizontally. Place on glass platter; set aside. Place cheese in 2-cup glass measure.

2. Microwave on WARM for 3 to 3½ minutes or until softened. Beat cheese until smooth. Spread between cake layer. Spread jam over top of cake.

3. Microwave on REHEAT for 2 to 3 minutes or until heated through. Sprinkle with almonds and serve.　　　6 to 8 Servings

Steamed puddings cook with the cake technique.

CHERRY NUT HOLIDAY PUDDING*

- ½ **cup butter or margarine**
- ¾ **cup orange marmalade**
- 2 **eggs**
- 1 **teaspoon almond extract**
- 2¼ **cups unsifted all-purpose flour**
- 1 **teaspoon baking powder**
- ¼ **teaspoon soda**
- ¼ **teaspoon salt**
- ¼ **teaspoon cinnamon**
- ¼ **cup maraschino cherry juice**
- ½ **cup chopped pecans**
- ½ **cup maraschino cherries, drained and halved**

  Confectioner's Icing:
- 1½ **cups powdered sugar**
- 1 **teaspoon almond extract**
- 2 **tablespoons milk**

1. Cream butter and marmalade in large mixer bowl; beat in eggs and almond extract. Stir in dry ingredients alternately with maraschino cherry juice. Fold in pecans and maraschino cherries.

2. Spread batter into greased and floured 1½-quart glass casserole. Cover with glass lid or plastic wrap.

3. Microwave on SIMMER for 10 minutes.

4. Microwave on HIGH for 2 to 3 minutes or until toothpick inserted near center comes out clean. Remove cover; let stand 5 minutes; unmold. Glaze with Confectioner's Icing. Garnish with maraschino cherries and pecans. Serve with Orange Sauce page 131.

4. Confectioner's Icing: Combine powdered sugar, almond extract and milk; mix well. 8 to 10 Servings

Cooked food is usually heated on REHEAT – fast warming without further cooking.

HEATING CANNED PLUM PUDDING

1. Remove 1 can (15 oz.) plum pudding from can. Place on glass platter.

2. Microwave on REHEAT for 3 to 5 minutes or until heated through. Serve with rum or brandy-flavored vanilla sauce. 4 to 6 Servings

---

FRESH AND DRIED FRUIT DESSERT KEY:
Fruit desserts cook quickly, never scorch, on Microwave HIGH.

Fresh fruit microwaves well — holding shape and retaining full flavor.

Desserts in which fresh fruit must hold shape are usually cooked, uncovered, in a glass baking dish or casserole.

Sometimes it's convenient to arrange fresh fruit desserts on a glass or pottery platter, microwave and serve. DO NOT use dishes with gold, silver, platinum or other metal paint and trim — it darkens and/or permanently damages trim.

Soften dried fruit in a glass casserole with a fitted glass lid or tight covering of plastic wrap.

When a recipe calls for standing time, follow directions carefully so dessert is cooked through. This is especially important to assure soft stewed fruit made from dried fruit.

BAKED APPLES

- 4 **medium cooking apples, washed and cored**
- ¼ **cup packed brown sugar**
- 2 **tablespoons butter or margarine**
- **Cinnamon**
- **Sweet or sour cream**

1. Place apples in 2-quart (8 x 8) glass baking dish. Place 1 tablespoon brown sugar and 1 tablespoon butter in center of each apple. Sprinkle with cinnamon.

2. Microwave on HIGH for 8 to 9 minutes or until apples are tender. Serve warm with sweet or sour cream. 4 Servings

TIP ● If apples have been sitting at room temperature, cooking time will be slightly shorter.

Serve with whipped cream.

APPLE CRISP

- 6 **cups cooking apples, peeled, cored and sliced**
- ½ **cup unsifted all-purpose flour**
- ½ **cup quick-cooking rolled oats**
- ¾ **cup packed brown sugar**
- 1 **teaspoon cinnamon**
- ¼ **cup butter or margarine**

1. Place apple slices in 2-quart (8 x 8) glass baking dish. Combine flour, oats, sugar and cinnamon in medium mixing bowl. Cut in butter until crumbly. Sprinkle evenly over apples.

2. Microwave on HIGH for 14 to 16 minutes or until apples are tender. 5 to 6 Servings

APPLESAUCE

> 8 medium cooking apples, peeled, cored and quartered
> ½ cup water
> 1 cup sugar

1. Combine apples and water in 2-quart glass casserole. Cover with glass lid or plastic wrap.

2. Microwave on HIGH for 10 to 12 minutes or until apples are tender. Stir in sugar; let stand, covered, 2 to 3 minutes to dissolve sugar. Stir before serving.   About 6 Servings

Easier to eat with a fork.

HOT PINK PEARS *

> 6 ripe winter pears
> 6 whole cloves
> 1 cup sugar
> ½ cup sweet vermouth
> ¼ cup water
> ½ teaspoon red food coloring

1. Peel pears, leave stem. Stick 1 whole clove into each pear. Combine remaining ingredients in 1½-quart glass casserole. Add pears. Cover with glass lid or plastic wrap.

2. Microwave on HIGH for 6 minutes; baste. Turn pears over and continue cooking on HIGH for 6 to 8 minutes or until pears are tender. Serve in individual bowls.   6 Servings

TIPS • Garnish with whipped cream.
• May be served as accompaniment for pork roast.

Flame sauce and serve over ice cream.

BANANAS ROYALE

> 6 tablespoons butter or margarine
> 6 tablespoons packed brown sugar
> ¼ teaspoon cinnamon
> ¼ teaspoon nutmeg
> ¼ cup light cream
> 4 medium bananas, peeled
> ¼ cup brandy, rum or flavored liqueur
> Vanilla

1. Place butter in 9-inch round glass baking dish.

2. Microwave on ROAST for 2 minutes or until melted. Stir in brown sugar, cinnamon, nutmeg and cream. Slice bananas once lengthwise, then once crosswise, into butter mixture. Stir to coat.

3. Microwave on ROAST for about 4 minutes or until bubbly. Measure ¼ to ½ cup brandy into 1-cup glass measure.

4. Microwave on HIGH for 15 to 20 seconds or until warm. Pour over dessert and ignite. Serve immediately over ice cream.   4 to 8 Servings

Cover and standing time are very important when stewing dried fruit.

APRICOTS BAKED WITH RAISINS

> 1 package (8 oz.) dried apricots
> 1 cup raisins
> 1½ cups water
> ¼ cup sugar
> ¼ cup dry sherry or water
> 1 teaspoon lemon juice

1. Combine dried apricots and raisins with water and sugar in 1½-quart glass casserole or bowl. Cover with glass lid or plastic wrap.

2. Microwave on HIGH for 10 to 12 minutes. Let stand, covered, 30 minutes to absorb liquid. Blend in sherry and lemon juice. Chill, covered.
                About 3½ Cups Sauce

TIPS • Make a thinner sauce by adding another ½ cup water.
• Pour over ice cream or serve topped with orange flavored yogurt.

Serve with dab of whipped or sour cream.

SPICY PRUNES

> 2 cups water
> 1½ cups dried prunes
> ¼ cup packed brown sugar
> 1 stick cinnamon
> ¼ teaspoon allspice

1. Pour water into 1½-quart glass casserole. Cover with glass lid or plastic wrap.

2. Microwave on HIGH for 5 minutes. Stir in remaining ingredients; recover, and continue cooking on HIGH for 6 to 7 minutes or until fruit is tender. Let stand, covered, 30 minutes to rehydrate. Chill, covered, 4 hours or overnight. Remove cinnamon stick.   4 to 6 Servings

TIPS • Start with hot tap water and speed cooking time.
• Use this method to "plump" dried apricots or dried mixed fruit.

CANNED FRUIT DESSERT KEY: REHEAT is the microwave setting for distributing heat evenly without making cooked canned fruit mushy.

Cooking techniques for canned fruit desserts are similar to those for fresh fruits — check the Fresh and Dried Fruit Dessert Key on page 151 for directions.

MINCED ORANGE DESSERT

  1 **can (11 oz.) mandarin oranges, undrained**
  1 **can (21 oz.) mincemeat pie filling**
  1 **can (29 oz.) pear halves, drained**
  Vanilla ice cream

1. Combine oranges and pie filling in medium glass bowl; mix well.

2. Microwave on REHEAT for 6 to 7 minutes or until hot in center; stir well to blend.

3. Place pear halves, cut side up, on individual glass serving plates or in bowls. Spoon ice cream into center of each pear half. Spoon hot fruit sauce over each serving.　　　　　8 to 10 Servings

CHERRIES JUBILEE

  1 **can (21 oz.) cherry pie filling**
 ¼ **cup currant jelly**
  1 **teaspoon grated orange rind**
 ¼ **cup rum**
 ¼ **cup brandy**
  Vanilla ice cream

1. Combine cherry pie filling with jelly, orange rind and rum in medium glass bowl; stir to blend.

2. Microwave on REHEAT for 5 to 6 minutes or until heated in center; stir.

3. Measure brandy into 1-cup glass measure.

4. Microwave on HIGH for 15 to 20 seconds or until warm. Pour brandy over cherry sauce and ignite. Immediately spoon over ice cream.
　　　　　About 4 Cups Sauce

PEACH ALMONDINE

  1 **tablespoon water**
 ¼ **cup sugar**
  1 **package (3 oz.) slivered almonds.**
  1 **can (29 oz.) peach halves, drained**
  1 **teaspoon lemon juice**
  2 **tablespoons dry sherry**
 ½ **teaspoon cinnamon**
  Vanilla ice cream

1. Combine water and sugar in 9-inch glass pie plate; mix well. Stir in almonds.

2. Microwave on ROAST for 2½ to 3 minutes or until almonds are glazed. Pour on wax paper to cool; set aside. Place peach halves, cut side up, in 8-inch round glass baking dish. Combine lemon juice, sherry and cinnamon in 1-cup glass measure; mix well. Pour equal amounts of sherry mixture on each peach half.

3. Microwave on REHEAT for 3 to 4 minutes or until very warm. Transfer warm peach halves to individual serving dishes. Place a scoop of vanilla ice cream in center of each peach half. Crumbled almond mixture on top of ice cream and serve.
　　　　　About 6 Servings

MIXED FRUIT AMBROSIA

 ½ **cup flaked coconut**
  2 **tablespoons graham cracker crumbs**
  1 **can (20 oz.) pineapple chunks, drained**
  1 **can (16 oz.) sliced peaches, drained**
  1 **can (11 oz.) mandarin oranges, drained**
  6 **maraschino cherries, halved**

1. Combine all ingredients in 2-quart glass casserole; mix well.

2. Microwave on REHEAT for 6 to 7 minutes or until hot.　　　　　6 to 8 Servings

---

SOFT CUSTARD DESSERT KEY: Soft custards and custard-base desserts call for eggs. So for the most part, cook on Microwave SIMMER to develop smooth texture and prevent curdling.

Scorching isn't a problem in a microwave oven because microwaves cook from all directions, not just the bottom of the dish.

Cook custard desserts in glass or pottery serving bowls or casseroles — without gold or other metal trim.

Sometimes it's convenient to measure, mix and cook custards right in a glass measure. Ingredients, however, should not fill the measure more than half full.

Stirring is important because the microwave oven cooks quickly. Recipes call for stirring custard during cooking so it stays creamy and lump-free.

Directions for stirring or beating after cooking make soft custards even smoother.

Dress up custards with fresh or cooked fruit slices, coconut or cookie crumbs.

Custard-base desserts use a soft custard plus other ingredients to develop light and creamy mixtures which are often served chilled and garnished with fruit and/or whipped cream.

TAPIOCA PUDDING *

  2 **cups milk**
 ¼ **cup sugar**
2½ **tablespoons quick-cooking tapioca**
 ¼ **teaspoon salt**
  2 **eggs, separated**
  2 **tablespoons sugar**
  1 **teaspoon vanilla**

1. Combine milk, ¼ cup sugar, tapioca, salt and egg yolks in 4-cup glass measure; mix well.

2. Microwave on SIMMER for 8 minutes. Stir and continue cooking on SIMMER for 6 to 7 minutes or until mixture boils.

3. Beat egg whites in small mixer bowl until frothy. Gradually add 2 tablespoons sugar, beating until mixture forms soft peaks. Beat in vanilla. Fold egg white mixture into pudding. Serve warm or cold.
　　　　　4 to 6 Servings

Microwave the custard for most any cooked custard ice cream recipe – use this one as a guide.

VANILLA CUSTARD ICE CREAM*

      2 **cups milk**
      2 **eggs**
    ¾ **cup sugar**
    ⅛ **teaspoon salt**
      1 **tablespoon vanilla**
      2 **cups light cream**

1. Combine milk, eggs, sugar and salt in 4-cup glass measure. Beat well with rotary beater.

2. Microwave on SIMMER for 8 minutes. Stir and continue cooking on SIMMER for 7 to 8 minutes or until mixture comes to a boil and thickens; stir well. Cool completely. Stir in vanilla.

3. Prepare ice cream freezer according to manufacturer's directions. Pour prepared custard into freezer along with cream. Freeze as directed by manufacturer.   2 Quarts Ice Cream

TIPS ● Make Chocolate Custard Ice Cream. Increase sugar to 1 cup. Add 2 envelopes premelted chocolate to custard sauce before cooking.

      ● Make Strawberry Ice Cream. Wash, hull and crush 2 cups (1 pt.) fresh strawberries. Stir in ¼ cup sugar. Omit vanilla from custard sauce. Add sugared berries to custard sauce with cream.

Soft custard bases create creamy chilled desserts.

CHOCOLATE MOUSSE*

      2 **squares (1 oz. each) semi-sweet chocolate**
    ⅓ **cup sugar**
      1 **envelope unflavored gelatin**
    ⅛ **teaspoon salt**
      3 **eggs, separated**
      1 **cup milk**
      1 **teaspoon vanilla**
    ⅓ **cup sugar**
      1 **cup whipping cream, whipped**

1. Place chocolate in large glass mixing bowl.

2. Microwave on HIGH for 2 to 3 minutes or until melted. Stir in ⅓ cup sugar, gelatin, salt, egg yolks and milk.

3. Microwave on SIMMER for 5 minutes. Stir and continue cooking on SIMMER for 2 to 3 minutes or until slightly thickened. Add vanilla; mix well. Refrigerate until cool.

4. Beat egg whites in small mixer bowl until soft peaks form. Gradually beat in ⅓ cup sugar until stiff peaks form, Fold egg whites and whipped cream into chocolate mixture. Spoon mixture into individual dishes or 9 to 10-inch chocolate cookie crumb crust. Chill about 3 hours or until set.   6 to 8 Servings

FRUIT MAGIC

Rewarm desserts made ahead of time quickly on Microwave REHEAT . Cover to speed heating. Check center for warmness.

Peaches peel easily after cooking on HIGH for about ½ minute, then standing several minutes.

Get more juice when you squeeze a lemon, orange or lime. Microwave unpeeled fruit on HIGH for about ½ minute. Fruit sizes vary time slightly.

Heat half a breakfast grapefruit in an uncovered sauce dish (without silver or other metal trim) on Microwave HIGH for 1½ to 2 minutes.

BAKED CUSTARD DESSERT KEY: DEFROST is the key microwave setting for baked custards and desserts with baked custard bases.

Eggs are the crucial ingredient — slow gentle heat keeps them from curdling this type of custard which is not stirred during cooking.

Mix and cook baked custards in glass serving casseroles or bowls without silver, gold, platinum or other metal trim. Only baked rice custards need a cover.

One-serving baked custards may be cooked in individual glass custard cups for make-ahead treats.

Remove individual custards from the oven as they finish cooking. Volume in each cup may vary and cause some custards to microwave faster than others.

If recipe calls for a cover, use a fitted glass lid or tightly-tucked plastic wrap.

Test for doneness as directed in each recipe.

Baked custards are not stirred – DEFROST (2) setting keeps them smooth.

SWEDISH RICE PUDDING

      2 **cups milk**
      2 **eggs, slightly beaten**
    ½ **cup sugar**
      1 **teaspoon vanilla**
    ¼ **teaspoon cinnamon**
    ½ **cup quick-cooking rice**
    ½ **cup raisins**

1. Measure milk in 4-cup glass measure.

2. Microwave on HIGH for 5 to 5½ minutes or until hot. Combine eggs, sugar, vanilla and cinnamon in 1½-quart glass casserole; mix well. Stir in rice, raisins and hot milk. Cover with glass lid or plastic wrap.

3. Microwave on DEFROST for 12 to 13 minutes or until set. Let stand, covered, 5 minutes before serving.   5 to 6 Servings

TIP ● Cover is used on rice pudding so rice stays soft and light.

Several microwave techniques combine to enhance this baked-custard-base dessert.

APRICOT CHEESECAKE

- ¼ **cup butter or margarine**
- ⅔ **cup graham cracker crumbs (about 12 crackers)**
- 2 **tablespoons all-purpose flour**
- 2 **tablespoons sugar**
- ¼ **teaspoon cinnamon**
- 1 **package (8 oz.) cream cheese**
- 1 **can (16 oz.) apricot halves, undrained**
- ⅓ **cup sugar**
- 2 **eggs**
- 1 **tablespoon lemon juice**
- 1 **can (16 oz.) apricot halves, undrained**
- 1 **envelope unflavored gelatin**

1. Place butter in 8-inch round glass baking dish.

2. Microwave on ROAST for about 1½ minutes or until melted. Stir in cracker crumbs, flour, sugar and cinnamon. Press mixture over bottom and halfway up sides of dish; set aside.

3. Place cream cheese in medium glass mixing bowl.

4. Microwave on WARM for 3 to 5 minutes or until cheese is softened; beat until light and fluffy.

5. Drain 1 can apricots and reserve juice. Puree apricot halves in blender or food mill. Stir into cream cheese along with sugar, eggs and lemon juice; beat until smooth. Pour into prepared crust.

6. Microwave on DEFROST for 23 to 25 minutes or until almost set in center. Chill 1 hour.

7. Drain second can of apricots and reserve juice. Arrange apricots on cheesecake. Pour gelatin and apricot juice from both cans in 4-cup glass measure; let stand 5 minutes.

8. Microwave on HIGH for 3 to 3½ minutes or until gelatin is dissolved; stir. Chill until consistency of unbeaten egg white, about 30 minutes. Spoon over cheesecake. Refrigerate about 4 hours before serving.　　　　10 to 12 Servings

Baked custards need gentle no-stir cooking for smooth texture.

BAKED CUSTARD

- 1¾ **cups milk**
- ¼ **cup sugar**
- 3 **eggs**
- ¼ **teaspoon salt**
- ½ **teaspoon vanilla**
- **Nutmeg**

1. Combine all ingredients, except nutmeg, in 4-cup measure. Beat well with rotary beater. Pour into four 6-ounce glass custard cups, filling each ¾ full. Sprinkle with nutmeg.

2. Microwave on DEFROST for 15 to 16 minutes or until knife inserted near center comes out clean. Let stand 5 minutes before serving.　　4 Custards

TIP ● Custards may cook at slightly different rates because amount of custard in each cup tends to vary. Remove custards from oven as they finish cooking.

PUDDING AND PIE FILLING MIX KEY: Use HIGH to microwave most pudding and pie filling mixes because a stabilizer in the mix keeps the pudding smooth and creamy.

ROAST is used for dry custard mixes with higher egg content. These mixtures tend to separate if cooked too quickly.

Prepare mixes as directed on packages.

Microwave any pudding mix in a glass container that holds at least twice the volume of the custard ingredients.

HOW TO COOK PUDDING AND PIE FILLING MIX

- Prepare mix as directed on package; mix well.
- Microwave as directed in chart.
- Pour into serving dishes.
- Chill to set.

DRY MIX	SIZE	GLASS CONTAINER	SETTING	MINUTES
PUDDING AND PIE FILLING MIX				
4 Servings	3¼-oz. pkg.	4-cup measure	HIGH	6 to 7
6 Servings	5½-oz. pkg.	1½-qt. measure	HIGH	8 to 9
GOLDEN EGG CUSTARD MIX				
4 Servings	3-oz. pkg.	4-cup measure	ROAST	10 to 11

Marvelous complement to American's sweet tooth — a microwave oven!

Discover what fun it is to make rich bars and big thin crunchy cookies, delectable candy or sweet nutritious snacks.

Two major microwave techniques are used in this chapter. One combines flour, sugar, shortening and flavorings into tasty cookies. The other develops syrup-y sugar mixtures that make great candy or snacks.

Both methods are simple enough so youngsters can enjoy making treats from this collection. **Do read the "grey box" keys** before starting a recipe.

Try cookies from a favorite recipe or bar and cookies from package mixes in the microwave oven. Use the chart on page 158.

Pictured top to bottom: Caramel Apples, page 161;
Cookie Bars from a Mix, page 158; Crystallized Orange
Nuts, page 160.

COOKIES, CANDIES & SNACKS

COOKIE/CANDY/SNACK
CHAPTER CONTENTS

COOKIE KEY: Bar cookies and individual cookies usually start cooking on Microwave ROAST to melt and blend shortening and sugar. Bars finish cooking on SIMMER so dense center of mixture cooks through without overcooking in spots.

Recapture the "just baked" flavor of stored or frozen individual bars and cookies, too. Place on a napkin and microwave on REHEAT for about 15 seconds if cookies are at room temperature, about 30 seconds if frozen. Time will vary according to fat and sugar content in the bar or cookie.

Bar cookies cooked in a microwave oven are a big time-saver because they cook so much faster than in a conventional oven.

Greasing a baking dish is the cook's decision — either way works; but do not add flour be-

cause it will combine with the grease to form a layer on the bottom of the cookie.

Many microwave-cooked individual cookies spread to big thin crunchy wafers — like those grandma always had in her cookie jar. Some are great dunkers.

Microwave individual cookies on wax paper. Space 1 to 2 inches apart. Experiment with one or two to find the best time and spacing. Do not remove cookies from the paper until cool and firm or they will break.

Commercial slice-and-bake refrigerator roll cookies are not successful in a microwave oven.

These recipes have been developed especially for microwave cooking. But next time you bake homemade cookies the conventional way, try a few in the microwave oven.

HOW TO MICROWAVE COOKIES AND BARS

• Prepare mix as directed on package.

• Grease baking dish, if desired, but do not flour as it will layer on bottom of bar.

• Microwave bars, uncovered, in a glass baking dish.

• Cool and cut bars as directed on package.

• Frost or glaze before cutting. Bars have a slightly irregular top.

• Mix cookies according to package or recipe directions.

• Microwave cookies on wax or parchment paper placed on oven floor.

• Allow enough space between cookies because they spread during cooking.

• Allow cookies to cool on wax paper; remove, and store.

COOKIE OR BAR	PACKAGE SIZE	CONTAINER	FIRST SETTING	MINUTES	SECOND SETTING	MINUTES
BROWNIE MIX*	16 oz.	glass (8 x 8)	SIMMER	7	HIGH	3 to 4
	22.5-oz.	glass (12 x 7)				4 to 5
DATE BAR MIX:	14 oz.	2-cup glass				
Filling		measure	HIGH	2		
Bars*		glass (8 x 8)	SIMMER	12	HIGH	2 to 3
PEANUT BUTTER CHOCOLATE CHIP BAR MIX*	21-oz.	glass (12 x 7)	SIMMER	8	HIGH	4 to 5
CHOCOLATE COOKIE MIX	10-oz.	parchment or wax paper				
4 Cookies			SIMMER	2 to 2½		
6 Cookies				3 to 3½		
12 Cookies				5 to 5½		
HOMEMADE COOKIES		parchment or wax paper				
4 Cookies			SIMMER	2 to 3		
6 Cookies				3 to 4		
12 Cookies				5 to 6		

These cookies shouldn't brown – and they won't in a microwave oven.

SURPRISE TEACAKES

> 1 **cup butter or margarine**
> 1 **egg**
> 1 **teaspoon vanilla**
> ½ **cup powdered sugar**
> 2⅓ **cups unsifted all-purpose flour**
> 1 **cup finely chopped nuts**
> 1 **package (5¾ oz.) milk chocolate kisses**
> **Powdered sugar**

1. Place butter in small glass mixing bowl.

2. Microwave on ROAST for about 1½ minutes or until softened. Beat in egg, vanilla and powdered sugar until light and fluffy. Blend in flour and nuts. Make teacakes by shaping 1 tablespoon dough around 1 unwrapped chocolate kiss. Arrange 12 teacakes on wax paper in oven, 1 inch apart.

3. Microwave on SIMMER for 5 to 6 minutes or until no longer doughy. Roll in powdered sugar and cool.   About 36 Cookies

TIPS ● Candied cherries can be substituted for chocolate kisses.

  ● If dough has been refrigerated, increase cooking time about 1 minute.

SUGAR COOKIES

> 1 **cup butter or margarine**
> 1 **cup sugar**
> 2 **eggs**
> 3 **cups unsifted all-purpose flour**
> 1 **teaspoon cream of tartar**
> ½ **teaspoon soda**
> ½ **teaspoon salt**
> 1 **teaspoon almond extract**
>   *1 tsp vanilla*

1. Cream butter in large mixer bowl until fluffy. Beat in sugar and eggs until well blended. Stir in remaining ingredients and chill. Shape into 1-inch balls; place on wax paper, 1 inch apart; flatten with glass dipped in water, then sugar. Place cookies on wax paper in the oven.

2. Microwave on SIMMER until tops have set appearance:

4 cookies — 2 to 3 minutes
6 cookies — 3 to 4 minutes
12 cookies — 5 to 6 minutes

Cool on wax paper; remove, and store in tightly covered container.   About 48 Cookies

TIPS ● Substitute 2 teaspoons anise seed or 1 teaspoon anise extract for almond extract.

  ● Form dough into 2 rolls, 2 inches in diameter, and freeze. Slice ¼ inch thick and place on wax paper. Microwave on SIMMER — 9 cookies about 4 to 5 minutes.

Pictured clockwise around the plate: No Fail Fudge, page 160; Sugar Cookies, this page; Brownies, this page; Fudge Frosting, page 143; in the center, Surprise Teacakes, this page.

Freeze for later – defrost quickly on REHEAT.

BROWNIES*

> 2 **squares or envelopes unsweetened chocolate**
> ⅓ **cup butter or margarine**
> 1 **cup sugar**
> 2 **eggs**
> 1 **cup unsifted all-purpose flour**
> ¼ **teaspoon baking powder**
> ¼ **teaspoon salt**
> ½ **teaspoon vanilla**
> ½ **cup chopped nuts**

1. Combine chocolate and butter in medium glass mixing bowl.

2. Microwave on ROAST for 1½ to 2 minutes or until melted. Stir in sugar; beat in eggs. Stir in remaining ingredients. Spread batter into 2-quart (8 x 8) glass baking dish.

3. Microwave on SIMMER for 7 minutes.

4. Microwave on HIGH for 3 to 4 minutes or until puffed and dry on top. Cool until set; cut into bars.
                                        24 Bars

TIP ● Top brownie squares with ice cream and chocolate sauce for a quick dessert.

CANDY KEY: Microwave candy on ROAST — a setting that allows sugar syrup to quickly boil and blend into a candy, yet needs little watching.

Mix and cook ingredients in a buttered glass mixing bowl or 4-cup glass measure.

Bowl or dish must be two to three times as large as the volume of the candy ingredients so candy syrup will not boil over.

Cover candy during cooking when called for in the recipe. Use a glass plate or stretch plastic wrap tautly across the bowl or glass measure; pierce plastic wrap so steam escapes during cooking.

There is no need to worry that candy will scorch because microwaves cook from all sides, not just the bottom.

Candy syrups are usually stirred once during cooking so heat is equalized and candy cooks smooth.

Do WATCH CANDY CLOSELY because a microwave oven cooks fast. A candy thermometer should register 236°F. (soft ball stage).

DO NOT put a candy thermometer into a microwave oven or it will be damaged.

Candy cooked in a microwave oven needs little stirring.

BUTTERMILK PRALINES*

- 2 cups sugar
- 1 teaspoon soda
- 1 cup buttermilk
- ¾ cup butter or margarine
- 1 teaspoon vanilla
- 2 cups pecan halves

1. Combine all ingredients, except vanilla and pecans, in buttered large glass mixing bowl. Cover with plastic wrap.

2. Microwave on ROAST for 15 minutes. Stir and continue cooking on ROAST for 13 to 15 minutes or until a soft ball forms in cold water. Add vanilla and beat until mixture forms soft peaks. Stir in pecans. Pour into buttered 2-quart (12 x 7) glass baking dish. Cool until firm; cut into pieces.

40 to 48 Praline pieces

TIP ● Individual candies may be dropped from a teaspoon onto wax paper.

Use an oblong dish so nuts can be turned and coated with glaze more easily.

CRYSTALLIZED ORANGE NUTS*

- ¼ cup orange juice
- 1 cup sugar
- 2 cups pecan halves

1. Combine orange juice and sugar in 2-quart (12 x 7) glass baking dish; mix well. Stir in pecans.

2. Microwave on ROAST for 6 minutes. Stir and continue cooking on ROAST for 8 to 10 minutes or until syrup crystallizes. Spread and separate glazed nuts on buttered cookie sheet to cool.

2 Cups Nuts

NO FAIL FUDGE*

- 3 cups sugar
- ¾ cup butter or margarine
- 1 can (5 oz.) evaporated milk
- 1 package (12 oz.) semi-sweet chocolate pieces
- 1 jar (10 oz.) marshmallow creme
- 1 cup chopped nuts
- 1 teaspoon vanilla

1. Combine sugar, butter and milk in buttered large glass mixing bowl. Cover with plastic wrap.

2. Microwave on ROAST for 10 minutes. Stir and continue cooking on ROAST for 5 to 6 minutes or until mixture forms a soft ball in cold water. Stir in chocolate pieces until melted. Fold in marshmallow creme, nuts and vanilla.

3. Pour into buttered 3-quart (13 x 9) pan. Chill until firm; cut into squares. 72 Fudge Squares

No scorching in a microwave.

TOFFEE PIECES

- 10 graham cracker squares
- ½ cup butter or margarine
- ¾ cup packed brown sugar
- ¼ cup chopped nuts
- 1 package (6 oz.) semi-sweet chocolate pieces

1. Place crackers on bottom of buttered 2-quart (12 x 7) glass baking dish; set aside. Combine butter and brown sugar in 4-cup glass measure.

2. Microwave on ROAST for about 2 minutes or until butter is melted. Stir in nuts. Pour syrup over crackers.

3. Microwave on ROAST for 4 to 5 minutes or until bubbly. Top with chocolate pieces and continue cooking on ROAST for about 1½ minutes or until chocolate is softened. Spread chocolate evenly over top. Chill for about 30 minutes or until cool; cut into bars. About 24 Bars

CARAMEL APPLES*

 1 package (14 oz.) caramels
 2 tablespoons hot water
 6 medium apples
 6 wooden sticks

1. Place unwrapped caramels in buttered deep medium-size glass bowl. Add water. Cover with plastic wrap.

2. Microwave on ROAST for 3 minutes. Stir and continue cooking on ROAST for about 2 minutes or until melted.

3. Skewer each apple with wooden sticks. Dip each apple in melted caramel mixture; turn to coat evenly. Place dipped apples on buttered cookie sheet or buttered wax paper.   6 Apples

TIPS • If caramel mixture thickens while dipping apples, return to oven and re-soften, covered, on ROAST

• Buttering cookie sheet or wax paper keeps caramel from sticking to cooling surface and pulling off apple.

GRANOLA*

 3 cups quick-cooking rolled oats
 1 cup shredded coconut
 ¾ cup wheat germ
 ¾ cup chopped pecans
 ¾ cup soybeans
 ½ cup sunflower seeds
 ⅓ cup sesame seeds
 ⅓ cup honey
 ⅓ cup cooking oil
 ¾ teaspoon salt
 ½ teaspoon vanilla

1. Combine all ingredients in large mixing bowl; mix well. Pour into 3-quart (13 x 9) glass baking dish.

2. Microwave on ROAST for 10 minutes. Stir and continue cooking on ROAST for 5 minutes. Stir again and continue cooking on ROAST for 5 to 6 minutes or until slightly crisp and flavors blend. Cool. Serve with milk.   About 8 Cups Granola

No worry about marshmallow scorching.

KRISPIE MARSHMALLOW TREATS*

 ¼ cup butter or margarine
 5 cups miniature or 40 large marshmallows
 5 cups crispy rice cereal

1. Place butter in 1½-quart (10 x 6) glass baking dish.

2. Microwave on ROAST for about 1½ minutes or until melted. Stir in marshmallows.

3. Microwave on ROAST for 1 minute. Stir and continue cooking on ROAST for about 1½ minutes or until marshmallows are softened. Stir until smooth. Mix in cereal. Press into baking dish. Cool until set; cut into squares. 24 to 30 Krispie Squares.

Make popcorn using a conventional method.

POPCORN: Cooking popcorn in a microwave oven is not recommended. There are too many variables — things such as time, temperature and age of popcorn.

Regardless of popcorn age, microwaves pop too few kernels to make the technique successful. Prolonged cooking does not yield more popped corn, but can cause fire or make the cooking dish too hot to handle and even break.

Never attempt to pop corn in a paper bag. Oil plus extended cooking can cause smoking and, eventually, fire.

Make tiny balls, wrap in plastic wrap and hang on the Christmas tree.

POPCORN BALLS*

 ⅓ cup light corn syrup
 ⅓ cup water
 1 cup sugar
 1 teaspoon salt
 ¼ cup butter or margarine
 1 teaspoon vanilla
 7 cups popped corn

1. Combine syrup, water, sugar, salt and butter in buttered 4-cup glass measure. Cover with plastic wrap.

2. Microwave on ROAST for 8 minutes. Stir and continue cooking on ROAST for 4 minutes. Stir and continue cooking on ROAST for 4 to 4½ minutes or until candy forms a hard ball (250°F.) in cold water. Stir in vanilla. Pour in thin stream over popped corn in large buttered bowl; mix well. Butter hands and shape into balls.   10 to 12 Balls

TIP • Popping corn is not a recommended microwave technique. Use a conventional method.

A freezer is one of the best things that's happened to busy modern homemakers — and a microwave oven is the perfect complement. Food defrosts and heats, defrosts and cooks or simply thaws in much less time that it does at room temperature or in a refrigerator. **See the "grey box" keys for tips.**

Many commercially frozen foods microwave right in their own cartons or trays. Homecooked food stays fresh and appetizing until ready to eat. Freeze in individual servings or family-meal quantities. Use the example recipes in this chapter as guides for other freezer-to-table foods from the supermarket or home freezer.

Pictured: Commercial and "made-at-home" frozen foods.

FREEZER TO TABLE CHAPTER CONTENTS

PRECOOKED FROZEN FOOD KEY:

Precooked frozen foods in this section range from commercially blanched vegetables, with or without instant-mix sauces, through homemade cooked main dishes and fried chicken. Thawing and heating is the technique used.

As with conventional food preparation, ingredients are a guide for freezer to table microwave cooking. So are the volume or amount of food to be thawed and heated, the density or compactness and whether the mixture includes a sauce.

Many precooked foods without critical ingredients thaw and heat quickly on REHEAT.

Precooked individual foods and main dish mixtures with mushrooms, cheese, sour cream and/or eggs thaw and heat on ROAST to prevent "popping," overcooking or separation.

Foods such as pizza and egg rolls which have crusts will retain a soft texture when cooked in the microwave oven.

Large volumes and/or quite dense precooked foods thaw on DEFROST until icy in the center, then usually heat on a higher setting for fastest to-table service. For example, gentle defrosting of large casserole dishes prevents overcooking at edges. Stirring is often called for to distribute heat evenly.

Note that volume, density and sauces may make similar foods vary in thawing and heating time as much as 5 to 10 minutes — even when these foods microwave at the same setting.

Use package labels on commercially frozen food to decide what microwave technique to follow. "From scratch" recipes and charts in other chapters may be used to figure out microwave oven settings for thawing and heating commercially prepared products.

Packages also instruct the user to "heat" precooked food and "cook" uncooked food. Check ingredient lists for "critical" ingredients before deciding on the thaw-heat setting to use.

Some frozen meals include a bread roll. Remove roll from tray before cooking meal. Return to oven during last 20 seconds of cooking.

Most commercially frozen food can be heated in its aluminum foil or plastic tray. Foil trays must be no more than ¾ inch high. Remove cover from tray; then slip food back into its carton or cover it with plastic wrap.

If food is placed in a cooking or serving dish, use glass or pottery without silver or other metal trim. Use a dish about the same size as the tray so sauces do not dehydrate.

Follow standing time directions to assure complete heating — a process that continues after food comes from oven. Stir when called for to distribute heat.

Different brands of frozen foods vary in size so heating times may vary slightly. Check food at lowest time given.

FROZEN EGG ROLL APPETIZERS

Remove 6 ounces frozen Egg Rolls from carton. Place on 8-inch glass pie plate or serving dish (without metal trim). Microwave on ROAST for 2½ to 3 minutes or until hot. Let stand 1 minute.

FROZEN BREADED FISH STICKS

Arrange frozen Fish Sticks on glass or pottery dinner or serving plate (without metal trim). Microwave on REHEAT until fish is hot and flakes easily when lifted with a fork near center — 4 Fish Sticks, 2 to 3 minutes; 6 Fish Sticks, 3 to 4 minutes; 8 Fish Sticks, 4 to 5 minutes; 12 Fish Sticks, 5 to 6 minutes.

FROZEN BREADED FISH PATTIES OR FILLETS

Arrange patties or fillets on glass dinner or serving plate (without metal trim). Microwave on REHEAT until fish is hot and flakes easily when lifted near center with a fork — 1 patty or fillet, 1½ to 2 minutes; 2 patties or fillets, 2½ to 3 minutes; 4 patties or fillets, 3½ to 4 minutes; 6 patties or fillets, 4 to 4½ minutes.

FROZEN FRIED CHICKEN

Heat either a frozen home-cooked 2½ to 3 pound cut-up fryer or a 32-ounce commercially frozen package of cooked chicken pieces. Place chicken pieces in 2-quart (12 x 7) glass baking dish. Microwave on REHEAT for 10 to 12 minutes or until hot. Let stand 3 minutes.

FROZEN COOKED MEAT SLICES

Place frozen meat slices on glass dinner plate or platter (without metal trim). Cover with plastic wrap. Microwave on REHEAT until hot — 1 slice, 30 to 40 seconds; 4 slices, 2 to 2½ minutes; 8 slices, 3 to 3½ minutes. Let stand, covered, 2 to 3 minutes. Note that thickness of meat slice and kind of meat make heating time vary. Use these times as guides.

FROZEN CORN DOGS

Remove frozen Corn Dogs from plastic wrap. Place in glass baking dish and microwave on ROAST until hot — 2 Corn Dogs, 2 to 2½ minutes; 4 Corn Dogs, 3 to 4 minutes.

FROZEN WIENERS

Remove frozen wieners from package. Place on glass plate. Microwave on REHEAT until hot — 2 wieners, 1 to 1½ minutes; 4 wieners, 2 to 2½ minutes; 6 wieners, 2½ to 3 minutes.

FROZEN HAM TV DINNER

Remove cover from 10½-ounce dinner. Leave food in foil tray if it is no more than ¾ inch high; slip back in carton or cover with plastic wrap. Microwave on REHEAT for 7 to 8 minutes or until hot. Let stand, covered, 2 to 3 minutes.

FROZEN SWISS STEAK TV DINNER

Remove foil cover from 10-ounce dinner. Leave food in foil tray if no more than ¾ inch high; slip back in carton or cover with plastic wrap. Microwave on ROAST for 8 to 10 minutes. Let stand, covered, 2 to 3 minutes.

FROZEN TURKEY TV DINNER

Remove foil cover from 19-ounce dinner. Leave food in foil tray if no more than ¾ inch high; slip back in carton or cover with plastic wrap. Microwave on REHEAT for 10 to 12 minutes. Let stand, covered, 2 to 3 minutes.

HOMEMADE FROZEN MAIN DISHES

Unwrap frozen main dish mixture and place in glass casserole or baking dish. Cover with glass lid or plastic wrap.

Microwave 2 individual (4 oz.) dishes on REHEAT for 7 to 10 minutes; let stand, covered, 3 minutes. Microwave 1-quart casserole on DEFROST for 8 minutes; then REHEAT for 12 to 14 minutes. Let stand, covered, 5 minutes.

Microwave 1½-quart casserole on DEFROST for 10 minutes; then REHEAT for 15 to 18 minutes. Let stand, covered, 5 minutes.

Microwave 2-quart casserole on DEFROST for 12 minutes; then REHEAT for 23 to 28 minutes; let stand, covered, 5 minutes. Stir 1 to 2-quart main dishes halfway through final cooking period.

FROZEN BEEF ENCHILADAS

Remove frozen Beef Enchiladas with Chili Gravy from plastic pouch. Place in 2-quart (8 x 8) glass baking dish. Cover with plastic wrap. Microwave on ROAST until hot — 12 ounces, 8 to 9 minutes; 22 ounces, 18 to 20 minutes. Let stand, covered, 3 minutes.

FROZEN SALISBURY STEAK *

Remove 32 ounces frozen Salisbury Steak with gravy from carton and metal container. Place in 2-quart (12 x 7) glass baking dish. Cover with plastic wrap. Microwave on ROAST for 15 minutes; turn over, and rearrange. Recover and continue cooking on ROAST for 12 to 15 minutes or until hot. Let stand, covered, 3 minutes.

FROZEN SHRIMP NEWBURG*

Remove 6½ ounces frozen Shrimp Newburg from plastic pouch. Place in 1-quart glass casserole. Cover with glass lid or plastic wrap. Microwave on ROAST for 5 minutes; stir. Recover, and continue cooking on ROAST 2 to 3 minutes or until hot. Let stand, covered, 3 minutes.

FROZEN SPAGHETTI SAUCE*

Remove 15 ounces frozen Spaghetti Sauce from plastic pouch. Place in 1-quart glass casserole. Cover with glass lid or plastic wrap. Microwave on REHEAT for 5 minutes; stir. Recover, and continue cooking on ROAST 3 to 5 minutes or until hot. Let stand, covered, 3 minutes before serving.

FROZEN STUFFED CABBAGE ROLLS

Remove 14 ounces frozen Stuffed Cabbage Rolls from foil container. Place in 1-quart glass casserole. Cover with glass lid or plastic wrap. Microwave on REHEAT for 11 to 12 minutes or until hot. Let stand, covered, 3 minutes.

FROZEN TURKEY TETRAZZINI*

Remove 12 ounces frozen turkey Tetrazzini from plastic pouch. Place in 1-quart glass casserole. Cover with glass lid or plastic wrap. Microwave on ROAST for 6 minutes; stir. Recover, and continue cooking on ROAST for 5 to 6 minutes or until hot. Let stand, covered, 3 minutes.

FROZEN WELSH RAREBIT*

Remove 10 ounces frozen Welsh Rarebit from plastic pouch. Place in 1-quart glass casserole. Cover with glass lid or plastic wrap. Microwave on ROAST for 4 minutes. Stir; recover, and continue cooking on ROAST for 2 to 3 minutes or until hot. Let stand, covered, 3 minutes.

FROZEN RICE OR PASTA DISHES

Place pouch of frozen rice or pasta mixture in glass casserole or baking dish. Slit top of pouch. Microwave mixtures with cheese, sour cream, eggs or cream on ROAST; others on REHEAT — 8 ounces Macaroni and Cheese, ROAST for 6 to 8 minutes; 22 ounces Lasagna, ROAST for 14 to 16 minutes; 14 ounces Spaghetti and Meat Sauce, REHEAT for 7 to 8 minutes; 12 ounces brown or white rice, REHEAT for 8 to 9 minutes. Let stand, covered, 2 to 5 minutes, depending on amount of food.

FROZEN SOUPS

Remove 8 ounces frozen soup from plastic pouch. Place in 1-quart glass casserole. Cover with glass lid or plastic wrap. Microwave on REHEAT for 4 to 6 minutes or until hot. Let stand, covered, 3 minutes.

FROZEN BEEF STEW

Remove 10 ounces frozen Beef Stew from plastic pouch. Place in 1-quart glass casserole. Cover with glass lid or plastic wrap. Microwave on REHEAT for 7 to 8 minutes or until hot. Let stand, covered, 3 minutes.

FROZEN CHUCK WAGON SANDWICH

Remove 2 (9 oz.) frozen Chuck Wagon sandwiches from carton and foil wrap. Place on paper towel or napkin. Microwave on ROAST for 3 to 3½ minutes or until warm.

FROZEN AU GRATIN POTATOES*

Remove 11½ ounces frozen Au Gratin Potatoes from plastic pouch. Place in 1-quart glass casserole. Cover with glass lid or plastic wrap. Microwave on ROAST for 8 minutes. Stir; recover, and continue cooking on ROAST for 4 to 6 minutes or until potatoes are cooked. Let stand, covered, 3 minutes.

FROZEN BAKED POTATOES

Remove 12 ounces frozen Baked Potatoes from carton. Place in 1-quart glass casserole. Microwave on ROAST for 10 to 11 minutes or until hot.

FROZEN CAULIFLOWER AU GRATIN*

Remove 10 ounces frozen Cauliflower Au Gratin from foil container. Place in 1-quart glass casserole. Cover with glass lid or plastic wrap. Microwave on ROAST for 6 minutes; stir. Recover, and continue cooking on ROAST for 4 to 6 minutes or until hot and tender. Let stand, covered, 3 minutes.

FROZEN SCALLOPED CORN

Remove 12 ounces frozen Scalloped Corn from foil container. Place in 1-quart glass casserole. Cover with glass lid or plastic wrap. Microwave on ROAST for 7 to 8 minutes or until hot and tender. Let stand, covered, 2 to 3 minutes.

POTATOES FORMED INTO 1-INCH LOGS, FRIED AND FROZEN

Remove potatoes from plastic bag. Place in glass casserole or baking dish. Microwave on HIGH until hot — 16 ounces, 8 to 10 minutes; 32 ounces, 12 to 14 minutes.

UNCOOKED FROZEN FOOD KEY: Uncooked frozen foods are handled in much the same manner as precooked. However times will be longer. See Precooked Frozen Food Key on page 164.

Note that uncooked frozen vegetables are cooked on HIGH . See How to Microwave Fresh and Frozen Vegetables, page 112.

Small pieces of frozen uncooked fish, as found in TV dinners, will cook on HIGH .

FROZEN PORK CHOPS*

Place 4 frozen pork chops (up to ½ inch thick) in 2-quart (12 x 7) glass baking dish. Season to taste. Cover with plastic wrap. Microwave on ROAST for 10 minutes. Turn chops over and continue cooking on ROAST for 6 to 8 minutes or until no longer pink. Let stand, covered, 3 minutes before serving.

FROZEN GROUND BEEF PATTIES

Place 4-ounce frozen pattie(s) in glass baking dish or plate in a single layer. Microwave on ROAST —
1 pattie, 2 minutes, turn over, drain, cook 2 to 3 minutes; 2 patties, 4 minutes, turn over, drain, cook 2 to 3 minutes; 4 patties, 5 minutes, turn over, drain, cook 3 to 4 minutes. Extra-thick patties take 1 to 2 minutes longer. Patties will continue to cook after being taken from oven.

FROZEN TURKEY ROAST*

Remove 2-pound frozen turkey roast from aluminum foil pan. Place in (8 x 4) glass loaf dish. Cover with plastic wrap. Microwave on ROAST for 25 minutes. Turn meat over and continue cooking on ROAST for 10 to 12 minutes or until microwave meat thermometer registers 175° F. Let stand, covered, 5 minutes. If roast is packaged with gravy mix, follow package directions for preparing gravy.

FROZEN MEATBALLS*

Place 18 to 20 (1-inch) frozen meatballs in 2-quart (8 x 8) glass baking dish. Cover with plastic wrap. Microwave on ROAST for 6 minutes. Turn meat over and rearrange. Continue cooking on ROAST for 5 to 6 minutes or until no longer pink. Let stand, covered, 5 minutes before serving. If cooked with sauce, cooking time will be longer.

FROZEN SCRAMBLED EGGS AND SAUSAGE

Remove foil cover from 6¼-ounce package of scrambled eggs and sausage. Leave food in foil tray if no more than ¾ inch high. Cover with plastic wrap or return to carton. Microwave on ROAST for 5 to 7 minutes.

FROZEN BREAKFAST LINKS

Remove 8 ounces links from plastic pouch. Place in 9-inch glass pie plate. Cover with plastic wrap. Microwave on REHEAT for 4 to 5 minutes or until hot. Turn links over halfway through cooking period. Let stand, covered, 2 minutes before serving.

FROZEN SOLE DIET TV DINNER

Remove cover from 18-ounce dinner. Place fish only in 1½-quart (10 x 6) glass baking dish or glass plate. Cover with plastic wrap. Microwave on HIGH for 5 minutes. Turn sole over; add vegetables. Recover and continue cooking on HIGH for 10 to 12 minutes or until fish flakes when lifted with fork.

FROZEN FRUIT PIE

Preheat conventional oven to 425° F. Remove 33-ounce frozen fruit pie from carton and aluminum pan. Place in glass pie plate. Microwave on HIGH for 15 minutes. Transfer pie to preheated conventional oven. Bake for 10 to 12 minutes or until crust is brown.

FROZEN PIE SHELL

Place 1 frozen (9-inch) commercial or homemade pie shell in glass pie plate; prick bottom and sides of dough. Microwave on ROAST for 7 to 8 minutes or just until brown spots begin to appear in crust.

THAWING FROZEN FOOD KEY: Microwave thawing on DEFROST takes the fuss and waiting out of defrosting food which stays freshest when stored in a freezer. Thawing times are short. Low heat allows defrosting without cooking.

Remove lids from jars and paper containers. Open cartons before putting these in the oven.

Place cookies, bars, cake squares and sandwiches on paper towel or napkin to absorb moisture.

Food may be thawed in a foil tray that is no more than ¾ inch high. Otherwise, remove food to a glass or pottery plate (without silver or other metal trim).

Thaw moist and liquid foods only until icy in the center. "Dry" foods like baked goods defrost until center is no longer icy. If food thaws completely in a microwave oven, edges will begin to dry and overcook.

Shake or stir liquids after taking them from the oven to distribute heat and finish thawing center.

Let foods stand a few minutes to complete thawing process.

Different brands of frozen foods vary in size so thawing times may vary slightly. Check food at lowest time given.

FROZEN EGG SUBSTITUTE

Thaw opened 8-ounce carton on Microwave DEFROST for 3 to 5 minutes. Let stand 3 minutes. Shake well before pouring into glass cooking dish.

FROZEN ORANGE JUICE

Remove lid and place container in oven. Microwave on DEFROST until icy in center only — 6-ounce can, 3 to 3½ minutes; 12-ounce can, 5 to 6 minutes. Let stand 2 to 3 minutes. Pour in pitcher; dilute and stir to blend as directed on container.

FROZEN NON-DAIRY CREAMER OR TOPPING (LIQUID)

Place opened ½-pint carton in oven. Microwave on DEFROST — 8-ounce, 3 to 4 minutes; 16-ounce, 8 to 9 minutes. Shake or stir to complete thawing. Let stand 2 to 3 minutes before using.

FROZEN PUDDING

Loosen lid on 17½-ounce container. Microwave on DEFROST for 7 to 9 minutes. Stir to blend. Let stand 2 minutes before serving.

FROZEN FRUIT

Remove lid or top from carton or jar. Remove fruit from a plastic package and place in 1-quart glass casserole; cover with glass lid or plastic wrap. Microwave on DEFROST until fruit is icy in center only — 10-ounce carton or package, 3 to 5 minutes; 16-ounce jar, 7 to 9 minutes. Stir to loosen fruit before serving.

FROZEN HOME-BAKED FRUIT-FILLED COOKIES

Place cookie(s) on paper napkin or towel. Microwave on DEFROST until warm — 2 cookies, 30 to 35 seconds; 4 cookies, 40 to 45 seconds; 6 cookies, 50 to 55 seconds.

FROZEN CHOCOLATE FROSTED BROWNIES

Remove foil cover from 13-ounce package. Place uncut baked brownies in oven on glass plate. Microwave on DEFROST for 2 to 3 minutes or until just warm on top and edges. Center will be cool. Let stand 5 minutes before serving.

FROZEN CAKE

Remove cake from carton. Place on glass or pottery serving plate (without metal trim). Microwave on DEFROST until cake is icy in center only. — 17-ounce Frosted Chocolate Fudge Layer Cake, 2 to 3½ minutes; 14-ounce Frosted Banana Cake, 2 to 2½ minutes. Let stand 5 minutes before serving.

Time saving, convenience and easy living are microwave bywords. Use this idea collection to help make full use of a microwave oven and stimulate new creative techniques.

HANDY LITTLE HELPERS

A microwave oven saves precious minutes in so many handy little ways. Try these — then discover others. Use only glass or pottery dishes (without metal trim) in a microwave oven.

MICROWAVE HIGH SETTING

● Melt chocolate: 1 square, 2 to 3 minutes; 2 squares, 3 to 5 minutes.

● Crisp 10 to 15 slices of pepperoni sausage for quick nibbling in about 1½ minutes.

● Warm almost any alcoholic beverage in a glass serving container — brandy snifter or cognac to a pitcher of wine punch. Heat only until warm enough to drink. Time will vary with quantity of liquid.

MICROWAVE REHEAT SETTING

1 pkg choc chips 3 5 min

● Heat 12¼-ounce jar of prepared ice cream topping in a serving pitcher for 2 to 2½ minutes.

● Freshen 2 cups potato chips or salted crackers for 30 to 45 seconds.

● Heat 1 cup syrup in a serving pitcher for about 1 minute.

MICROWAVE ROAST SETTING

● Melt butter or margarine: 2 to 4 tablespoons, 1 minute; ½ cup, 1 to 1½ minutes; ¾ cup, 2 to 2½ minutes.

● Mix a quick bread crumb topping: Melt 2 tablespoons butter 1 to 1½ minutes; stir in 2 tablespoons dry bread crumbs and 2 tablespoons Parmesan cheese, if desired.

MICROWAVE SIMMER SETTING

● Use this setting to speed up the simmering process needed to blend flavors in sauces or soups — and to tenderize less tender meats.

MICROWAVE DEFROST SETTING

● Defrost ½ gallon opened carton of frozen milk for 5 to 8 minutes. Let stand 5 minutes. Stir, center will be icy.

MICROWAVE WARM SETTING

● Soften unwrapped cream cheese: 3-ounce, 1 to 2½ minutes; 8-ounce, 3 to 5 minutes.

● Soften 8-ounce uncovered jar of cheese spread for 1½ to 2½ minutes.

● Warm 8-ounce baby bottle of milk for 3 to 6 minutes.

● Keep 1½ to 2-quart covered cooked main dish warm for about 1 hour without overcooking.

● Soften 1 stick (½ cup) butter or margarine for 1 to 2½ minutes.

● Raise bread dough quickly. See Yeast and Quick Breads chapter.

NECESSARY ACCESSORIES

● Check and organize cupboards so the glass and pottery measures, cooking containers and covers are stored together for easy microwave use. Glass covered casseroles and extra glass measures are especially handy.

● Invest in a microwave meat thermometer. DO NOT use a conventional thermometer of any kind in a microwave oven as it will be damaged.

● Keep pot holders handy. Although microwaves won't heat the dish, the hot food will during longer cooking periods.

BUY AND STORE FOR EASY MICROWAVE MEAL PREPARATION

● Live alone? Buy a beef round steak when the "price is right." Divide and freeze in pieces, strips and cubes for future microwave meals. Use more tender top round for steak pieces; less tender bottom round for strips and cubes. At least 4 "singles" meals can be cut from a 2½ to 3-pound beef round steak.

● Ask the meat man to saw a large package of frozen fish into individual servings. Keep frozen at home; use one at a time.

● Order a larger piece than needed when buying a standing rib roast, boneless sirloin tip roast, pork loin roast or ham for company. Have the meat man slice off 1 to 3 individual steaks or chops for future use.

● Season a pound of ground beef, then shape and freeze individual patties — microwave as needed.

● Freeze individual portions of meat in flat single layers. When ready to use thaw quickly on DEFROST.

● Freeze left-overs in single-serving-portions for a few days on a paper plate placed in a plastic bag. Heat on uncovered plate on REHEAT.

● Freeze individual portions of soup in glass jars twice the size of the ingredient volume. Remove metal lid; cover loosely with plastic wrap, and heat soup in jar on REHEAT.

● Make party appetizer mixtures or dips ahead. Refrigerate or freeze until party time. Put toppings on crackers just before heating so crackers stay crisp. See Appetizers and Beverages chapter for ideas.

COOKING KNOW-HOW

● "Mix well" means just that. Blend liquids completely to avoid separation during cooking.

● Stir food thoroughly and/or turn it over, when specified, to assure rearrangement of mixtures in cooking containers. Microwaves cook first at the edges of a dish.

● Avoid possible steam burns. Slit or pierce plastic wrap covers before removing from hot dishes.

● Cover dishes and casseroles with a glass plate or saucer (without metal trim) if no glass lid, plastic wrap or wax paper are available.

● Evaporation is minimal in microwave cooking. When adapting favorite recipes, find a model recipe in this book because less butter and liquid will probably be needed.

● Trim excess fat from all meat to prevent fatty meat juices and oven spatters.

● Small cubes and thin strips of meat cook and tenderize fastest.

● Cut pot roasts in half or quarters. Rearranging is easier and even cooking is assured.

● Bone and fat cause variations in meat roast cooking time. Use the meat roasting chart on page 50 as a guide. A meat thermometer, however, is the only accurate test for doneness. Only a microwave meat thermometer can be used in the oven during cooking.

● Do not try to cook eggs in the shell in a microwave oven. Pressure builds up inside shell and can cause egg to burst.

● Make a big pot of coffee for breakfast. Remove grounds and let coffee cool. Microwave cup-by-cup as needed, thus avoiding bitter flavors that often develop when coffee is kept hot over long periods of time.

● When heating several cups of beverage at once, place them on a glass tray or in a shallow glass dish to move them easily in and out of the oven.

● Marshmallows melt beautifully when added to a cup of cocoa during the last 15 seconds of heating. Let the kids each add their own and watch the process.

● Heat a snifter of brandy or a glass of wine — enjoy superb aroma and flavor.

● Barbecuing for a crowd? Grill meat out of doors ahead of time. Finish cooking and heating in the microwave oven when guests arrive — or reverse the procedure.

● Poach eggs in individual dishes so every person has his done "exactly right."

● Toast bread for hot sandwiches in a conventional toaster. Bread has more body and doesn't get soggy during heating.

● Cooked meat heats most evenly if thinly sliced and layered in sandwiches.

● Reheat individual servings of meat or main dishes quickly on a dinner plate.

● Warm leftover custards and pour over unfrosted cake for a dessert change.

● Freshen or heat a piece of leftover pie right on a glass serving plate.

● Defrost or freshen cookies in a wink on a paper napkin or paper-doilie-lined glass serving plate (without metal trim).

SUBSTITUTION GUIDE

EQUIVALENT AMOUNTS

1 pound apples	=	3 medium or 3 cups sliced
1 pound butter	=	2 cups
1 cup broth	=	1 teaspoon or cube instant bouillon + 1 cup water
4 ounces cheese	=	1 cup shredded
8 ounces cottage cheese	=	1 cup
6 ounces chocolate pieces	=	1 cup
4 ounces shredded coconut	=	about 1⅓ cups
½ pint whipping cream	=	1 cup, or 2 cups whipped
8 ounces sour cream	=	1 cup
1 medium lemon	=	1 tablespoon grated peel and 3 tablespoons juice
1 pound shelled nuts	=	about 4 cups
1 medium onion	=	½ to ¾ cup chopped
1 medium orange	=	2 tablespoons grated peel and ⅓ to ½ cup juice

WEIGHTS AND MEASURES

U.S. Measure

3 teaspoons	=	1 tablespoon
16 tablespoons	=	1 cup or 8 fluid ounces
5⅓ tablespoons	=	⅓ cup
4 tablespoons	=	¼ cup
2 cups	=	1 pint
2 pints	=	1 quart
4 quarts	=	1 gallon
16 ounces	=	1 pound

Metric Measure

1 gram	=	0.035 ounces
1 kilogram	=	2.21 pounds
1 ounce	=	28.35 grams
1 pound	=	453.59 grams
1 cup	=	236.6 milliliters
1 liter	=	1.06 quarts or 1,000 milliliters

EMERGENCY SUBSTITUTIONS

1 cup buttermilk	=	1 tablespoon vinegar or lemon juice plus milk to make 1 cup
1 tablespoon chopped chives	=	1 teaspoon freeze-dried chives
1 tablespoon cornstarch	=	2 tablespoons all-purpose flour
1 clove garlic	=	⅛ teaspoon instant minced garlic or garlic powder or ½ teaspoon garlic salt
2 tablespoons green pepper	=	1 tablespoon dried pepper flakes
1 teaspoon dried leaf herbs	=	¼ teaspoon powdered herbs
1 teaspoon grated lemon peel	=	½ teaspoon dried lemon peel
1 teaspoon grated orange peel	=	½ teaspoon dried orange peel
1 small (¼ cup) onion	=	1 tablespoon instant minced onion or onion flakes, ¼ cup frozen chopped onion or 1 teaspoon onion powder
1 tablespoon snipped parsley	=	1 teaspoon dried parsley flakes
1 package active dry yeast	=	1 scant tablespoon dry or 1 cake compressed yeast

CONTAINER	POSSIBLE USE	EFFECT FROM MICROWAVE
China plates and cups	Heating dinners and coffee	Generally, no effect.
China plates and cups with metal trim	Not recommended	Arcing (sparking) which will tarnish the trim permanently. Will not necessarily damage oven.
Paper plates, cups and napkins	Heating leftovers, coffee, hot dogs, donuts and rolls	Suitable for microwave. Absorbs moisture from baked goods.
Melamine dishes	Not recommended	Will become hot, often too hot to handle. Food will take longer to cook.
Soft plastics such as dessert topping cartons and Tupperware®	Storage of leftovers, then used for reheating	Will withstand most lower temperatures reached in reheating. Will distort or melt if used for cooking or reheating foods with high fat or sugar content.
Pottery mugs, plates and bowls	Coffee, dinners and soups	Generally, suitable for microwave. If pottery is unglazed, it may absorb moisture. Moisture may cause it to heat up.
Earthenware (ironstone) mugs, plates and bowls	Heating dinners, coffee and soup	Generally, suitable for microwave. Thickness has no effect on ability for microwaves to penetrate. If dish is refrigerated, may take longer to heat food, since it will absorb heat from food.
Special plastic roasting racks	Roasts, chickens and sandwiches	Suitable for microwave. Allows juices to drain away from meat. Juice can be used for gravy later.
Cooking pouches	Vegetables, rice, meats and other frozen foods	Suitable for microwave. Slit pouch so steam can escape. Seal on bag is made to withstand low pressure — will not explode if bag is not slit.
Wax paper	Used for wrapping corn on the cob and covering casseroles	Microwaves have no effect on wax. However, hot food temperature may cause some melting. Will not adhere to hot food. (Remember, chocolates that you eat are often part paraffin.)
Plastic Wrap	Used for covering dishes	Suitable for microwave. Always puncture to allow steam to escape. Otherwise, could cause steam burn.
Oven film and cooking bags	Roasts or stews	Material is suitable. Do not use metal twister (use rubber band); it will spark (arc) and melt bag. Bag itself will not cause tenderizing. Do not use film with foil edges.

CONTAINER	POSSIBLE USE	EFFECT FROM MICROWAVE
Deep metal pots and pans	Not recommended	Depth of metal would cause microwaves to penetrate through top opening only. No time advantage when cooking does not occur from all sides.
T.V. dinner trays (metal)	Frozen dinners or homemade dinners	Shallow metal, ¾", is suitable. However, microwaves still penetrate from the top only, and food will receive heat from the top surface.
Metal spoons (not silver)	Stirring puddings and sauces	If there is a quantity of food, there is no arcing. Handle may become warm to the touch. Do not leave in oven with small amounts of food.
Wooden spoons	Stirring puddings and sauces	Material can withstand microwaves for short periods of cooking.
Wooden cutting boards and wooden bowls	Not recommended	Microwaves will cause natural moisture in wood to evaporate, causing drying and cracking.
Corningware® casseroles	Cooking vegetables, casseroles, desserts and main dishes	Suitable for microwave. This material can be used on surface units, oven and broiler as well, with no breakage.
Pyrex® casseroles	Cooking vegetables, casseroles, desserts and main dishes	Suitable for microwave. Do not use dishes with metal trim, or arcing will occur.
Centura® dinnerware	Not recommended	This absorbs microwaves and can become too hot to handle. Eventually can break or crack.
Corelle® Livingware dinnerware	Heating dinner, coffee and soup	Suitable for microwave. Closed-handle cups should not be used.
Micro-Browner™ grills and skillets	Searing, grilling and frying small meat items	These special dishes absorb microwaves and preheat to high temperatures. A special coating on the bottom makes this dish unique.

NOTE: *If a dish tends to become warm during cooking, two things may result:*
1) It will take longer to cook the food since the dish is absorbing microwaves rather than allowing them to pass through with no effect.
2) If used for extended *periods of time, may become so hot that scorching of the dish (plastics) or cracking of the dish (glass) may occur.*

ADAPTING RECIPES

FOODS	WHAT TO EXPECT
FRUITS AND VEGETABLES	Tender-crisp end results. Penetration of microwaves uses natural moisture in fruits and vegetables to cook. They do not depend on thermal transfer of heat from water. Very little additional water needed. Microwaves cook fruits and vegetables, and steam conducts heat for even cooking. No scorching. Suggested variable power setting: HIGH.
FISH AND SEAFOOD	Fish will be more moist because of lack of dry heat. Excellent results because it is a tender, high-moisture product, often cooked in sauces, which create excellent results. Suggested variable power setting: HIGH.
POULTRY AND GAME BIRDS	Microwaves increase surface temperatures because of attraction to fat. Good tender poultry. Skin will be soft except for more fatty birds, such as duckling. Golden brown rather than crispy brown. Suggested variable power settings: HIGH and ROAST.
MEATS Roasting tender cuts such as rib, leg of lamb, pork loin	Microwaves increase surface temperatures because of attraction to fat, causing browning. Meat will brown somewhat but not as much as with conventional cooking. Standing time is important, as some cooking occurs after removing from oven. This happens by conduction of heat, occurring from the outside toward the center. Use meat thermometer for doneness. Suggested variable power setting: ROAST.
Braising less tender cuts such as chuck, heel or round roast	Not as much browning as conventional cooking. Variable power lower cooking setting allows for tenderizing of meat fibers: the longer the cooking, the more tender the results. Complementary cooking by pre-browning on top of conventional range will enhance results. Suggested variable power setting: SIMMER.
Stewing less tender cuts such as stew beef	Some ingredients tend to cook at different rates. Acceptable results in minimum time. The longer the cooking, the more tender the results. Use less liquid for stew than in conventional cooking, as no evaporation occurs. Suggested variable power setting: SIMMER.
Frying tender cuts of meat such as bacon, steak, chops .	Bacon will brown because of high fat content. No searing occurs on steak and chops without browning grill; best browning on first side. Breaded products will not be as crisp because of the steam rising to the surface of foods, resulting in a moist surface. Suggested variable power setting: HIGH.
Baking tender cuts such as meat loaf and ham	Good results. Not as much crisping on outside as with conventional cooking. Cured meat must be watched carefully, as overcooking may happen easily because microwaves concentrate in spots with food containing sugar. Suggested variable power setting: ROAST.
APPETIZERS AND SANDWICHES	Toasted bread gives better results. Do not assemble canapés until ready to microwave, or crackers and toast will be soggy because moisture has no dry heat source to drive it off. Appetizers with crust do not microwave well; pastry is pale because of lack of dry heat. Heated dips in microwave are smooth and free from scorching, since cooking occurs from all sides of the dish. Suggested variable power settings: HIGH and ROAST.
EGGS, CUSTARD AND CHEESE	The high fat content of the yolk will cook faster than the white. Do not do eggs in the shell because egg will explode. Scrambled eggs are light and tender. Poached eggs are successful, especially on lower setting. Fried eggs can be done on microwave browning grill. Souffles and puffy omelets cannot be done because of moist condition in microwave oven. There is no heat to hold and dry structure. Custard requires low power setting to avoid curdling. Cheese must be melted or cooked in recipes at a low power level. Stirring helps in cheese sauce and fondue. Process cheese has better melting properties. Suggested variable power setting: ROAST.
RICE AND PASTAS	Rehydration must be done through time. Minimal time-saving items. Add 1 tablespoon cooking oil to boiling water to prevent boilovers. Use large dish, or rub oil around edge of dish. Suggested variable power setting: DEFROST.
SAUCES AND FILLINGS thickened by starch	Blend thickening agent well at beginning. Exceptional results. Stir halfway through cooking to prevent lumpiness. Scorching is no problem because cooking occurs from all sides at once. Use slightly less liquid than conventional recipes because evaporation does not occur. Suggested variable power setting: HIGH.
FROSTINGS AND CANDIES	Use buttered large bowl. Requires very little stirring. Check temperature with candy thermometer after cooking periods. Microwaves are attracted to sugar mixtures and cook fast. Very excellent results. Since this food reaches high temperatures, use a heat-proof dish. Suggested variable power setting: ROAST.
CAKES, QUICK BREADS, YEAST BREADS AND COOKIES	Lack of dry heat source develops these products in a unique way. Since they are not restricted by a crust, they are fluffier. Top of cakes will be moist and wet-looking after cooking, as steam rises to surface. Do not overcook to remove this moist appearance from these baked goods, as they will toughen. When adapting a conventional recipe, use about half the amount of baking powder and soda. Baked products will be pale (except chocolate) and not crusty. Low power setting may help prevent irregular-shaped top. Will not bake angel food and chiffon cakes. Select cookies such as bars that need no browning and are soft. Suggested variable power setting: SIMMER.
PIES	Flaky crust but does not brown. Acceptable. Cook crust first before adding wet filling to be cooked to prevent sogginess. Complementary cooking gives excellent results by starting in the microwave and finishing conventionally. Suggested variable power settings: HIGH and ROAST.
FROZEN FOODS	Reheat well in microwave. More moisture than with conventional cooking. Better results on lower settings. Important to use dish that conforms to shape of frozen food to prevent overcooking of melted food. Breaded foods do not get crisp. Suggested variable power settings: REHEAT, ROAST and SIMMER.
COMBINING FOODS	Several foods cooked at same time in a microwave will cook at a different speed. Cooking time will at least double from the fastest cooking item. Remove food as it gets done. Suggested variable power setting: HIGH.